From Father's

Property to

Children's Rights

From Father's Property to Children's Rights

Mary Ann Mason

The History of Child Custody in the United States

Columbia University Press | *New York*

Columbia University Press
New York   Chichester, West Sussex

Library of Congress Cataloging-in-Publication Data
Mason, Mary Ann.
    From father's property to children's rights: the history of child
custody in the United States / Mary Ann Mason.
        p.   cm.
    Includes bibliographical reference and index.
    ISBN 0-231-08046-8
    1. Custody of children—United States—History.   I. Title.
KF547.M37   1994
    346.7301'7—dc20
[347.30617]   93–34524
                                                        CIP

Casebound editions of Columbia University Press books are
printed on permanent and durable acid-free paper.

Printed in the United States of America
c 10 9 8 7 6 5 4 3 2 1

For my children, Tom and Eve

Contents

Acknowledgments   ix

Introduction   xi

1. *Fathers/Masters: Children/Servants: Child Custody in the Colonial Era*   1

2. *From Fathers' Rights to Mothers' Love: The Transformation of Child
Custody Law in the First Century of the New Republic, 1790–1890*   49

3. *The State as Superparent: The Progressive Era, 1890–1920*   85

4. *In the Best Interest of the Child? 1960–1990*   121

5. *The Ascendancy of the Social Sciences*   161

Afterword   187

Notes   195

Index   225

Acknowledgments

There were many people whose support was critical to completing this book—whether or not they realized it. These of course include my always supportive family: husband Paul Ekman, children Tom and Eve Ekman. My colleagues at the School of Social Welfare, University of California, Berkeley, were most helpful in suggesting funding possibilities and publishers. These include Ralph Kramer, Neil Gilbert, James Leiby, Harry Specht, and Jewelle Taylor Gibbs. I owe a great deal to Eleanor Maccoby, Michael Wald, and the students in the Child Custody Seminar at Stanford Law school for stimulating the ideas that are incorporated into the last two chapters, particularly regarding the influence of social scientists on custody disputes. I am particularly indebted to Dr. Judith Wallerstein for her many wonderful observations about custody from a child-centered point of view, and for her comments on part of an earlier draft. My students in the Children and Law class that I teach at the School of Social Welfare have also provided me with important insights into child custody from a child welfare perspective.

The University of California at Berkeley Committee on Research was generous in providing research assistant funding for two years. With this funding I was able to employ several law students from Boalt Hall, without whom this book would not have been completed within my lifetime. These very competent, enthusiastic law students made the process of writing this book most often a pleasure. They clearly enjoyed their work and were my best sounding boards and critics. These wonderful research assistants include Laurie Culp, Al Zarate, Marlene Saks, Steve DeSalvo, and Serena Eisenberg.

Introduction

The relationship between parents, children, and the state is arguably the most fundamental relationship in a society. The social attitudes and legal norms embedded in this triangle determine the way we raise our children and provide the basis of social continuity within a nation. This relationship usually goes unexamined. Only when the family breaks down, by virtue of the death of one or more parents, divorce, or parental incompetence or abuse does the state intervene to carry out and make explicit society's values. Temporarily, and sometimes permanently, the state becomes involved with the issue of custody and control of the child. And, at times, the triangle is transformed into a more complicated matrix involving fourth parties: masters (of indentured servants and child slaves), stepparents, foster parents, and grandparents. These parties, too, often seek legal recognition in custody disputes.

This book traces the historical development of the American family, and focuses specifically on the evolution of legal rules determining who shall have custody and control over a child. In examining child custody it is charting new territory. While the history of the American family is slowly being told, legal history relating to children is almost unknown. In modern times we automatically think of child custody in the context of divorce, and, indeed, in the last half of the twentieth century divorce has been the setting for the vast majority of custodial disputes. However, custodial disputes have surfaced far more frequently on other occasions: the death of a father, or both parents, the incompetence or financial inability of parents to care for their children, the birth of illegitimate children, the voluntary indenturing of children by their parents or the involuntary indenture of children with no competent parents, and the sale of slave children. Today, of course, indentured servants and slaves exist no more, and parents are more likely to survive beyond their children's childhood. However, many children today are temporarily removed from the custody of their parents on grounds of abuse or neglect. Often parental rights are terminated and the children are adopted by others. Abuse and adoption, as well as divorce, will continue to be the major social issues involved in the custody of children.

The law relating to child custody has dramatically changed over the course of our history. This book, which begins with the colonial period, examines overall themes relating to child custody but concentrates on pivotal points of change. There are a few themes to which the reader should be alerted. First, for much of our history, society viewed the child as an economic asset. Children were not considered property under common law, as it has become fashionable to expound, but a child's labor was a valuable resource to parents and other custodial adults. Use of this resource was supported by the law until fairly recently. Second, a two-tiered system of dealing separately with poor children and with children whose parents can support them characterizes the history of child custody. The law and the courts have treated indigent children differently from middle-class children of divorce, and this trend continues. Third, the contemporary emphasis on biological parenthood, including unwed parents and sperm and egg donors, is new. Until recently biological parenthood was deferred to in a custody dispute only when the parents were legally married. Finally, a persistent theme is the interdependency of the status of women and the custody rules regarding children. This relationship is the single most important factor in explaining the wide swings in custody law.

Focusing on pivotal historical eras, the colonial period is perhaps the most difficult to reconstruct for a historian and is the most unfamiliar to today's reader. The legal system then was not as formally constructed as it is today, and colonial courts, far more than today's remote institutions, were at the center of the community, settling everyday quarrels and disputes. Children were viewed as important economic producers then, and therefore the courts became principally involved in issues of the custody and control of children when they were asked to approve contracts for indentures or to resolve conflicts regarding child labor. The rights and obligations of fathers and masters overlapped; both depended upon child labor and both were required to provide education and moral training in addition to ordinary sustenance. Fathers and masters had similar paramount rights to the custody and control of the children in their household. A colonial mother had no legal right to her children when her husband was alive, and only restricted rights upon his death. For the most part English common law prevailed, except for the unique American experience of slavery, which allowed masters to sell children as chattel. Divorce was an unusual event. The courts, however, dealt frequently with the punishment of unwed mothers and fathers and the disposition of their offspring.

In the first hundred years of the new republic, from 1790 to 1890, after the end of the colonial period, there was a dramatic shift away from fathers' common law rights to custody and control of their children toward a modern emphasis on the best interests of the child, with a presumption in favor of mothers as the more nurturing parent. Slavery was abolished and indentured servitude for children was increasingly frowned upon. The trend favoring mothers was manifest in custody following divorce, testamentary guardianships, bastardy law, apprenticeship law, and the new laws creating adoption. The changing status of women—their acquisition of greater property rights and the elevation of their position within the family—was a critical factor in this transformation.

Toward the beginning of the twentieth century, in the historical period known as the Progressive era, the state assumed a decisively more active role, irrevocably reducing parental control by means of legislation that insisted upon compulsory education, strict controls on child labor, and standards for parental competence. If parents violated these laws they risked losing custody of their children. At the same time the state, for the first time, considered aiding poor but "worthy" mothers rather than removing their children when they were unable to support them. These state actions established the structure for the modern child welfare system. The earlier judicial trend preferring mothers in custody disputes following divorce became nearly universally established in case law and was ratified by many state legislatures.

Beginning in the 1970s a major swing in custody law sharply reversed what had been a well-entrenched preference for mothers. Most states adopted laws conferring an equal status on the custodial rights of mother and father with a favorable attitude toward joint custody. Biological parents gained rights over the growing numbers of nonbiological parents, particularly stepparents and foster parents, who were, in fact, raising the children as traditional families broke down. The state took a more active role in monitoring standards of parental conduct, frequently intervening to take temporary or permanent custody of the child. On the other hand, the state supported an ever-growing population of single parents, allowing them to maintain custody of their children. New reproductive technology, separating conception and childbearing, blurred the concept of biological parenthood and challenged the ingenuity of lawmakers.

Finally, the determined entrance of the social and behavioral sciences into custody issues toward the end of the twentieth century changed not only the legal rules governing custody but the proceedings themselves. Overwhelmed by the volume of divorce cases and frustrated by indeterminate standards after the abolition of the maternal preference lawmakers and judges increasingly looked to social and behavioral scientists to provide guidelines for what constituted the best interests of the child, employing expert witnesses to evaluate the relationship between the parent and the child.

Focusing on child custody offers us a unique window from which to view American history. It provides an intimate view of childhood and parenting, but also allows us to see how the law in this arena responds to social change. Among the many factors that affect a society's view of children, the changing status of their mothers is perhaps the most important. Both the organized movement for women's rights and the changing role of women in the economy have affected the way society views children and thus have critically impacted child custody law.

The move from a colonial household economy to an urban economy separated the father from the home and elevated the mother to the role of primary child raiser. The same urban middle-class culture encouraged the growth of the first wave of feminists, dedicated to more rights for women, including the right to the custody of their children. The vision of the first wave of feminists, however, was focused on middle-class mothers, not poor mothers. It was the second wave of feminists, the social feminists of the Progressive era, who introduced the concept that society should support "worthy" poor mothers in their efforts to retain custody of their children. In the late twentieth century the abolition of the maternal preference coincided with the movement of women out of the home and into the labor market. Indeed, the abolition of the maternal preference was advocated by the third wave of feminists who, in seeking equal rights for women, rejected special preference for women in divorce and custody.

Perhaps the reason that their mothers' status has been so determinative in custody issues is that children have no voice of their own. In this story of child custody children are seen but rarely heard. Court records offer sparse details about children, usually omitting their names, while providing lengthy accounts of the conduct and misconduct of their parents. Still, these court decisions are our ear to the wall behind which the human dramas that create custody disputes occur. The judges' reasoning also permits us to understand the values and judgments of past and current eras.

In addition to court records I have relied upon legislation and legal commentators of the time. I have also utilized a wide variety of primary and secondary sources that illuminate custody issues at different historical periods. These include some lively scholarship on families and children and a small sample of the growing body of scholarship on the women's movement.

This historical examination should expand our limited understanding of families, children, and the law in the past, but also illuminate current controversies. The custody of about half of American children is at issue at some point in their lives today. The rights of stepparents, foster parents, and other nonbiological parents are being reexamined without a grasp of their historical development. Basic questions are being asked about resolving custody disputes that could be guided by historical understanding. Is a mother a more appropriate custodian for young children than a father? What voice should the child have in custody disputes? Under what conditions should the state intervene to remove children from their parents? And finally, Should the law relinquish its role as decision maker in favor of the social and behavioral sciences? These questions of today and the future are difficult to answer, but an understanding of the underlying historical foundation may help to build our future.

From Father's

Property to

Children's Rights

Fathers/Masters:
Children/Servants:
Child Custody in the
Colonial Era

In 1620 the Virginia Company complained to Sir Robert Naunton, principal secretary of James I, that London street children were unwilling to be sent to Virginia colony as apprentices.

> The City of London have by act of their Common Council, appointed one hundred children out of their superfluous multitude to be transported to Virginia: there to be bound apprentices for certain years, and afterward with very beneficial conditions for the children. . . . Now it falleth out that among those children, sundry being ill disposed, and fitter for any remote place than for this city, declare their unwillingness to go to Virginia, of whom the City is especially desirous to be disburdened, and in Virginia under severe masters they may be brought to goodness.[1]

In response, the English Privy Council granted the Virginia Company permission to do whatever necessary to force the children into the ships.

And if any of them shall be found obstinate to resist or otherwise to disobey such directions as shall be given in this behalf, we do likewise hereby authorize such as shall have the charge of this service to imprison, punish, and dispose any of those children . . . and so to ship them out for Virginia with as much expedition as may stand with conveniency.[2]

This exchange of letters between the Virginia Company and the Privy Council suggests several salient facts regarding children and custody in the colonial era: first, the Virginia Company was desperate for child labor and went to to great lengths to import unwilling youths; second, while it is not clear whether or not they had parents, these children certainly emigrated without them and were placed in the custody of the masters to whom they were apprenticed; and third, neither the Virgina colonialists nor the English showed any concern for the best interests of these children, nor, for that matter, for basic due process before punishment—rights guaranteed adult Englishmen, but apparently not children.

Children who came to America as indentured servants without parents were an important part of the story of the colonies' settlement. More than half of all persons who came to the colonies south of New England were indentured servants, and, according to historian Richard B. Morris, most servants were less than nineteen years old. The average age was between fourteen and sixteen, and the youngest was six.[3] By contrast, most children who emigrated to the New England colonies did so as a member of a family.

While most children were not forcibly imported to the New World without parents, separation from parents and forced labor were common in all the colonies. Children were critical to the colonial labor force; after the age often children were often employed like adult workers, and many, if not most, did not remain in the custody of either parent until adulthood.[4] While some came without parents, many others lost both parents through death or abandonment. Parents very often apprenticed or sent out their children to serve another family at around age ten. Children born out of wedlock were routinely separated from their mothers upon weaning and "bound out" to a master. Slave children, who comprised about one-fifth of all children by the end of the eighteenth century, could be sold away from their parents at any time. Sentimentality about children and childhood, which bloomed in the nineteenth century, was nearly absent in this practical, struggling era. And, as we shall see in the following section, in the hierarchical structure of the colonial household the relationship between child and father overlapped the relationship between slave and master.

The harsh manner in which colonialists treated children reflected the English tradition. Colonial family law and employment law were still firmly tied to their English origins. Common law relating to indenture contracts for children, custody following divorce or the death of a parent, and the disposition of orphans and bastards traversed the ocean virtually unchanged. Sometimes these laws were modified in practice by the colonialists. For the most part, however, these laws were well suited to the New World experience, where the demand for labor exceeded the available supply of adult workers. These laws did not formally change until the nineteenth century. Only the unique experience of slavery created custodial arrangements for children that were unknown to common law.[5]

Since children were viewed as important economic producers, the courts became principally involved in issues of the custody and control of children when they were asked to approve contracts for indenture or to resolve conflicts regarding child labor. The dockets of the ordinary courts were filled with such cases. Courts regulated the abuse of child indentures—including the selling of children—settled disputes between father and the masters to whom their children were apprenticed, returned runaway indentured children, and bound out orphans and indigent children to relieve the community of the financial burden of maintaining them. In the southern states, by the eighteenth century, judges typically settled disputes regarding the selling or devising (gift by will) of slaves, including slave children.

Custody disputes between mother and father following divorce or separation, which loomed as the major custodial issue in later centuries, received scant attention in this era, when women had few rights and divorce was rare, even forbidden in some colonies. Far more common was widowhood, where the rights of custody and control of children by the surviving mother could be assigned by the father testamentarily or given by the court to a male guardian. Also prevalent was illegitimacy, where both mother and putative father were subject to punishment and fines and the fate of the illegitimate child was determined by the court.

Courts frequently were asked to intervene into families on grounds of abuse or neglect, particularly in New England, but they often focused on neglect that was labor oriented. Masters and fathers risked losing the children if they failed to adequately prepare them for a role in the labor economy. Parents also lost their children if they were not able to provide economic support. All these children were quickly recycled into the labor force as apprentices in other households.

The Colonial Household: Parents and Children

Functional rather than blood ties were frequently the basis of relationships between adults and children in the colonial era. Thus the primary unit of social and economic organization during the colonial era was not the family but rather the multipurpose colonial household. All the important interactions between adults and chilren occurred within this self-contained unit; there, children were born, raised, schooled in religion, and, as soon as they were productive, put to useful labor. These children could be blood relatives or merely be hired help. Understanding the colonial household, then, is central to our understanding of child custody arrangements of that period.

This examination of child custody begins with a glance at the colonial household as a unit, followed by a deeper analysis of the roles of each of the members of that household and their relationship to the household's children. Within the hierarchy of the household the adult roles relevant to child custody, in descending order, included: father, master, putative father, guardian, stepfather, married mother, mistress, widow, stepmother, unwed mother, and slave mother. Children could be sons or daughters, apprentices or servants, orphans, bastards, or slaves. Other relatives and nonrelatives might fill out the household, but their roles in relation to the custody and control of children were usually peripheral.

Households in New England and the Chesapeake colonies were similar in many respects. Both performed the same dual functions of socialization and economic production, and both were most likely to be nuclear rather than multigenerational. Yet, they were demographically quite distinct throughout the seventeenth century. New England was settled mostly by families, who, with the exception of a few notable epidemics, enjoyed good health and relatively low infant mortality. The New England household, therefore, was more likely to comprise a mother, father, and several children of their own, with the addition of one or two servants or apprentices not their own.[6]

By contrast, the Chesapeake colonies were settled mostly by single people, usually male and under twenty-one. More than half of the settlers came as indentured child servants without parents.[7] These colonies were a "death trap" for early child immigrants and were not conducive to infant survival. By one estimate as many as one-fourth to one-third of all children died before their first birthday, and 45 to 55 percent died before their twentieth birthday.[8] Most children who survived could expect to lose one or both their parents by the time they reached adulthood. These factors contributed to smaller and more unstable households, which could include orphans, stepbrothers, and sisters, half-brothers and sisters, as well as the children who had immigrated as indentured servants. The head of the household may have been an uncle or stepfather, not necessarily the biological father of any of the children.[9]

The demographic differences between New England and Chesapeake households also grew as the South became more dependent upon slavery. Slave children became a common presence in southern households, although usually housed in separate slave quarters. In several colonies slaves comprised half or more of the population; on large plantations slave children greatly outnumbered all other children. Slavery certainly complicated the legal relationships between adults and children in the Chesapeake household, and affected the quality of the childhood experience. Nevertheless, the existence of slavery in the South had little effect on the basic function of the colonial household. As a production unit the household in both the New England and Chesapeake colonies was arranged in a system of hierarchical mutual obligations. The father/master, clearly at the pinnacle of the hierarchy, was obliged to provide adequate sustenance, vocational training, and, with some variation between the colonies, rudimentary education and religious training to all children (except the slave children) in his custody. The mother was obliged to assist him in these tasks. Children were obliged to be obedient and to provide labor as fit their age and legal status. The labor of a child, even a nonslave, was a commodity that could be sold or hired out by fathers and assigned by masters. Slave children, like their natural parents, were sold as a chattel. All children were looked upon as current or potential economic producers; in the labor-hungry colonies, small hands could not be idle.

Fathers: Rights and Responsibilities

All Parents and Masters of Families are obliged by themselves or others, to Teach or Cause to be taught, all their Children, so much Learning as they may be able to Read perfectly the English Tongue, upon penalty of 20s. for every Offence.

All Masters of Families, are to teach their Children and Apprentices, the knowledge of the Capital Laws, on penalty of 20s. for Every Offence.

Masters of Families are to Catechize or cause to be Catechized, their Children and Apprentices at least once a week, on the Grounds and Principles of religion. A. 1642.   (seventeenth-century Massachusetts Bay Colony statute)[10]

In labor-scarce America the services or wages of a child over ten was one of the most valuable assets a man could have. Thus fathers, without dispute, had almost unlimited authority of custody and control over their natural, legitimate children, leaving almost no room for maternal authority, at least during the fathers' lifetime. This authority was enshrined in the common law. For example, a father's right to custody was firmly established in English common law as the right to the association and services of his legitimate children. Association was defined as physical custody as against all parties, including the mother, and services included not only the labor of the children for his own use, but their wages, if they worked for another. A father had the right to maintain an action for the seduction of his daughter or the enticement of a son who left home, since this deprived him of services or earnings.[11] The existence of these common law rights have led some contemporary legal historians to conclude that the law regarded children as a property right, to be treated as chattel.[12]

Yet, as indicated by the Massachusetts Bay Colony statute, the relationship between fathers and children was far more complex than these legal historians might have us believe. While fathers had almost absolute control over their children, fathers also had considerable responsibilities, both to their own children and to children legally bound to them as apprentices. In that sense the relationship between father and child was more that of master and servant than of owner and chattel. A master-servant relationship, although not equal, required that master give something to servant in exchange for the servant's labor. In addition, a master could not injure the servant, while an owner theoretically might dispose of the his chattel in any manner, including extermination.

Commentary writer James Kent, frequently cited by early nineteenth-century jurists, emphasized the mutuality of the relationship. Kent wrote that because of the father's "obligation . . . to provide for the maintenance, and, in some qualified degree, for the education of his infant children, he is entitled to the custody of their persons, and to the value of their labour and services."[13] The right to a child's labor therefore was seen as recompense for the father's obligation of support. This mutuality was a relatively recent development in the father-child relatioship. Ancient English tradition initially required only that the father control the child's education and religious training. The Elizabethan poor laws and, later on, common law and statutes, added the duty of maintenance and support.[14] Mutuality was contrary to Roman law, where the father enjoyed absolute power, and in the early Roman republic, according to the historian Dionysius, "the atrocious power of putting his children to death, and of selling them three times in an open market, was vested in the father." [15]

Colonial America expanded and enforced these mutual obligations beyond the English tradition. The duty to educate and provide religious training was enlarged to include vocational training. In New England local governments insisted that parents train their children to be literate, religious, and economically productive citizens. As an early Massachusetts law dictated:

> This court [the court serving in its law-making function], taking into consideration the great neglect in many parents and masters in training up their children in learning, and labor, and other employments which may be profitable

to the commonwealth, do hereupon order and decree that in every town the chosen men appointed for managing the prudential affairs of the same shall henceforth stand charged with the care of the redress of this evil . . . especially of their ability to read and understand the principles of religion and the capital laws of the country.[16]

The New England father was responsible for making his child a productive member of the community, either by his own teaching or by apprenticing his child to another master for training. Fathers were not allowed to exploit their children by assigning them only menial work, such as tending livestock, but were expected to prepare them to perform skilled tasks. Laws instructed town officials to assign work to children that taught skills. "They are to take care that such are set to keep cattle be set to some other employment withal, as spinning . . . knitting weaving tape, etc."[17]

Although the father was squarely at the head of the household, those elected or appointed by charter to enforce community standards carefully supervised the household. In New England these town officials could enter the household, interrogate the children to determine the level of their education and skill, and remove the children from the home and apprentice them to another master if the father was found wanting the teaching of his children. According to an early Massachusets law,

The Select Men of every Town, may examine the Children and Apprentices, in any Family within their respective Towns, and if they find them Rude and Ignorant they shall admonish the Parents and Master, and in case of continued neglect, may with the consent of two Magistrates, or the next county court, take such children from them, and placed them with such other Masters as will reduce them to Government and Instruction. [18]

Following an unsatisfactory inspection by selectmen the Suffolk County Court decreed, "William Scant of Braintree being bound over to this court to anser for his not disposing of his children as may be for their good educatin, and for refusing to consent to the Selectment of Braintree as the law directs . . . doth leave it to the prudent of the Selectment of Braintree to dispose of his children to service so far as the necessity of his family will give leave."[19]

In the Chesapeake colonies intrusion by public officials into households was less frequent, although the expectations were similar, at least with regard to religious and vocational training. A series of Virginia acts from 1631 to 1645 required fathers and masters to provide compulsory religious education to all children and servants by sending them weekly to church. If the heads of households ignored the warning of ministers and failed to send the children, they were subject to a penalty of five hundred pounds of tobacco for the use of the parish, "unless sufficient cause be shewn to the contrary."[20]

Virginia, like New England, worried about "sloathe and idelnesse wherewith such young children are easily corrupted." Beginning in 1646 the legislature passed a series of ambitious laws to create workhouses for "the relief of such parents whose poverty extends not to give them good breeding." Children would be taken from their homes to live in the workhouses where they would learn "spinning, weaving, and other useful trades."[21] While there is no firm evidence that these workhouses were actually established, the laws clearly endorsed the need for vocational training.

Unlike New England, Virginia compelled masters and guardians to provide book learning, but not vocational training, to orphaned, poor, illegitimate, and, sometimes, mulatto children. The first law requiring masters or guardians to provide such education did not appear in Virgina until 1705. However, an education requirement frequently was included in the indenture contract during the seventeenth century. Fathers in Virginia were never legally compelled to provide nonvocational education for their own children. The assumption was that fathers would attend to the education of their own children and did not need to be forced by law.[22]

Fathers were expected to work hard to provide food and shelter for their wife and children in all the colonies, and it was the community's responsibility to enforce this obligation. In New England the same town officials who supervised the proper education and religious training of the children also monitored their father's diligence as provider. In Watertown, when Hugh Parsons was found lacking as breadwinner for his family, "he was Sent For, and advised to imploy his time to the better providing For his Family, and for his incouragement, he was supplied with some present Corne."[23] If fathers did not mend their ways they could be punished by imprisonment, as was the case with Samuel Mattock, indicted by the grand jury of Suffolk "for Idleness and neglecting his Family," and sentenced "to the house of correction for an idle person and to pay fees of Courts."[24]

In Virginia the vestrymen of each parish supervised family welfare, following the English model. After 1676 these vestrymen were chosen by the freeholders. They were to investigate cases of immorality and disorder and to administer the poor laws. At the same time the English Poor Law Act of 1601 firmly established the obligation of the father to support his children until they reached majority at the age of twenty-one. This law also emphasized the system of apprenticing poor children. Virginia, with its large population of orphans and illegitimate children and its insatiable labor needs, eagerly embraced the apprenticeship model.[25]

While the community was willing to advise and supervise households, its patience was not infinite. Ultimately, in all the colonies, communities were unwilling, and usually unable, to subsidize poor families. Following the tradition of the English poor laws, fathers who could not adequately maintain their family lost custody of their children to poor law officials. These officials routinely "bound out" the children to a master who could support them. The preamble of a Virginia "Act of 1672 for Suppressing of Vagabonds and Disposing of Poor Children to Trades" expressed regret for previously straying from the English laws.

> Be it Enacted and it is hereby ordained that the justices of peace in every County do put the Laws of England against Vagrant Idle, and desolate Persons into strict Executions: And that the Respective County Courts shall and hereby are authorized and impowered to place out all Children whose Parents are not able to bring them up, apprentices to Trades: The males till one and twenty years of Age, and the Females to other necessary imployments until eighteen years of Age and no longer.[26]

Similarly, a Massachusetts Act of 1642 authorized the town officials, with the consent of any appropriate court or magistrates, "to put forth as apprentices the children of such as shall not be able and fit to employ and bring them up."[27]

While all colonial fathers were clearly responsible for training and taking care of the material needs of their children, New England fathers also had to raise them to be obedient, rather than "rude, stubborn or unruly,"[28] but were not permitted to use excessive physical force to accomplish this goal. At first glance the infamous "stubborn child laws," as they have been referred to, imply that any amount of force could be used to control a disobedient child. As the act of the General Court of Massachusetts decreed in 1646:

> If a man have a stubborn or rebellious son, of sufficient years and understand-ing, viz. sixteen years of age, which will not obey the voice of his Father or the voice of his Mother, and that when they have chastened him will not harken unto them: then shall his Father and Mother being his natural parents, lay hold on him, and bring him to the Magistrates assembled in Court and testify unto them, that their son is stubborn and rebellious and will not obey their voice and chastisement, but lives in sundry notorious crimes, such a son shall be put to death.[29]

Similar laws were enacted in Connecticut in 1650, Rhode Island in 1668, and New Hampshire in 1679.[30]

Two important facts should be noted regarding these laws, which were not based on English common law or tradition, but on the Old Testament, Deuteronomy. First, they do not authorize the father to unilaterally punish the child; rather, the child first must be judged by the court. Second, there is no evidence that the extreme punishment of death was ever imposed upon a rebellious child.

These laws reflect the intention of New England Puritans to live in a strictly governed moral community in order to satisfy the people's covenant with God. They also illustrate the seamless web between private and public life in the Puritan colonies. Defying one's parents was an offense against the community and against one's parents, and was therefore punishable by the community rather than by the father alone. While the community never imposed the ultimate punishment of death, it routinely meted out other forms of punishment, especially public whipping, to rebellious children.

In a Connecticut case the court called "Young Mistress How" (age unspec-ified) who, witnesses testified, had turned over a page of the Bible and declared it not worth reading. The witnesses also testified that when her mother called her, she said, "a pox of the devil, what ails this mad woman?"

The court ordered that she pay ten shillings for swearing "and for her cursing speeches and rebellion to her mother, and profane speeches of the scriptures, tending to blasphemy," and further ordered that "she be corrected publicly by whipping suitable to her years, and if this be not a warning but that she go on in these course, it will come to a higher censure."[31]

While a child had a clear obligation to be obedient toward his or her parents, the father had a mutual obligation to control the child. If the father could not raise the child properly, and if, following the town officials' warning that the child (or servant) was found "rude, stubborn and unruly," the town officials had the right to remove the children from the parents and "place them with some masters for years . . . which will more strictly look unto, and force them to submit unto government according to the rules of this order."[32]

If fathers dealt with their children too harshly, however, they risked punishment or loss of custody of their child. For instance, the Ipswich Quarterly Court sentenced John Perry of Newberry Massachusetts "for abusive carriage to his wife and child, bound to good behavior and to sit one hour in stocks at Newbery next lecture day,"[33] while in Salem, Massachusetts "Henry Phelps . . . was complained of at the county court at Boston, July 31, 1660 for beating his son, John Phelps, and forcing him to work carrying dung and mending a hogshead on the Lord's day, also for intimacy with his brother's wife and for entertaining Quakers."[34] As punishment his son John Phelps was to be taken away from him and given to his uncle to place him with a religious family as an apprentice. No mention was made of a mother.

Clearly, New England fathers walked a tight line between effective control and overbearing behavior. If they erred in either direction, their children could be removed from their custody and apprenticed to a more worthy master. Their children were obliged to demonstrate obedience and respect or risk public whipping. Outside New England, however, no strict supervision of this kind existed. As we shall see, while the law protected indentured servants from abuse by their masters in all colonies, town officials outside of New England did not monitor the discipline of fathers over their own children. Nor were children outside of New England held to the Old Testament standard of obedience where infractions were theoretically punishable by death and in practice punished by public humiliation.

Colonial fathers, then, had obligations as well as paramount rights to the association and labor of their children. This almost total legal emphasis on the role of the father to the exclusion of the mother may seem, by today's standards, out of touch with reality. Nevertheless, the colonial father did perform many of the tasks that today are shared or handled only by the mother. The vast majority of seventeenth- and eighteenth-century fathers were farmers, the rest were mostly artisans or tradesmen who also worked at or near home. Thus, even at work, most fathers were not far from their children. According to historian John Demos fathers were not only a daily visible presence but also took charge of their children's education and moral supervision. Children turned to their fathers for guidance, not to their mothers. While mothers played a larger role with infants, and necessarily worked closer with their daughters, they were not the central figure in their children's life that they became in the nineteenth century when the father's work often took him away from home. As examples of mothers' peripheral role, Demos cites letters of children, always to their fathers, with only perfunctory mention of their mothers, often asking only to be "remembered" to their mother.[35]

Demos suggests that the centrality of the father in the child's life, particularly his role of moral supervisor, created the common law right of child custody for the father in case of marital separation. While in the context of daily seventeenth- and eighteenth-century life this explanation has merit, the father's custodial rights must also be seen as only one of the many legal rights that the father enjoyed and the mother did not under a patriarchal system.

Mothers: Reverence and Respect

A mother's place in the hierarchy of the colonial family was clear. She fulfilled a critical social and economic role in the governance of the household, but she was definitely second in command. As Puritan minister Samuel Willard expressed it:

> If God in his Providence hath bestowed on them Children or Servants, they have each of them a share in the government of them: tho" there is an inequality in the degree of this Authority over them by God: and the Husband is to be acknowledged to hold a Superiority, which the Wife is to allow; yet in

respect of all others in the Oeconomical Society, she is invested with an Authority over them by God: and her Husband is to allow it to her, and the others are to carry it to her as such.[36]

Colonial mothers had few enforceable rights to the association and labor of their children. Blackstone stated the English common law simply: the father had a natural right to his children and the mother "was entitled to no power [over her children], but only to reverence and respect."[37] Fathers, not mothers, held the rights of association and the right to the wages of their children. The right to association included the right to send the child to live with a relative or another family, or to apprentice the child; the father was not required to obtain the mother's consent for either action.

The colonial mother also had few obligations toward her children. In contrast to the father, who was obliged to maintain and support his children and teach them civic and religious duties, a New England mother was obliged only to assist the father in teaching the children (and servants) to read. The *enforcement* of this and other obligations, however, fell only upon the father. Only the father was fined and subject to removal of the child from his custody. In seventeenth-century Virginia the obligations differed somewhat. Women in Virginia were were included in the duty to provide religious education; "all fathers, mothers, masters and mistresses shall cause their children, servants and apprentices which have not learned the catechism to come to church." If they neglected their duties, they could be "cursed by the corts in those places holden."[38] However, if neglect persisted beyond multiple warnings, the master alone was legally liable for the "500 pounds of tobacco for the use of the parish."[39]

A mother's lack of power over her children was an aspect of the general legal impotence of married women. Under English common law a married woman (*femme couvert*) could not own property, either real or personal. All that she brought to her marriage became her husband's. He could spend her money, sell her slaves and her jewelry. Married women could not make a legally binding contract, and they had no right to execute a deed of gift or write a will unless the husband consented.[40] There is a robust scholarly debate on whether or not marriage settlements (prenuptial agreements), as enforced by equity law in both English and American courts, greatly mitigated the inequalities of common law. The leading proponents of the ameliorating power of settlement agreements, R. B. Morris and Mary Beard, insist that if a marriage settlement allowed women to own property, make contracts and write wills, then women were nearly their husbands' equal before the law.[41] Marilyn Salmon's recent study of marriage settlements in South Carolina, however, indicates that while marriage settlements were successfully enforced in courts of equity, they were rarely used. She suggests that there is evidence that women were fearful of antagonizing men with such a device.[42]

While the extent of a colonial woman's control of her property and general legal status may be disputed, the role of a colonial woman in child custody issues is not in question. Marriage settlements did not give custody to the mother, or even confer equal custodial rights. They dealt with children only so far as to secure their inheritance from their mother. It was not until the nineteenth century that the newly developing women's rights movement attempted to include equal custodial rights and powers of testamentary guardianship for mothers in their state legislative campaigns to win property rights for all married women.[43]

Married women in colonial America, then, had no claim to the custody of their children during the marriage either at common law or in courts of equity. This powerlessness apparently extended to divorce. Although the examination of colonial divorce is by no means complete, existing studies give no indication that women attempted to challenge their husband's right to the custody of their children in divorce actions.[44]

The right to divorce was not uniformly established in colonial America. South Carolina, for example, did not grant its first divorce until 1868. Colonies like New York and Virginia followed the English tradition where full divorce was an ecclesiastical affair and only rarely granted. English law, until 1753, retained the principle of Canon law that no marriage can be destroyed. In those states, following English tradition, divorce could be obtained by a private bill in the legislature, but it appears in most cases this kind of divorce did not include the right to remarry. In New England divorce laws were more liberal, as marriage fell under the jurisdiction of the civil courts and legislatures. Following what they believed to be the laws of God, they granted divorce (with the right to remarry) when either party to a marriage could prove that the other had neglected a fundamental duty. The usual grounds for divorce were adultery, desertion, and absence for a length of time determined by the government. Connecticut developed the most liberal divorce policy and, not surprisingly, experienced the highest rate of divorce. Its statute specified "adultery, fraudulent contract, or willful desertion for three years with total neglect of duty, or seven year's providential absence being not heard of after due enquiry made and certifyed" as being acceptable grounds for divorce.[45] The ambiguous term "total neglect of duty" apparently meant failure of economic support, as evidenced by three divorces granted for desertion and nonsupport.[46]

The two most divorce-prone states, Massachusetts and Connecticut, have been fairly well studied. Twenty-seven divorces were granted in Massachusetts between 1639 and 1692. From 1692 to 179%, when all petitions were heard by the governor and his council, 115 petitions for divorce, 11 petitions for annulment, and 17 petitions for separate bed and board were filed, with a success rate of 68 percent for husbands and 58 percent for wives. In Connecticut the total numbers are unclear, since court records are incomplete, but the existing records provide good clues as to the patterns of divorce in that state.

Overall, in Connecticut and Massachusetts more women than men filed for divorce. The leading grounds for divorce were adultery and desertion. Men, however, were more likely to be granted a divorce for adultery alone than were women. Not until the 1770s in Massachusetts was the husband's adultery alone (without additional causes) considered adequate grounds for divorce. Property settlements were rarely mentioned, indicating that there was no property, that the issue had been resolved privately, or that the wife did not believe she had any claim to it.[47]

The most important aspect of these divorces is that children were not considered at all. In no cases do the courts speak about the best interests of the children, or indeed, show any concern for the children. Children were mentioned only in a peripheral context. For example, in Massachusetts, of the 229 eighteenth-century petitions for divorce, children were mentioned in only about one-third, usually to emphasize that this was a longstanding marriage with offspring that the offending spouse had ruined.[48] Sometimes children were mentioned because the children, generally infants, were pointed to as proof of the wife's adultery. Usually this occurred when the husband was absent for more than nine months, as with Walter Gustin of Connecticut, who testified that he left home on February 11, 1772, to visit his farm "160 Miles distance from Said Colchester and did not Return untill the 20th of December 1772 when he found Said Betty with Child in Adultery by Another man." Further testimony was offered by witnesses who were present at the birth of the baby on January 17; other witnesses attested to Walter's absence during the months he claimed to be visiting his farm. The divorce was granted.[49]

The absence of dispute over the custody of the children, which became a prominent issue in the nineteenth-century divorce cases, has at least two possible, not mutually exclusive explanations. The first is that mothers believed they had no chance to gain the custody of their children and therefore did not even advance this cause. There is anecdotal evidence that some women avoided divorce because they feared their husbands would take the children away from them. Nancy Shippen Livingston, from a prominent Philadelphia family, endured a loveless marriage in which her husband forced her to turn the baby over to his family to be brought up. Since she was living in New York, she could obtain a divorce only by a private bill in the legislature, which was a notoriously difficult feat. She considered hiring the dashing lawyer, Aaron Burr, to plead her case with the legislature, but lost courage when she realized that if she won the divorce her husband would gain complete custody and she could be prevented from ever seeing her child again.[50]

The belief that they had no legal right to their children was enforced by English precedent. The first known instance where an English Court of Equity gave custody to a mother rather than an unfit father did not occur until 1774, the very end of the colonial period. In Blisset's Case the chancellor, Lord Mansfield, allowed a mother to keep her six-year-old child when the father, a bankrupt, mistreated mother and child.[51] Lord Mansfield put forth the innovative notion that "the public right to superintend the education of its citizens necessitated doing what appeared best for the child, notwithstanding the father's natural right." This case, however, did not establish any change in direction. Twenty-five years later, in Rex v. DeManneville (1804), a mother ran away from an allegedly brutal husband, but Lord Ellenborough of the King's Bench, emphasizing a father's paramount right to custody of his children, returned the child to her father, even though "she was an infant at the breast of the mother."[52]

A second explanation for the absence of custody disputes during the colonial period is that mothers often got custody of the children without a fight. Women were most often granted divorces in cases of adultery or desertion, and it is unlikely that the father deserted with children in tow. In fluid, expanding colonial America, the father most likely "went West" in search of new opportunities and failed to send for his family. More than likely, many deserted wives never took the matter to court at all.

While the question of child custody following divorce is certainly an interesting one, it affected relatively few mothers and children, since divorce was rare in colonial America. The death of a father, however, was common, and in such instances the right of the surviving mother to custody and control of her children was legally and practically complicated. As noted earlier, survival rates, particularly in the seventeenth-century Chesapeake colonies, were grim. Of those children who survived to maturity, about half could expect to spend part of his or her childhood in the home of a stepfather or other guardian. While survival conditions were more favorable in New England, the death of a father was not uncommon.[53]

In the evolving common law tradition followed by the colonies, the mother was the natural guardian of her children upon the death of the father.[54] This simple rule, however, did not always apply if the father appointed someone else in his will, the mother remarried, the father left a large estate, or, conversely, left his family impoverished. The rule was further complicated by the fact that common law allowed for separate guardians of the person and the estate of the child.

An orphan in colonial America was defined as a child whose father had died, even if the child had a surviving mother. To facilitate the supervision of the large numbers of orphans, some colonies set up orphan's courts, and others handled orphan matters through the general courts, where supervision was perhaps not as keen. The two most active orphan's courts appear to have been in Maryland and Virginia; both were colonies where fathers did not enjoy a long life span. The purpose of these courts was to protect the person and property of the orphans. The surviving mother could be, and most often was, the guardian of the orphan's person, but unless she could find the sureties to pay for a bond to safeguard the child's portion, she could not be the guardian of the orphan's estate. If the mother remarried (and in colonies where women were scarce, she usually did so quickly), she once again became *femme couvert* and lost her ability to act as an independent legal being. The stepfather then was required to post a bond and submit to the court's supervision.

This process could be subverted, however, by the living father through the instrument of his will. Perhaps fearing a future unscrupulous stepfather or perhaps the limitations of his own wife, a father could appoint anyone as guardian, and the courts were bound to respect his testamentary wish. Theoretically, he could appoint someone other than the mother as the guardian of the child's person as well as estate, giving that guardian the right of custody. An English parliamentary act of 1660 codified the existing practice, providing that a father might "by deed executed in his lifetime, or by last will and testament in writing dispose of the custody of his minor children," and that this disposition should be "good and effective against all and every person claiming the custody and tuition of such children."[55] Statutes in Virginia and Maryland narrowed this principle to the guardianship of the orphan's estate, stating: "Concerning orphans' estates, be it enacted that all wills and testaments be firm and inviolable, unless the executors or overseers do refuse to execute the trust reposed in them by the testator."[56]

There is no evidence that it was common in colonial America for a father to give physical custody to any other than the mother, as long as she lived. Fathers, however, frequently appointed a male guardian for the orphan's estate, even when he was survived by his wife. It was a widespread practice to appoint a male relative to control the child's estate until the child reached twenty-one or, in the case of a girl, until she married. He could do this without the mother's consent.[57] Furthermore, courts might appoint a guardian for the child's estate if the father died intestate and the widow was not capable of raising a bond or simply did not want the responsibility of supervising the estate. In New Amsterdam, while still under Dutch rule, courts customarily appointed a guardian in all cases where the father died. In the seventeenth century fathers could die in great numbers, often with little warning. Following an Indian massacre in 1655 the burgomasters, as orphanmasters, appointed a guardian for all of the minor children left fatherless:

> The Burgomasters of this City as Orphanmasters have deemed it necessary, that following the usages of our Fatherland guardians be appointed for said child, in order that neither the child nor the widow may be injured in their rights and inherited property.[58]

In this case, the wishes of the widow were considered in the appointment choice.

In most instances, however, it appears that when a father left an inheritance for the child mothers or stepfathers retained custody of both the child and the child's estate. A study of Prince George County, Maryland Orphan Court records for the years 1696 through 1705 gives some indication of the guardianship procedure upon the death of the father. Of forty-six men whose estates went through probate, orphan's proceedings were held for the children of twenty-four. The fate of the children, if any, of the remaining twenty-two men is unknown. In the orphan's proceedings the court bound out the children of four landless men; the other twenty were landowners. The court took security for the bonds of seventeen of these twenty landowners, in most instances, from a mother or a stepfather. Besides these forty-six men, twenty-three landless men whose estates were not probated left orphans who were bound out to service.[59]

This study suggests that while mothers and their new husbands most often kept full custody of children with estates, mothers of children without estates were very likely to have their children bound out to another family because they could not support them. Sometimes the community would support the widow and her children for a short time, but this was usually a temporary measure until the children could be placed out. An order by the mayor's court of New York City in 1731 illustrates this custom:

> Orders the Church Wardens Visit Jane Mackintosh Widow whose husband was lately, unfortunately drownded and who is left with four small Children and nothing to Support herself or them and if they find them Objects of Charity to support them as they Shall see needfull until such time as the Children Can be put out or till further Order.[60]

In Prince George County, Maryland, children without estates far outnumbered children with estates. The court records of all colonies are filled with case of both widows and poor law officials indenturing orphans of all ages. Undoubtedly, most of these are children without estates. The laws of Virginia and Maryland insisted that children bound out as orphans by the Maryland orphans court should be taught a trade, but there is evidence in Virginia and other colonies that orphans were often simply put out to service, which meant they could be put to performing any kind of menial labor, with no hope of developing specific skills.[61]

A formal indenture contract usually bound boys until twenty-one or twenty-four years and girls until eighteen years. During this period mothers could presumably visit the children but could not regain custody. The indenture contract abolished parental rights to custody and control. Some mothers chose instead to pursue more temporary arrangements, at the end of which time they could regain custody of their children if they were capable of doing so. In one such arrangement, witnessed as a formal contract and recorded by a Maryland court, the widowed Elenor Empson gave Richard Dod two heifers to maintain her daughter Mary Empson for two years. The contract reflects that this was a desperate measure: "Note that I, the said Elenor Empson, am constrained to dispose of the said child above specified for the present relief, otherwise it might have perished in the condition I am left in."[62]

Stepfathers

Since many widows with children remarried, the role of stepfather is prominent yet unclear in colonial America. Under seventeenth-century English common law, as indeed under modern American family law, the stepfather stood in an uncertain legal position with regard to his stepchild. Under common law the mere relationship of stepfather and stepchild conferred no rights and imposed no duties. If, however, the stepfather voluntarily received the child into the home and treated it as a member of the family, the reciprocal rights and duties of the parent-child relationship were established and continued so long as the relationship lasted. If a man died intestate his stepchildren would not inherit from him.[63] Beyond that the law is mostly silent. We do have evidence that, as heads of households, the stepparent took on virtually all the rights and responsibilities of natural fathers. Certainly all the colonial laws requiring fathers, parents, and masters to maintain, educate, and train children and servants applied to stepfathers, who may well have had natural children in the household as well. There are also many references to stepfathers apprenticing their stepchildren, a role normally reserved for fathers. Of course, the mother of the children, *femme couvert* once again upon remarriage, lost the legal ability to make indenture contracts in her own right.

Stepfather, however, were limited in their rights and responsibilities. As heads of households, they were obliged to support the child they had accepted into the household, but not if the natural father was available. If the child was illegitimate the natural father still had to pay maintenance for the child, which he gave directly to the stepfather. In one such case the putative father was forced to make payments for his sexual transgressions both to the stepfather and to his wife's natural father. A Massachusetts county court decided:

> Joseph Hall of Lyn, charged by Elizabeth wife of Nathll Eastman of Salisbury, as being the father of her child before her marriage, and the charge having been proved true, was ordered to pay 121i. [pounds] toward the child's maintenance to the husband of Elizabeth, in provisions within two years. Hall was also to pay 51i. [pounds] according to the law to Jonathan Hudson, father of Elizabeth, for enticing her and frequenting her company contrary to her father's warning.[64]

The putative father, however, had only the obligation to support but no rights to the custody of the child as against the stepfather.

If the stepchild's mother died, the rights of the stepfather were greatly weakened. In a legal tradition that relied heavily upon legitimate bloodlines for purposes of inheritance, adoption was not a legal option. Not until the second half of the nineteenth century did child welfare become a central concern in custody matters, when the legal instrument of adoption was created by state legislatures. If the natural father had appointed a testamentary guardian to serve upon his wife's death, the courts could then be obliged to support this choice. The mother could not appoint a testamentary guardian in her own right until late in the nineteenth century, and therefore could not offer this legal advantage to the stepfather.[65] Even if the father had not appointed a testamentary guardian, the stepfather's claim was ambiguous. The stepfather could be confronted by other relatives vying for the custody of his stepchildren. Labor was scarce and healthy children were an important asset, a fact not ignored by the courts. Petitions on behalf of the stepfather before the Maryland orphan's court that argued for custody of the child as against the claims of the grandparents did not mention the best interests of the child but rather stressed the investment the stepfather had already made in the maintenance of the children and his need for their services.[66]

In practice most children remained with their stepfather, if he chose to keep them, but the community continued to keep a close watch on stepfathers. Court records are filled with accusations about stepfathers squandering the children's estate or mistreating the child. Under guardianship law a minor could appoint his own guardian of the estate at age fourteen. At that age Aaron Prother asked the Maryland court permission to choose his own guardian since "he has had the mishap sometime since to fall under the lash of an unfortunate father in law [stepfather]."[67] Neighbors and town officials also monitored the behavior of stepfathers as they did of fathers, but courts appeared more willing to remove a child from a stepfather than from a father for what was frequently referred to as "evil usage" or "hard usage" of their stepchildren.[68]

Stepmothers

Since widowers remarried just as did widows, stepmothers constituted a large class in colonial America. There is very little to say about the legal status of stepmothers because, like natural mothers, they were *femme couvert*, and had a legal existence only in the shadow of their husband. They, of course, would have assumed the mother's role in the household, and, presumably had a claim to the legally unenforceable "love and respect" due to natural mothers. Upon the death of her husband a stepmother had a weaker claim to the custody of their stepchildren than would a stepfather, since her economic and marital future was uncertain. Only if the father had made a will appointing the stepmother as the guardian of his children could a stepmother have a strong claim.

In some cases the court chose a blood relative over a stepmother. In Connecticut the stepdaughter of Edward Clark's widow was bound out to her aunt against the widow's objection. This could mean that, in the court's judgment, the stepmother was unable to maintain the girl and the nearest relative offered to do so. Although adoption was not yet a legal concept, binding out resembled adoption. It did not confer all the rights that legal adoption later offered, but it gave the relative a firm legal hold on the child until the child reached majority. It could also mean that the court chose the aunt because she was a blood relative and the stepmother was not.

In other instances, however, stepmothers prevailed against blood relatives. In a Maryland dispute the widow of Matthew Magbee fought for the custody of her stepchildren when they had been lured away by their maternal grandfather. The court initially granted the children to the stepmother, since she needed their help and was of "a Generall good character." When the children left to live with the grandfather who made them "fair and insinuating promises," the court ordered the grandfather to immediately return the children "which he by soe Claindestine and unjust manner Detaine[d]."[69]

These contradictory decisions indicate both the lack of clear legal principles regarding stepparents' rights and the practical strategy followed by the courts in placing the children where they could provide critical labor. Matthew Magee's widow had, in fact, other children who were still small. The court may have been concerned that the rest of the family would fall upon poor relief without the help of the older children.

Illegitimate Children

Neither the mother nor the father had a legal right to the custody of a child born out of wedlock in colonial America. English common law defined a bastard as *filius nullius*, the child and heir of no one, bearing no legally recognized relations with either parent. A bastard had no right to inheritance or maintenance. Furthermore, English common law refused to follow the Continental civil code practice of allowing the parents to legitimize their offspring with a subsequent marriage. Blackstone justified this policy by explaining that allowing subsequent legitimization "is plainly a great discouragement to the matrimonial state; to which one main inducement is usually not only the desire of having children, but also of procreating lawful heirs."[70] In an expansion of this harsh policy offspring from void or annulled marriages were also considered illegitimate.

The most important change in bastardy law occurred with the passage of the English Poor Law Act of 1576, which decreed that parents (both mother and father) had to pay for the upbringing of a bastard, thus relieving the public of those costs. This act also included criminal penalties for the parents' illegal sexual acts. This change in bastardy law was obviously not brought about for the benefit of the parents or the best interests of the child but rather as an economic measure to relieve the burden of public support and to deter future liaisons that would produce an economic burden. Fiscal motives determined policies treating bastards and their parents in the colonies as well. English bastardy law was imported more or less intact to the colonies. The harshness of the law, particularly the criminal penalties for fornication, suited the needs of the colonies to impose social control on a mobile and diverse population. It also met the financial needs of struggling communities, which did not need more mouths to feed.

Under English law, since an illegitimate child was not legally part of the mother's family, a bastard's place of settlement was the town in which he or she was born. That town then became responsible for the child and could assume custody. If an indigent mother gave birth in a town where she was not a resident, the poor law officials could theoretically separate the mother from the child and send the mother back to her original town of residence, which was the mother's place of settlement.[71] However, towns made decisions based on what was economically feasible and that usually included keeping a mother with a nursing child.

All the colonies adopted civil laws for support of the child and criminal penalties to discourage fornication. Massachusetts passed the criminal laws against fornication first, and not until 1660 did the state pass the law requiring putative fathers to maintain their children. This law, representative of those passed in other colonies, gave no rights to the father, only responsibilities.

> It is therefore ordered, and by this court declared, that where any man is legally convicted to be the father of a bastard child, he shall be at the care and charge to maintain and bring up the same, by such assistance of the mother as nature requireth and as the Court, from time to time (according to circumstances), shall see meet to order.[72]

If the putative father denied his fatherhood, evidence could be brought against him. Particularly damning was the accusation of the mother while giving birth; this was considered highly credible by the courts.

There is some evidence that the father could make the choice to take the child and bring it up himself or pay support to the mother or a foster mother, in which case he was obliged to post a bond with the poor law officials, "that the county may come to no charge." The mother, however, apparently was given no choice in the matter of whether the child was given to the father or remained with her. Judges also put pressure on the father to marry the mother, thereby relieving the community of its responsibility. In one such case the jury decided that Arthur Turner must either pay so many pounds of tobacco a year to Lucy Stratton for the child's support or bring up the child himself. Dissatisfied with this decision of the county court Turner appealed to the provincial court. The provincial court overturned the decision, because Turner had in fact asked Lucy to marry him after the birth the child. The provincial court decreed that since she had refused, Lucy must bring the child up herself, with no allowance from Turner.[73] If Lucy had agreed to marry Turner the problem of support would have been solved as far as the poor officials were concerned, but the child would still not be considered legitimate for purposes of inheritance.

The Chesapeake colonies, with their vast population of indentured servants, had particular problems with bastards, and passed laws to accommodate these problems. Since the birth of a bastard by a servant woman was considered an economic burden to the master, a Virginia statute mandated that she serve two more years beyond her indentures or pay two thousand pounds of tobacco to her master.[74] Apparently, this law had unintended negative consequences.

> Whereas by act of Assembly every woman servant having a bastard is to serve two years and late experience show[s] that some dissolute masters have gotten their maids with child and yet claim the benefit of their service, and on the contrary, if a woman got with child by her master should be freed from that service it might probably induce loose persons to lay all their bastards to their masters.

As a compromise, the legislature decreed that the servant must first complete her indentures. Thereafter, church wardens of the parish "where she lived when she was brought to bed of such a bastard," could sell her services for two years and use the wages for the parish.[75] This law illustrates that the responsibility for the bastard was in the hands of the poor law officials where the bastard was born. It also indicates that mothers were obligated to contribute to the support of their illegitimate children.

Colonial laws punishing fornication and demanding support by fathers were not simply prescriptive—they were widely enforced. Courts frequently ordered fathers to pay for maintenance of their bastard child. These orders sometimes included whippings for fornication, particularly applied to mothers. A survey of Prince George County Maryland records during the years 1696 to 1699 reveals important details of bastardy proceedings. During this period ten female servants were found guilty by the court of "bastardizing." In seven cases corporal punishment was imposed upon the mother, ranging from ten to thirty lashes (thirty for a third offender, and twenty-six for a servant bearing a mulatto bastard). In one case the offender was cleared of corporal punishment when the putative father paid the fine instead, and in another the court determined the bastard was born in another county and, therefore, the court had no jurisdiction.[76] In no case was a father whipped.

In several cases the court ordered the offending servant to serve an additional year or half year for the disgrace and trouble to her master's house and ordered the child to be bound out until the age of twenty-one, the party to the bond being obligated to teach the child to read and write and to furnish him, at the expiration of his time, with two suits and two of a sort of all necessary apparel. In one such instance the child was only thirteen months old.[77] A bond might be required of the master (twenty lb) or the father, and a second security (twenty lb) to indemnify the county against the maintenance of the child. The sheriff kept the mother in custody until all fees were paid.[78]

In two cases the alleged father of the bastard was presented at court. The fate of one putative father is not clear, but the other offender, found guilty by a petty jury, was fined twenty shillings and ordered to pay the damaged master eight hundred pounds of tobacco for the trouble to his house. He was ordered held in custody until he could pay the fines. In two other cases, an order was sent out for the alleged father to appear, but no indication of his appearance is recorded.

Several striking facts emerge from this admittedly scanty sample. First, none of these women were freewomen, which is not a surprise given the time and the place; most settlers to the Chesapeake colonies came as indentured servants. It is also possible that free women who had bastards might have been better able to settle the problem outside the law. The second noteworthy fact is that apparently none of these mothers kept custody of their children, and certainly none of the fathers took custody. In most cases the father was not identified, and in all such cases the child was apprenticed to another as soon as was feasible. One mother was given a reprieve while nursing: "Ruth Sansbury brought a Child of Stephen Ashbees (who is runneway)" and the court determined "it being not weaned . . . that it Continue with her the Said Ruth to have twelve Hundred pounds of Tobacco per year for Nurseing or it."[79]

The servant mother of the mulatto bastard in this sample was punished more severely than the other mothers, but it is unknown whether her bastard was required to serve longer than the other bastards or whether the term of the mother was extended. According to a law of Maryland (1664) the white mother of a mulatto child could receive more lashes as punishment of her fornication but could also lose her child to slavery if the father were a slave. In addition, she could be held to serve the same term as her "husband." While all the colonial laws eventually decreed that the child inherited the mother's and not the father's slave status, an exception apparently was made in Maryland for a period of time.[80]

And, forasmuch as divers freeborn English women, forgetful of their free condition and to the disgrace of our nation, do intermarry with Negro slaves . . . [they] shall serve the master of such slave during the life of her husband and that all the issue of such freeborn women so married shall be slaves as their fathers were.[81]

In Virginia a "free Christian white woman" who had a child by a mulatto or Negro was required to pay a large fine or serve an additional five years.[82] Her bastard child was apprenticed until the age of thirty-one rather than twenty-one. Moreover, if that child were female, her children were also mandated to serve until thirty-one.[83] These laws effectively placed mulatto children who were not slaves into a twilight zone between regular apprenticeships and lifetime slavery.

Most mothers who had children out of wedlock probably lost custody once they were weaned. In that sense they were treated no differently than poor widows and impoverished parents, whose children were removed by the poor officials and bound out to families who could maintain them. Unwed mothers, however, were subject to whippings and the social shame attached to illegitimacy, and if they were servants their service usually was extended to compensate for the expense and inconvenience to their master. Their children would endure a lifelong stigma as bastards. As already noted, adoption was not a legal option until the late nineteenth century; the only option for bastards was indentured servitude. While some families were undoubtedly kind to their servants, bastards usually were not treated as natural children. Even as an indentured servant among other indentured servants, the child's identity as a bastard would travel with him or her. One complaint brought before the orphans court in Maryland alluded to the status hierarchy among child apprentices. In this instance the neighbors complained that William Watt's orphans were "putt to unreasonable Labour, supposing them to have been bastard Children much orphans that had an Estate left them."[84]

Signs of change began to appear at the end of the colonial period. Both Virginia and Rhode Island passed statutes granting bastards inheritance rights from their mothers.[85] The Virginia statute declared that bastards "shall be capable of inheriting or transmitting inheritance on the part of their mother, in like manner as if they had been lawfully begotten of such mothers."[86]

Probably not prompted by child welfare concerns, these laws reflected the sweeping changes in feudal inheritance laws that preceded and followed the birth of the new republic. It was not until the nineteenth century that concern for child welfare slowly spread to include bastards as well as natural children. By the end of that century almost every state had passed legislation declaring that a bastard child was a member of its mother's family (not his father's), with a right to inherit from the mother, the same as a legitimate child.[87]

Masters and Servants

A very large proportion of children in the colonial era did not spend their whole childhood under the custody and control of their own parents or step-parents. These children were put under the custody and control of masters (and sometimes mistresses), to whom they were indentured. "Binding out," "putting out," or "apprenticing" were all variations on the well-established English custom of placing children in the home of a master who was obliged to provide ordinary sustenance and some training in return for services. This training could be as specific as teaching a skilled craft or it could be as general as instruction in basic reading and the catechism. Laws under common law differed pertaining to articles of indenture for servants and for apprentices. In the New World the distinction between indentures for servants and apprentices was less clear. Binding out or apprenticing became a catch-all concept that both provided a controllable and skilled labor force to the new country and parent figures to thousands of children who had no parents. Whatever the terms of the indenture contract, it was ratified and supervised by the local court.

The master-servant relationship established by the indenture contract closely reflected the parent-child relationship. Master and servant shared mutual obligations, as did parent and child, and for the most part these obligations were the same; courts often described the master as serving in loco parentis. While the affectional bonds between a father and his child may have been of an entirely different nature, the legal responsibilities of father and master were not. Many laws, such as the Massachusetts Bay Colony law referred to earlier, assigned identical duties to fathers and masters regarding the care and training of the children in their charge. In return masters could expect labor from their charges, just as fathers could. Blackstone clearly supported this analogy. "The father has the benefit of his children's labor while they live with him and are maintained by him; and this is no more than he is entitled to from his apprentices or servants."[88]

In a society where production relied on the economic services of children, the law strongly supported this master-servant relationship. In the absence of social workers and children's protective services, the courts cooperated with poor officials in creating and supervising the indentures of orphaned or impoverished children. They also settled the disputes between parents and masters over the treatment of apprentices and ordered runaway apprentices back to their masters if they could not prove gross abuse. While courts rarely, if ever, heard custody disputes following divorce, colonial courts everyday struggled with problems relating to the "placing out" of children.

Courts supervised a broad variety of indentures, roughly divided into two categories: 1. voluntary apprenticeships, where a parent voluntarily arranged with a third party, usually to train the child in a specific trade in exchange for the child's services; and 2. involuntary apprenticeships, where the parents were dead or unable to properly raise their children and the town poor law officials placed them with a master, primarily in order to relieve the town of the financial burden. In the absence of the legal form of adoption involuntary apprenticeships were also used to ratify the legal position of close relatives who took in a child upon the death of the child's parents. Both types of indenture contracts were under the jurisdiction of the county court and were usually not enforced by other courts if the master moved.[89]

Involuntary Apprenticeships

Children who came to America as indentured servants without parents provided critical labor for the settlement of the colonies. More than half of all persons who came to the colonies south of New England were indentured servants, and most servants were under nineteen years old.[90] Whether these children who came alone to the colonies came as voluntary or involuntary servants is unknown. Certainly, some of the older children voluntarily signed their own indentures, as did adults, in hopes of a fresh start in an uncrowded country. However, many children were orphans, or children of the poor, and their indentures, like those of all impoverished children, were not voluntary.

In 1617 the Virginia Company actively solicited the lord mayor of London to send poor children to settle the colony. The lord mayor complied by authorizing a charitable collection to grant five pounds apiece for equipment and passage money, while the children were to be apprenticed until the age of twenty-one and afterward to have fifty acres of land in the plantation to be held in fee simple at a rent of one shilling a year.[91] This arrangement apparently worked well, and was initiated again in 1619 for "one hundred children out of the multitude that swarm in that place to be sent to Virginia."[92]

The children, like all settlers, did not survive long in deadly Virginia, and the London City Council once again complied with a request in 1622 for the transportation of another hundred children, "being sensible of the great loss which [the plantation] lately susteyned by the barbarous cruelty of the savage people there."[93]

A similar process occurred in New Netherland (later named New York), where the directors of the West India Company asked for and received several shiploads of poor and/or orphaned children from Amsterdam. An official of Fort New Amsterdam asked for more children in 1658 but specified their age: "Please to continue sending others from time to time: but, if possible, none ought to come less than fifteen years of age and somewhat strong, as little profit is to be expected here without labor."[94]

Other children, many of whom were not orphans or under the control of the poor law officials, were tricked into indentured servitude by "spiriters" who gained a healthy profit for each suitable child (or adult) they could deliver to the colonies, where they sold their indentures. The custom grew out of hand by the middle of the seventeenth century; victims often were blatantly kidnapped and held prisoner for a month or so until sent off to sea. One father obtained a warrant to search the ship for his eleven-year-old son whom he claimed had been spirited away. The search uncovered nineteen servants, eleven of whom had been taken by "spirits," most against their will.[95] The spirit trade provoked public outrage and fear. Petitioned by merchants, planters, and masters of ships, the attorney general of Charles II established in 1664 a central registry recording the contracts of all servants leaving for the colonies. This remedy was supplemented by fierce prosecution of those caught spiriting.

Given the circumstances of immigration, many children arrived with irregular indentures or none at all. The law required the would-be master to bring the child before the court to determine the terms of the indenture. Most common was the term set by the Virginia legislature: "Such persons as shall be imported, having no indenture or covenant, either men or women, if they be above sixteen years old shall serve four years, if under fifteen to serve till he or she shall be one and twenty years of age, and the courts to be judges of their ages."[96] Other colonies fixed eighteen years of age or marriage as the termination date of indentures for girls.

The law did not require that masters teach these child immigrants a specific trade but rather allowed them to put the children to whatever service they wished. At the termination of the indenture, however, the law required masters to provide the servant with a suitable wardrobe and some provisions. A North Carolina law specified: "Every Christian servant shall be allowed by their master or mistress at the expiration of his or her time of service three barrels of Indian corn and two new suits of apparel of the value of five pounds at least or, in lieu of one suit of apparel, a good well-fixed gun, if he be a man servant."[97]

In the New England colonies and in colonies south of New England, following the first decades of intense immigration, children were most often involuntarily apprenticed when their parents were unable or unwilling to care for them properly. Adoption was not then a legal option, and orphanages and asylums for children were rare until the end of the eighteenth century. The town of the child's "settlement" was responsible for the child's welfare. Elaborate laws determined how "settlement" would be carried out, since no town was eager to take on an unnecessary burden. Generally, the child's place of the birth was its settlement if neither his mother nor father had one. However, if the father or the mother had a town of settlement, that was the child's, in that order of preference.[98] Bastards, however, as *filius nullius*, had only the town in which they were born.

The officials of the child's town of settlement charged with administering the poor laws took charge of these children and, with appropriate approval of the court, "bound them" to an appropriate master who gained full custody and control of the child, but under continued court supervision. Once the child was bound out the parents, if alive, lost any legal claim to its custody. In the case of orphans the child was often bound out to a close relative, providing the legal custodial authority to the relatives that was not available by adoption. If the child was an infant poor law officials might pay a family to nurse the child until it was old enough to bind out. In this instance poor law officials maintained legal control of the child. These infants were often bastards. The records for one parish in Virginia between 1748 and 1753 indicate that fully half of the poor relief paid out went to families for the purposes of keeping a bastard child for a year.[99]

The conditions of indenture or apprenticeship for children who were bound out by poor law officials were very similar to those of immigrant children. There was, however, one notable departures from this tradition; they often included a covenant to provide basic education. Moreover, poor law officials made an effort to insist upon specific vocational training as well as elementary reading, writing, and arithmetic. Colonial laws gradually supported education of poor involuntary apprentices, with laws mandating this as early as 1642 in Massachusetts but as late as 1705 in Virginia.

Marcus Jernegan's examination of the indenture records of two Virginia parishes in the mid-eighteenth century indicates the type of child that was involuntarily apprenticed and the nature of the indentures. Orphans constituted 38.1 percent of all child apprentices; 39.3 percent were classified as poor children, 11 percent were described as illegitimate, and 12.6 percent were termed mulatto. Boys were most often apprenticed to learn the trade of carpenter, shoemaker, blacksmith, planter, or farmer. Girls were usually apprenticed as domestic servants with no trade mentioned. Out of 163 apprentices, all but forty-two had some education requirement in their indentures. Of those forty-two without educational requirements fourteen were mulatto children and 4 were children of free Negroes.[100]

The reality was that many poor apprentices often had to settle for less than their indentures specified. In some cases there was a bargaining process about the conditions of the apprenticeship; usually that meant exchanging time served for a specific training. For instance, in Pennsylvania "William Cope brought a boy whose name is Thomas Harper, who was adjudged to serve five years and three quarters, if he be taught to read and write, or else to serve but five years, to him or his assigns."[101]

Some aspects of the articles of indenture resembled a contract for chattels more than an employment contract. If the master died the remaining years of the indenture were often counted in his estate. When the sheriff of Kent County was ordered to seize the property of Elllis Humphrey to the extent of ten thousand pounds of tobacco for the benefit of the lord proprietary, the appraisers listed one servant boy with four years to serve, eleven poor, weak cows, a handmill, and a grindstone. The servant boy was valued at twenty-eight hundred pounds of tobacco.[102] Many indentures, like that of Pennsylvanian Thomas Harper noted above, specifically stated that the apprentice's time belonged to his heirs. Some indentures included even more elaborate estate planning. A Connecticut court bound John Gennings to Jeremiah Adams in 1661, ordering that Gennings would finish his term with Adams's widow if he died, with another relative if they both died, and if it became necessary to "otherwise dispose of Gennings the benefit is to return to Jer[emiah Adams] or his assignees."[103] On the other hand, many children were returned to their parents or to the charge of the poor law officials upon the death of the master.

Although a master could devise the custody of his apprentice following his death to specified heirs, he could not assign his apprentice to another during his life without the consent of the poor law officials and the approval of the court. The assignment was made in consideration for payment by the second master, thereby constituting a form of child selling. Statutes regulating masters and servants in several colonies indicated that this approval was necessary. With approval, however, custody was transferred, and "said assignee, upon accepting such assignment, shall be equally bound to the said apprentice, according to the tenor or the said indenture as the original master or mistress was."[104] In many southern states indentures forbade masters to move out of the original jurisdiction with their apprentices. Others allowed this only with the consent of the servant and the approval of two justices of the peace.[105]

These restrictions represented effort on the part of the poor law officials and the court to provide continuing supervision of the child's welfare.

The relationship between master and apprentice was set by statute and enforced by the courts. The law strongly supported the enforcement of indentures, since apprentices were a major factor in the labor force, and dealt harshly with apprentices who disobeyed their masters or ran away. The penalty for runaway apprentices was to extend their indentures from three to five times the number of days they were absent. Rewards were given for those who turned in runaway apprentices. According to a Pennsylvania statute, "Whoever shall apprehend or take up any runaway servant, and shall bring him or her to the sheriff of the county, such person shall, for every such servant, if taken up within ten miles of the servant's abode, receive ten shillings: and if ten miles or upwards, twenty shillings reward."[106] Striking a master was a punishable crime while, when the master disciplined the apprentice, courts often gave the benefit of the doubt to the master. Even when masters treated their servants with unusual cruelty they were let off lightly. In Salem, for instance, Philip Fowler was accused of abuse his servant, Richard Park, by hanging him by his heels. The court determined that while any person was was justified "in giving meet correction to his servant, which the boy deserved . . . they do not approve of the manner of punishment given in hanging him up by the heels as butchers do beasts for the slaughter, and cautioned said Fowler against such kind of punishment."[107] If the master actually killed his apprentice through cruel treatment, he could be appropriately tried and punished for manslaughter or murder and could be executed, as was William Franklin of Boston, who "by sundry cruel stripes and other kinds of ill usage" caused a boy to die "under his rigorous hand, and that (by a strange providence of God and his own folly) at Boston, as if God meant to bring him on the stage for an example to all others."[108]

Voluntary Apprenticeships

Voluntary apprenticeships occurred when the parent or guardian entered into an agreement with a third party (master) for the apprenticeship of their child or ward. These agreements were approved by the local court. Voluntary apprenticeships were sought 1. when the parents or guardians themselves felt that they could no longer support or raise a child, and 2. when the parents or guardians sent the child to a master to receive specialized training in order to prepare them for a career as a skilled artisan. Edmund Morgan, in his study of the Puritan family, suggests that Puritan parents had a third reason: to prevent parents from loving their children too much and God less.[109] This final reason, however, is not evident in the testimony of the court records, while the first two are.

There was little practical difference between impoverished or incapable parents binding out their own children or waiting until the poor law officials took over the chore. Town council proceedings are filled with pleas for parents to take this responsibility. For instance, Robert Styles of Dorchester, Massachusetts, was admonished for not attending public worship, neglecting his calling, and not submitting to authority. He was ordered to "put forth his children, or otherwise the selectmen are hereby empowered to do it according to law."[110] Fathers were not the only ones authorized to bind out children they were not able to keep. Widows also had that authority, unless there was a testamentary guardian, and putative fathers were frequently enjoined by the court to bind out their bastard or pay the town maintenance. Stepfathers and other male relatives performed the function when necessary. In a country where long and unpredictable ocean voyages were a necessary part of commerce with the motherland, fathers sometimes just disappeared. In one such case William Chicester of Salem had left his wife Mary with several children and no means to bring them up. Her father was forced to apprentice her ten-year-old son James to Frances Scerry of Salem. Scerry agreed to send him "to schoole untill he can write a leagable hand, to give him one ewe lamb to keep, to pay him ten pounds at the end of his time in corn or cattle and a suite of clothes for Lord's day and one for working days."[111]

The second type of voluntary apprenticeship was the more truly voluntary act of securing appropriate vocational training for a child. This practice stemmed from medieval practice, as institutionalized in the Statute of Artificers of 1562. In England the purpose of apprenticeships was to control competition among trades by requiring all workers to have completed their apprenticeship. In labor-hungry America these requirements could not be enforced, and apprenticeships offered a general trade education, not a guild certificate. Boys usually entered their apprenticeship between the ages of ten and fourteen and served for seven years or until they were twenty-one. Girls served until eighteen or marriage. The apprentice lived in the master's household and saw his own family only with the master's permission.[112] The parent relinquished custody and control of the child under the indenture contract, and this right as well as the responsibilities that adhered to the father passed to the master.

In the Puritan colonies the issue of vocational training was taken very seriously; the choice of an apprenticeship for a child was a decision not lightly taken. The Puritans believed that every individual had a religious calling that directed him or her toward God and a personal calling that determined his or her employment. Puritan minister Cotton Mather advised his congregation: "See to it, O Parents, that when you choose Callings for your Children, you wisely consult their Capacities, & their inclinations: lest you Ruine them. and, Oh! cry mightily to God, by Prayer, yea with Fasting and Prayer, for His Direction when you are to resolve upon a matter of such considerable consequence.[113]

The language of indentures for this formal training was very much like that of involuntary indentures, with the addition of the obligation to train the child in a specific trade. The major difference between voluntary and involuntary indentures, however, was that the indentures were entered into between the apprentice (if the apprentice were old enough, at least twelve) and the master, with the consent of the parents. Therefore it was up to the parent, not the poor officials, to supervise and enforce the indentures. The parents had lost the right to custody and governance of their children, but they could still pursue their child's welfare by suing for strict enforcement of the indenture contract.

Parents sued masters frequently, e.g., for abusing their child, for failing to teach their child a trade, for not instructing them, for having the child work on Sunday, or for not caring for them when they were sick. Masters also brought actions against parents when their apprentice returned home, for interfering with business, and for lost services. The standard of care expected from the master was not always clear. Certainly he had the right to punish an apprentice as a parent would, but the degree of punishment was unclear. Jan Van Hoesem of New York sued Joachim Wesselson for kicking his daughter, rendering her unable to work. Wesselson answered that Van Heosem's daughter "was admonished by his wife to mend her ways as she was a young maiden, whereupon she, making some retort, the woman was moved to chastize her."[114] On the other hand, when children returned home to their parents masters could successfully sue on the contract, unless they could be shown to be failing in their duties. The court in Plymouth severely rebuked parents whose five-year-old son frequently wandered home, and ordered that if the parents "do receive him, if he shall again [depart] from his said master without his lycense, that the said Frances, and Chrisian his Wyfe, shall be sett in the stocks every lecture day during the tyme thereof, as often as he or shee shall so receive him."[115]

Children and Slavery

When the War for Independence began in 1776 about one in five American children was a slave. In some of the southern states the majority of children were slaves (slaves constituted two-thirds of the population in South Carolina). Already by 1700 slaves constituted the bulk of the agricultural labor force in Virginia, Maryland, and South Carolina, and their numbers exploded almost fifteenfold during the following three decades leading up to the revolution.

Indentured Servitude to Slavery

While a good deal of scholarly attention has been paid to the role of slavery in the development of the colonial labor force, very little study has focused specifically on black children and their role in this labor force. There is, in fact, a clear continuum from indentured child servants and apprentices to child slaves. All of these children were essential elements of the labor force and all were under the control of masters who had almost unlimited rights to the custody and control of their persons. With slave ownership as with contracts of indenture, natural parents forfeited all legal rights to their children to the master. While masters of slave children could sell the children without legal restriction, masters of apprentices could assign the time remaining on their contract for money (usually with the approval of the local court). Unless a child's indentures specified a particular trade, the master of an apprentice or an indentured servant could put the child to work at any task and for any length of time. The condition of indentured servitude could be in force during the whole span of childhood, since many children were "put out" as infants and not released until they turned eighteen or twenty-one.

The continuum between indentured servitude and slavery is demonstrated in the laws for the gradual abolition of slavery, initiated by conscience-stricken legislators in the northern states during the last part of the eighteenth century. Recognizing the property interest of slaveholders, these statutes did not free the adults already in slavery, but set terms of freedom for their children, which were like those of indentured servants. The first such law, passed by the Pennsylvania legislature in 1780, decreed that all children who would have been born into slavery then were required to serve their owner "until such child shall attain unto the age of twenty-eight years, in the manner and on the conditions whereon servants bound by indenture for four years are."[116] The designation of twenty-eight years rather than the usual twenty-one placed these children of slaves in a middle ground between child apprentices and lifetime servants.

To emphasize the similarities between the condition of children in various forms of servitude does not detract from the central fact that, both legally and conceptually, slavery was a distinctly different condition than indentured servitude. The central legal distinction was that indentured servitude was a contractual employment arrangement with rights and obligations adhering to both master and servant, while slavery was a form of property ownership where the slave held a legal status most closely akin to chattel. This meant that, short of murder, the master could use or abuse him as he could a horse. The master of an apprentice, as we have seen, was limited in the degree of physical punishment he could inflict upon his servant and was required to provide adequate food and shelter and, in most cases, elementary literacy and training in religion.

Conceptually, indentured servitude had a built-in termination date, and while the condition of servitude may have lasted until adulthood, the child and the adults in control of the child both understood its limits. The child would someday become the legal equal of the adult. Another distinction is that the condition of slavery only adhered to black children, who were looked upon as permanently inferior. While an apprentice might sit at the same table and be treated the same as the natural children of the master's household, a slave child would almost never be treated with such respect.

Race, of course, played a central and complicated role in this continuum of child labor arrangements in the colonies. Not all black children were born to slave mothers. There was always a sizable number of free blacks in the North and smaller numbers in the southern colonies. Even in the southern colonies the children of free blacks were not automatically "put out" unless their parents could not support them. As a Kentucky court observed:

> The mere fact that these are colored persons does not put them out of the protection of the law, nor subject them to be dealt with or disposed of with a view merely to the interest of individuals. There must be some ground of necessity, in view of the requirements of the law, to authorize the binding out of these children.[117]

Mulatto children were automatically determined to be slaves if their mothers were slaves, but if their mothers were free white women, they were often placed in a "twilight zone" between normal indentured servitude and slavery. Mulatto children of white mothers were treated more harshly than free black children, since there was a widespread fear and loathing of miscegenation. As noted earlier, it was possible, at least in one state for a period of time, to consider the offspring of slave fathers and free white mothers as servants for life. There was a great increase of illegitimate mulatto children in the eighteenth century, which the law attempted to curb by punitive means. Generally, the law in the southern colonies dictated that all mulatto children, whether born of free or servant white women, must be bound out to service, usually until thirty or thirty-one years of age.[118] The punishment did not stop with the child of the offender: it was extended to future generations.

Where any female mullato, or indian, by law obliged to serve 'till the age of thirty or thirty-one years, shall during the time of her servitude, have any child born of her body, every such child shall serve the master or mistress of such mullato or indian, until it shall attain the same age the mother of such child was obliged by law to serve unto.[119]

American Indians offered yet a another classification problem. Some Indians were taken as slaves following their capture in war but they proved unsatisfactory. Not only could they slip back into the wilderness and survive, but they could also inspire their tribe to undertake a bloody revenge attack.[120] Although they were discriminated against in many ways, few of their children were raised as slaves, and, for most of the same reasons that they were not suitable for slavery, they did not make reliable apprentices. Therefore, Indian children were far more likely than black or mulatto children to be raised by their own parents, outside of white settlements. At least in some states when Indians were indentured, they were placed in the same twilight zone of thirty to thirty-one years of service along with mulatto children.[121]

Mothers and Slavery

The "peculiar institution" of slavery posed peculiar custody issues for slave children and their parents. Perhaps the most peculiar was the legal and practical connection of the slave child to its mother and the complete repudiation of the father; the reverse of the situation in a free white family.

> I Cuthbert Fenwick, in consideration of the unfained love and affection that I bear unto Mrs. Jane Maryson . . . Do by these points give, grant confirm and endow . . . for & behalf of the said Jane, Three negro servants (VIZ) Two negro men, & One negro woman, to say, William Allington and Tom Payne and Nan: & all their issue both male and female, Six Milch Cowes & Three Heyfers with their encrease, Two young Mares, and a Stone horse, with their increase.[122]

This Maryland will, executed by Cuthbert Fenwick before his marriage to Mrs. Jane Maryson in 1649, both illustrates the attitude of masters toward children born into slavery and the confusion of the law as to how to deal with this new legal institution. The master, Cuthbert Fenwick, clearly considered unborn slave children as property even before their birth and classified them with the potential issue of his cows and the horses. Since there was no precedent for slavery under English common law, courts split on whether one could actually devise children not yet conceived. As one Virginia court put it, "I have mentioned of Possibilitys Cases in Point cannot be expected there being no Slaves in England." That court found the devise of unborn slave children void on the general principle that "it is a known rule that a bare possibility cannot be devised."[123] Since the devise of future slave children was common in colonial wills, it may be assumed that it was most often allowed or simply not contested.

Another puzzling part of this agreement was that the unborn children in question were the issue of the two male slaves, William Allington and Tom Payne, as well as one female, Nan. Slave children were owned by their mother's master. Unless Fenwick owned the mothers as well as the fathers, he could not give away the children of male slaves. The designation of the child's slave status through the child's mother, not father, was one aspect of the development of the institution of slavery in the New World that might have gone differently. It contradicted the general English common law principle that a child's status was inherited from the father. In fact, a short-lived Maryland statute in 1664 decreed that "the condition of children of slaves was fixed after that of their fathers."[124] Early on, however, it became apparent that white men, particularly white masters, would frequently impregnate slave women. It would be a significant property loss if these children were recognized as free according to their father's status. Therefore, all southern states eventually followed the lead of Virginia, which in 1662 declared: "Whereas some doubts have arisen whether children got by any Englishman upon a negro woman should be slave or free. Be it therefore enacted . . . that all children born in this country shall be held bond or free only according to the condition of the mother."[125]

By severing the connection of a child's legal status from that of its father, the legal institution of slavery, as it became established in colony after colony, made fatherhood an irrelevancy. By contrast to the complete dominance that free white fathers held over their children, the institution of slavery totally ignored fathers. This is not to say, of course, that a slave mother had legal rights to the custody and control of her children, but the practicalities of slavery gave the mother a certain degree of protection in maintaining physical, if not legal custody of her children until they were around ten years old. In fact, it may be argued that slave women had a somewhat better chance of holding onto their children than did mothers of illegitimate children or impoverished widows, whose children were often "put out" after weaning to relieve the public of their charge.

The economics of slavery inadvertently strengthened the role of slave mothers. According to historian Allan Kulikoff, investigator of the origins of the African-American family, planters kept women and their small children together but did not keep husbands and teenage children with their immediate family.[126] It made sense for planters to keep the valuable asset of their future labor supply alive and healthy. Young children sold separately from their mother would have had little value, and less chance of being raised to successful adulthood. As the African slave trade was cut off toward the end of the eighteenth century, children became even more valuable as the only source for replenishing the labor force.[127] By contrast, town poor officials, faced with supporting the child of an unwed mother or of a poor widow, were motivated to find someone else to take the child and support it.

In addition to economic incentives, there was moral pressure on masters to keep mothers and young children together. While the law certainly allowed planters to sell the children away from their mothers, since their status was akin to chattels, some judges seemed influenced by moral pressure as well, and were reluctant to enforce such sales. For example, when a Kentucky heir objected to the sheriff's sale of the mother and three-year-old child together, the court responded,

> The mother and child were indeed physically divisible, but morally they were not so: and the sheriff in selling them together certainly acted in conformity to the dictates of humanity, and probably in pursuance of the interest of the owner. If the child had been sold separately from its mother, it is pretty certain its value would have been greatly diminished.[128]

Slave families, then, tended to cluster around the mothers, and would sometimes be more geographically stable than the white families that owned them, since they were often bequeathed or sold with the land. For instance, Daphne was born on a large plantation in Prince George, Maryland, in 1736. From that date until 1787 she had six different masters, but she still lived where she was born. Daphne lived with her mother until her mother's death, and with her ten children until 1779, when two of her younger children were sold to a farm several miles away. She continued to live on the plantation with her older children and grandchildren and had contact with her younger children as well.[129] In this manner a large extended family of kin developed between nearby plantations.

There were, however, significant variations in time and place with respect to who raised slave children. The initial wave of Africans were mostly young adult males who were placed on small plantations. They were likely to be sold off, and children, originally few in number, were kept with their mothers. Later, when plantations grew larger in some southern colonies and more women and children were present, the family was less likely to be separated. In his study of very large Maryland plantations in the second half of the eighteenth century, Kulikoff found that 47 percent of households with children contained both husband and wife. On the other hand, only 18 percent of the families with eight or fewer slaves in the same county contained both mother and father.[130] While this does not represent definitive evidence of the condition of all plantations in all colonies, it makes economic sense that small plantations would not be able to support burgeoning families. While mothers and children under ten would probably remain as a unit, any slave could be sold at any time.

Ironically, slave children in northern colonies, where there was a strong humanitarian sentiment against slavery, were more likely than southern slave children to be separated from both mother and father. Black slaves represented only a very small fraction of the eighteenth-century northern population, but, in contrast to southern blacks, many lived in households near urban and commercial centers where there were only a few slaves. In such an environment maintaining slaves was expensive, and masters viewed children as an economic liability rather than an asset. Since slave marriages were discouraged, most women slaves married "abroad," the term for marrying outside the household. Therefore, a child was not likely to be raised with its father, and the child had a good chance of being separated from its mother as well. It was common for masters to sell infants or to apprentice older children to avoid the expense of raising them. One New England master offered to give away a slave child free of charge to anyone who would take the baby off his hands.[131]

Conclusion

Overall, the economic needs of the colonies determined the custodial arrangements of children, superceding child nurturing and often biological parenthood. Childhood, even for those children raised by their natural parents, was a time for work, and for preparation to become adult workers. Vast numbers of children were orphans, bastards, or had parents too poor to care for them. They were quickly "put out" to provide labor in another household and to relieve the community of any burden of support. In the eighteenth century increasing numbers of children were born as slaves, whose only function in life was to provide labor for their master.

The mutual obligations of a master-servant relationship, rather than a parent-child relationship in the modern sense, best describes the legally enforceable bonds between the adult, who held custody and control of the child, and the child, who held rights similar to those of an employee. The head of the household, whether he wore the hat of father, or master of indentured servants, had complete rights to the labor of the children in his custody and had strictly enforced obligations as to their training and education. When the children in his custody were slaves the master held further rights, including the unconditional right to sell them, and was burdened with few responsibilities. The mother played only an assistant's role to this master, and held few enforceable rights or responsibilites toward her children. A free white mother could lose her children completely on account of poverty, divorce, widowhood, or illegitimacy. A slave mother's child could be sold away from her at any moment.

While individual children may have been loved, protected—even spoiled, the law principally enforced the labor relationship and paid little heed to the needs of children for nurturing. The "best interests of the child" slowly developed as a legal concern in the new republic, when, at least for a growing class of parents, child labor needs were less urgent, and children were assigned an emotional value, enhanced by the romanticization of their mothers.

2

From Fathers' Rights to Mothers' Love: The Transformation of Child Custody Law in the First Century of the New Republic, 1790–1890

Maria Barbour, age nine, was indentured to Benjamin Gates in 1865 by her mother, a widow. Under the contract of indenture Maria was to remain with Gates until she reached eighteen, but after three years her mother, in better position, asked to have the child returned to her. She claimed that the indenture contract was technically defective, since the judge was not a proper justice of the peace, there was no revenue stamp, and the postage stamp was not canceled.

Dismissing the defects of the contract, the judge found that the mother did indeed sever her right to legal custody by indenturing her child, but nonetheless found the mother the better custodian, "because of all the affection she must feel for her offspring."[1] The court returned the child to her mother, claiming, "The laws of nature have given her an attachment for her infant offspring which no relative will be likely to possess in equal degree."[2]

In this decision the court rejected well-established indenture law, under which the child, like the subject of any contract, has no rights and the parent, as contractor, can sue only on the terms of the contract.[3] The judge looked to the interests of the child, rather than the technical imperfections or performance of the contract, and determined on the basis of natural law that the child's nurturing was best performed by her mother.[4]

The legal and social status of the child was transformed during the first century of the new republic. While the transformation came slowly in contrast to the fast pace of political events or economic development, it was nevertheless relentless. The colonial view of children as helping hands in a labor-scarce economy gave way to a romantic, emotional view of children, who were no longer legally akin to servants, under the complete control of their fathers or masters, but instead were deemed to have interests of their own. Increasingly, these interests became identified with the nurturing mother.

This significant shift in perspective altered the legal forms of custody in the nineteenth century, but change did not occur smoothly or completely. At the end of the century many judges were still reciting the common law maxim that "the natural right is with the father, unless the father is somehow unfit."[5] However, the laws regarding bastardy, custody following divorce, testamentary guardianship, and voluntary and involuntary apprenticeship were fundamentally altered by this new attitude toward children. In addition, the modern legal arrangement of adoption was developed to meet the newly recognized needs of children for family nurturing.

Most of these changes favorable to children, however, were confined to the sphere of private law, where the law settled disputes over custody of a child between private parties. Children who were dependents of the state because of their parents' death, abandonment, or poverty did not fare as well, nor did slave children freed during the Civil War. Relieving the economic burden of a public charge rather than catering to the best interests of the child, was still the guiding principle of most communities until late in the nineteenth century. Poor law officials wielded almost unlimited custodial control with little supervision by the legislatures or the courts.

Motherhood and Women's Rights

While a few legal historians have noted the changes in the law that emphasized the child's interests and effectively shifted the presumption from father to mother during this century, there has been only a limited attempt to explain the complex historical factors that prompted this change.[6]

In private law the changing status of their mothers was the single most important factor contributing to the new consideration for children's needs, and to the corresponding changes in their legal status. The status of mothers was transformed by two conflicting historical movements: the cult of motherhood and the campaign for women's rights.

The cult of motherhood describes the new emphasis that society put on the role of the mother in raising children. According to historian Maxine Margolis, one of the most striking features of the child-rearing advice of the mid-nineteenth century is the disappearance of references to fathers.[7] Colonial fathers were given advice, mainly in the form of sermons, about their responsibility to supervise the secular and religious education of their children. Both parents were admonished to set good examples and take care of the everyday well-being of their children. However, in the nineteenth century the primacy of mothers became the theme of the professional child-rearing manuals and parents' magazines that proliferated. Mothers were extolled in the burgeoning mass circulation women's magazines and popular novels, and biographies of famous men stressed motherhood themes and the pivotal role of a mother in shaping her child's destiny.

The elevation of motherhood has been explained as a result, in part, of the waning of home industry and the declining birthrate.[8] The colonial household was a busy hive of productivity, with all members of the family, including children, working together to produce the material bases of their everyday life: food, clothes, shelter, with a little left over for trade. The nineteenth-century family, however, depended increasingly on adult men going outside the home to find work in developing urban industry or trade in order to support the family. The home, no longer a workplace, gradually became a retreat from the demands of the competitive world, and affectional bonds dominated economic bonds in the skein of family relationships.[9]

During the nineteenth century the birthrate dropped sharply, perhaps because children had less productive value where family farms were giving way to urban industries. Between 1800 and 1900 the average number of children born to white women fell from 7.04 to 3.56.[10] Mothers had fewer children and, consequently, more time to give to each of them. Fathers were out of the home more often and were therefore less involved with the everyday tasks of child raising. Children, who previously had been viewed, at best, as miniature adults, and, at worst, as small creatures possessing evil tendencies that must be firmly tamed, began to be viewed positively as innocent beings who were naturally closer to God.[11] Thus, it was the mother's role, as conveyor of moral values, to ensure that her child was not corrupted by the world.

While this explanation certainly applies to the new urban middle class, it does not adequately take into account the fact that in 1850 eighty percent of the population still lived in rural areas, and by the end of the century the majority still remained rural.[12] In rural areas the labor of children and, indeed, of the whole family, would still be an economic necessity. Nevertheless, by the second half of the century courts from throughout the country, from the deep rural south to pioneering California, displayed concern for the welfare of the child and endorsed the nurturing nature of mothers.

My own explanation of why even judges from rural areas shared this growing solicitude toward children and their mothers is the development of a uniform middle-class culture based on mass circulation magazines and books. Between 1784 and 1860 at least one hundred new magazines were published, most of which were devoted to women's interests.[13] In the colonial period communication among the colonies was limited and cultural differences and social values developed independently. In contrast, the newly united republic began to develop its own mass culture, which extended from fashion to child raising. This urban middle-class culture was aimed at the literate urban housewife who had the leisure to read. Even so, literate women in small towns and on farms read the magazines as well. [14]

Judges were certainly part of this new middle-class elite, even if they lived in the small towns of predominantly rural areas.[15] Their wives and daughters probably subscribed to *Godey's Ladies Book* or the *Ladies' Magazine*, two of the most popular magazines of the nineteenth century. They would have been exposed to such flowery phrases in support of mothers as these, offered by a writer in *Ladies' Magazine*, describing the modern woman: "[She is] forming the future patriot, statesman, or enemy of his country, [but] more than this, she is sowing the seeds of virtue or vice which will fit him for Heaven or for eternal misery."[16]

The attitude of the judiciary toward women as mothers was clearly expressed by the U.S. Supreme Court in an opinion that supported the denial of the admission of women to the Bar:

> Man is, or should be, woman's protector and defender. The natural and proper timidity and delicacy which belongs to the female sex evidently unfits it for many of the occupations of civil life. The constitution of the family organization, which is founded in the divine ordinance, as well as in the nature of things, indicates the domestic sphere as that which properly belongs to the domain and functions of womanhood. The harmony, not to say identity, of interests and views which belong, or should belong, to the family institution is repugnant to the ideas of a woman adopting a distinct and independent career from that of her husband.
>
> . . . The paramount destiny and mission of woman are to fulfill the noble and benign offices of wife and mother. This is the law of the Creator.[17]

The cult of motherhood, portrayed as a romantic, even spiritual ideal, worked to women's favor in obtaining custody of their children after of separation, divorce, or death of a husband. Judges' decisions increasingly noted the superior role of mothers in their decisions, thwarting the father's common law right to control and custody of his children. Judges, however, did not give mothers legal rights of their own but rather gave custody to them based on the growing judicial view that placing children in their mothers' care was in the best interests of children.

In contrast, the organized women's movement, which developed rapidly in the second half of the century, noted the moral superiority of mothers, but primarily viewed child custody as only one item in the struggle for married women's property rights.[18] This struggle was carried on in the state legislatures, not the courts.[19] In essence the women's movement perpetuated the old common law tradition of children as economic assets as opposed to the emerging modern notion of children as emotional treasures whose interests came before those of their parents.

Women fought for property rights of their own that were, at that time, held exclusively by their husbands. These rights encompassed the right to control their own wages and their own inheritance, and, additionally, the right to equal control of the custody of their children while their husbands were alive and complete control if their husbands were dead. Other custodial rights included an equal right with their husband to make contracts of indenture that bound their minor children[20] and an exclusive right to make indenture contracts and to receive the wages of their children if their husbands were dead.[21]

Thus, a fundamental ideological conflict developed between a women's rights strategy, which sought legal and civil rights for women directly, and a judicial deference to the cult of motherhood, which gave women limited benefits only in relation to their children's interests. This conflict was played out in all areas of custody law, but was particularly evident in custody disputes following divorce

Custody of Children Following Divorce

While all facets of child custody, including bastardy, testamentary guardianship, apprenticeship, and, of course, the status of slave children, were severely altered during the nineteenth century, it was the dispute over custody of children following separation and divorce that received the greatest attention in the courts. Several hundred published court decisions deal with child custody following divorce or separation between 1790–1890.[22] They represent only a small fraction of the number of lower court decisions, since most decisions were never published. This is in contrast to the colonial era, where divorce was uncommon or forbidden in most colonies and custody of children following divorce was almost never addressed in published decisions.[23]

The growing number of custody disputes probably reflected two trends: the rise in divorce and the uncertainty of the laws governing custody. Obtaining a divorce became easier in most states, and by the second half of the nineteenth century many people were taking advantage of this new opportunity. A Census Bureau study on divorce reveals a rapidly escalating pattern. While there were 53,574 divorces granted in the years 1867 to 1871, this figure nearly tripled to 157,324 between 1887 and 1891.[24] In about 40 percent of the divorces children were involved. Another 20–40 percent of the divorces did not report either the presence or absence of children.[25] These figures do not take into account the couples who separated but never divorced. In a culture where a strong stigma was attached to divorce, this unknown number of couples was probably much larger than those who sought legal termination.[26]

Custody following divorce or separation, as in all matters governing the family, was decided by each state. The relationship between state legislatures and the state judiciary in changing the nature of custody law following divorce illuminates the complex and sometimes contradictory origins of these changes. In fact, these two branches of state government represented two different perspectives: the legislatures were reacting to demands, spearheaded by women's rights advocates, to expand the property rights of married women, while judges were responding to the growing idealization of women as mothers and to the romanticization of children. The legislatures were influenced by the lobbying efforts of women's rights advocates, while the judges were probably more influenced by social values promoted by the popular culture as manifested in popular magazines and child-raising manuals. Both were persuaded by flexible natural rights arguments that could be used in favor of either mother or father.

The Legislatures

Although there is a great deal of controversy about why the women's rights movement in America began when it did,[27] there is strong evidence that it first emerged in New York with the fight for the first Married Woman's Property Act.[28] The Polish-American reformer Ernestine Rose led the movement by stumping from door to door in New York City to collect petition signatures for the act. She enlisted Elizabeth Cady Stanton and Paulina Wright, small-town reformers who had been active in the antislavery movement, to join the cause. All three appeared as delegates to the 1846 New York Constitutional Convention and lobbied for the act's successful passage in 1848.[29]

The act cracked the common law concept of coverture, by which a woman was considered united to her husband with no civil or property rights of her own. This act allowed women the right to control property received by gift, grant, devise, or bequest, but it left the question of a married woman's right to her own wages unsettled.[30]

In that same year, 1848, Elizabeth Cady Stanton, fresh from the successful legislative campaign, was a chief organizer of the first Women's Rights Convention at Seneca Falls, New York. The concept of custody rights for women following divorce or separation was included as one of the important items in the general plea for expanded property and civil rights. This priority is illustrated in the following passage from the Seneca Falls Convention Declaration of Rights and Sentiments:

> He [the legislative and judicial patriarchy][31] has so framed the laws of divorce as to what shall be the proper causes, and in the case of separation, to whom the guardianship of the children shall be given as to be wholly regardless of the happiness of women—the law in all cases going upon the false supposition of the supremacy of man, and giving all power into his hands.[32]

The idea of women's property rights, fired by the New York law, spread quickly. Between 1869 and 1887 the legislatures of thirty-three states and the District of Columbia granted married women control over their own wages and earnings, while thirty of the states specifically provided for a separate estate for women. During those same years Louisiana, Texas, New Mexico, Arizona, and California adopted the law of community property, wherein the property of a married couple was held in equal shares by husband and wife. In the great majority of states women were given the right to make contracts and bring suit.[33] These dramatic changes in the law were painstakingly pursued in behind-the-scenes activities by the legislative committees of women's clubs, which moved away from their purely social focus to pursue political change.[34] However, the actual law making still rested with all-male legislatures.

It was not necessarily sympathy for the cause of women's rights that prompted men to vote for women's property rights but rather, according to Women's Club spokeswoman Rheta Dorr, "because they perceived plainly that their own wealth, devised to daughters who could not control it, might be easily gambled away, or wasted through improvidence, or diverted to the use of strangers."[35]

While most states expanded married women's rights to wages, bequests, and gifts, few states expanded women's rights to their children. New York State enlarged the Married Women's Property Act in 1860 to include women as the "joint guardian of her children along with her husband, with equal powers, rights, and duties in regard to them, with her husband."[36] The lawmakers retreated, however, in 1862, requiring that husbands only obtain their wives' consent before appointing testamentary guardians or indenturing the children.[37] In addition, New York judges in the aftermath of this act were unwilling to interpret the law as applying to women who were separated from their husbands. The New York Supreme Court claimed that there must be a "legally recognized head" to protect the family from the "controversy for power and supremacy in a dual-headed family."[38] By the end of the century only nine states and the District of Colombia gave mothers the statutory right to equal guardianship.[39]

This refusal to grant women legislative rights to custody illustrates the barrier of fear that restricted the advance of women's rights. Most men, and even some women's rights advocates, feared that too many rights would tempt women to leave the family. Again, according to Rheta Dorr, the California legislature defeated an equal guardianship bill with the argument that "if women had the guardianship of their children, would anything prevent them from taking the children and leaving home?"[40]

The organized women's movement remained split through the next century over how far to push women's rights without destroying the family. Elizabeth Cady Stanton represented one extreme when she argued, "I think divorce at the will of the parties is not only a right but that it is a sin against nature, the family, the state for a man or woman to live together in the marriage relationship enduring continual antagonism, indifference, disgust."[41] Most women's rights activists were more cautious. They feared that easy divorce would hurt women by leaving them without support. Lucy Stone, a cofounder of the women's rights movement with Stanton, stated that Mrs. Stanton was "sincere in her antagonism to inequitable laws as between men and women," but mistakenly sought an "equal license accorded to both, instead of equal restraint imposed on both."[42]

The Courts

While organized women had little success in gaining custody rights for mothers through property rights legislation, the courts increasingly awarded children to their mothers in custody disputes—not under the dangerous doctrine of women's rights but rather under the newly developing rule of the best interests of the child.

Custody disputes were brought before the court in two ways: as part of a divorce proceeding or, more frequently, by a writ of habeus corpus, where one party claimed that the child was being wrongfully held or imprisoned. Habeus corpus actions were most often brought by the noncustodial parent following divorce or when the couple was separated. Because of the successful crusade to obtain property rights, women who were still technically married could bring suit on their own in most states.

Since the beginning of the republic judges wielded a great deal of individual discretion in all matters of family law. They established what historian Michael Grossberg terms a "judicial patriarchy," in which they relied on their own judgment to interpret English common law rules and their own state's legislative mandates. The use of this individualized power was supported in tradition by the English courts' increasing use of chancery courts to determine the welfare and property of minors under the doctrine of parens partriae. Beginning in the eighteenth century the English chancery courts sometimes used their equitable powers to override common law provisions, which gave fathers paramount control, in order to provide protection for children whose fathers were grossly immoral or heretical.[43]

In America the equitable tradition of the chancery court was gradually extended by judges to consider the interests of the children against those of their parents, even when there was not gross abuse. The patterns of judicial decisions across the states show that judges were not simply idiosyncratic in determining the best interests of children. With some slight regional differences, judges in all parts of the growing nation shared the same emerging middle-class values about the role of the family, the need for child nurturing, and, especially, the special moral and religious capacities of women as mothers.

Common Law Origins

Early in the republic judges were more likely to rely upon English precedents regarding custody disputes rather than their own newly emerging case law.[44] Fortunately, English precedents offered choices, allowing judges to be flexible. The two most frequently cited English cases were Rex v. DeManneville (1804)[45] and Blisset's Case (1774).[46] DeManneville exemplified the doctrine of a father's paramount right to his children. In this case the mother had run away from an allegedly brutal father, but Lord Ellenborough of the King's Bench returned the child to her father, even though "she was an infant at the breast of the mother." By contrast, a quarter of a century earlier, Lord Mansfield allowed a mother to keep her six-year-old child when the father, a bankrupt, mistreated mother and child.[47] Lord Mansfield held that "the public right to superintend the education of its citizens necessitated doing what appeared best for the child, notwithstanding the father's natural right." Thus he planted the germ of what was to become the best interest standard in the new world.

American courts soon created their own precedents, although by the end of the century they still differed about which rule to follow, even within the same state. Some judges followed the tradition of Blackstone and DeManville, giving custody to the father. One court justified its decision by stating that the language of the law places the husband and father at the head of the household, to serve "the peace and happiness of families and to the best interests of society." The court continued, "By the common law the legal existence of the woman is suspended during the marriage. . . . The obligation imposed on the husband to provide for their wants and protection, makes it necessary that he should exercise a power of control over all the members of his household."[48] However, even courts that gave superior rights to the father doctrine usually conceded that he could lose this right if custody "should be inconsistent with the welfare of his children, which is a paramount consideration."[49]

The tradition of judicial discretion became so firmly imbedded that many judges often gave no more than lip service to precedent, or even to legislation in their own state, but instead sought to probe tangled fact situations to discover the best interests of an individual child.[50] Practical, rather than legally correct results, were often the consequence. One judge, challenging the paternal rights doctrine by awarding the daughter to the mother, stated that when the duties of "supporting and maintaining the child" are assumed by the mother the parents "stand upon a footing of perfect equality." In this case the mother had cared for the daughter following the desertion of the father.

Early American Cases

With the earliest American cases the best interest of the child was associated with the mother's special capacity to guide and nurture young children. In 1809, in Prather v. Prather, the first published decision in the new republic to defy the paramount rights of fathers, the court awarded the youngest child, a five-year-old girl, to the mother.[51] In this case William Prather, after ten years of marriage, turned his wife Jennett out of the house and brought in another woman, with whom he lived in open adultery. This South Carolina court, clearly incensed by the injustice done to the mother, who the court described as "a prudent, discreet and virtuous woman," was fearful of defying the weight of common law. In deciding to give the young child to the mother, the court passed the responsibility of strictly enforcing common law to higher courts. "The Court is apprised that it is treading on new and dangerous grounds, but feels a consolation in the reflection that if it errs, there is a tribunal wherein the error can be redressed."[52]

Other courts strode more boldly into this new territory. In 1842 New York's highest court, in the oft-cited Mercein v. People, went so far as to replace the common law tradition of paternal authority with a natural law argument in favor of mothers, stating: "By the law of nature, the father has no paramount right to the custody of his child."[53] The court awarded custody of a three-year-old sickly daughter to her mother, explaining that

> the law of nature has given to her an attachment for her infant offspring which no other relative will be likely to possess in an equal degree, and where no sufficient reasons exist for depriving her of the care and nurture of her child, it would not be a proper exercise of discretion in any court to violate the law of nature in this respect.[54]

In a vivid illustration of the seesawlike ambivalence of nineteenth-century courts in choosing between the traditional common law rights of father and the natural rights claim of the mother, the New York Supreme Court modified the custody decree in People v. Mercein two years later and delivered custody of the little girl to her father. This court clearly rebuked the natural rights reasoning of the previous court, claiming that father's right should prevail, since "it has not been denied that he is the legal head of the whole family, wife and children inclusive; and I have heard it urged from no quarter that he should be brought under subjection to a household democracy. All will agree, I apprehend, that such a measure would extend the right of suffrage too far."[55] A second judge, who joined in the opinion, took a further swipe at the previous court's dangerous application of natural rights, and invoked divine law instead. "It is possible," he wrote, "that our laws relating to the rights and duties of husband and wife have not kept pace with the progress of civilization. . . . But I will not enquire what the law ought to be . . . I will, however, venture the remark . . . that human laws cannot be very far out of the way when they are in accordance with the law of God."[56]

Evolution of Best Interests Standard and Tender Years Doctrine

Judges continued to be torn between applying common law rights of the father and the more modern rule of the best interest of the child. Eventually, however, the trend favored the latter.[57] The best interests of the child, particularly for very young or female children, became increasingly associated with the child's mother. This tendency of courts to award infants to their mothers later became known as the "Tender Years Doctrine." In awarding a four-year-old boy to his mother the court, in People ex rel. Sinclair v. Sinclair stated:

> Nature has devolved upon the mother the nurture and care of infants during their tender years, and in that period such care, for all practical purposes, in the absence of exceptional circumstances, is almost exclusively committed to her. At such periods of life courts do not hesitate to award the care and custody of young infants to the wife as against the paramount right of the husband where the wife has shown herself to be a proper person and is able to fully discharge her duty toward the child.[58]

While maternal nurture was the most prominent factor in considering the best interests of the young child, some courts also gave weight to the child's gender, particularly with older children. Courts favored placing an older child with a parent of the same sex, despite the fact that this often resulted in separating siblings.[59] An Alabama court justified this preference by stating that "no greater calamity can befall an infant daughter, than a deprivation of a mother's care, vigilance, precept and example."[60] The initial decision could be modified as the child grew older, but there are few published decisions on this subject. In one rather unusual case, however, the court recognized the father's claim of change of circumstance and ordered the boy delivered to his father's custody when he reached age five, stating, "A boy of three years is deemed to be of such tender age that consideration of his welfare call for his having a mother's care, but the same cannot be said when the child has reached the age of five."[61]

Not surprisingly, courts also considered the relative wealth of the parties in the custody dispute in a best interests analysis, especially if one party was barely able to supply the mean necessities.[62] However, mere poverty or insolvency did not furnish an adequate ground for depriving parents of their children, and if the child was young this consideration most often was overriden by a tender years argument.[63]

Many appellate courts followed the same route: the common law was routinely asserted and then bypassed, presumably in the best interests of the child. For example, the New Jersey court ruled that the general common law rule is that "the father, as head of the family is entitled to custody and control of his legitimate children, but may be denied if he is cruel, corrupt, immoral etc., or if the child is of tender years, or if the child is female or of sickly constitution."[64] The court stated further that "it has broad discretion, is not arbitrary, and makes decisions based on sound principles."[65] In this case, since Mrs. Stigall could not prove her allegations that Mr. Stigall was abusive and cruel, the court divided the three children, Elizabeth (aged one), Robert (aged three) and Charles (aged five), giving Charles to the father.

Parental Fitness

The almost universal exception to the growing rule of awarding children of tender years to their mother occurred when the mother was considered unfit.[66] Fitness was sometimes determined by the party considered at fault in the divorce action, particularly if the ground was adultery.[67] Many states had divorce legislation that indicated that the party not at fault be awarded custody.[68] Judicial discretion, however, still prevailed.[69] Often, the couples were separated but not divorced, and in some the instances the immoral behavior occurred after the divorce. This gave judges further room for discretion.

The very high moral standards attributed to mothers in the nineteenth century allowed judges to view them more positively in custody disputes, but it also meant that judges turned harshly against them when they strayed from conventional moral standards. The two transgressions that most frequently caused women to lose custody of their children were adultery and leaving their husbands without, in the opinion of the judge, just cause.

Adultery was considered an inexcusable act for mothers, but not necessarily for fathers. In Lindsay v. Lindsay the mother claimed that she was not living in an adulterous relationship since she believed her ex-husband had obtained a total divorce. Furthermore, she argued that she left him because of his adulterous affair while they were still living together. Nevertheless, the court gave their four-year-old daughter to the father, stating, "there may be no difference in the sin of the man and the women, who violate the laws of chastity. . . . But we do know, that in the opinion of society, it is otherwise . . . for when she sins after this sort, she sins against society . . . her associations are with the vulgar, the vile and the depraved. If her children are with her, their characters must be, more or less, influenced and formed by the circumstances which surround them." [70]

Courts were so offended by adulterous mothers that they most often denied them visitation rights and cut off all obligations for support by the husband. In New York the same state court that had recognized the natural law rights of the mother in the Mercein case refused an adulterous mother any contact with her eight-year-old daughter. The court explained, "The idea that the court should interfere and impose upon the father husband the duty of admitting her within the privacy of the family is repugnant to every sentiment of virtue and propriety."[71]

Judges also were very unsympathetic to women who left their husbands, even when they seemed to have just cause. In Alabama Mrs. Bryan, mother of two small children, ages two and four, claimed that she left Mr. Bryan because of his excessive drinking, occasional physical violence against her and her daughter, admitted adultery, and use of profane language. The court listened to a great deal of testimony regarding these allegations and found that, although the husband was a heavy drinker and was "often rude, harsh, and indecorous," there was insufficient proof on the charges of physical violence and adultery and therefore the wife had no good reason to leave.[72]

Clearly, fathers were not held to the same high moral standards by which the courts judged mothers. Adultery alone does not usually appear in nineteenth-century cases as a reason for granting custody to the mother over the adulterous father. Indeed, in an 1881 Iowa case a six-year-old boy was taken away from his mother and delivered to his father, whom the mother had divorced on the proven grounds of adultery. The mother, a respectable music teacher, was found to be "imprudent" in her conversations with her son with regard to the adultery charges and the father's "criminal conduct" and disposition.[73] A New York court, citing the English DeManneville case, where the eight-month-old baby was given to the father, reasoned, "Even a father living in adultery is entitled to custody, so long as the child does not come in contact with the adulteress."[74]

A father could be denied custody if he clearly abused his wife and children (abuse was most often defined as proven physical injury)[75] or if he deserted and did not support them.[76] Simple bad behavior or adultery alone, however, were not usually sufficient.

Guardianship Following the Death of a Parent

Nonparents were not often awarded custody in cases of separation or divorce if both parents were alive and at least one considered fit.[77] The rule changed, however, if the father died or the custodial mother remarried.

Marion Goerlitz, aged seven, lost her father in the Civil War. On his deathbed he gave Marion to his mother, the child's paternal grandmother, since his wife, nearly destitute, had younger children to care for. Immediately afterward, all the children contracted scarlet fever and only Marion survived.[78] The Pennsylvania court was forced to choose between the mother and the grandmother. The legal dispute involved the testamentary right of the father to determine a guardian upon his death, in light of the emerging "natural right of the mother." The situation was complicated by the fact that the grandmother in fact had cared for the child for several years. The court finally asked Marion to indicate her preference. Marion chose her grandmother, and the court decided to leave her with the grandmother for one year. The court indicated they would give her to the mother after one year if she could improve her circumstances.

Marion Goerlitz's dilemma illustrates the unpredictability of life for children living in the nineteenth century. Tens of thousands of children lost fathers in the Civil War and suffered disrupted family lives. While divorce became an increasing problem toward the end of the century, a marriage was far more likely to end by death than by divorce. For instance, in the year 1860 almost thirty out of one thousand existing marriages were dissolved by death or divorce, with divorce accounting for only 4.1 percent of the total.[79]

When a parent died the surviving parent normally took custody and the courts were not called upon to settle a dispute. Sometimes, however, the father appointed a guardian other than his wife for his minor children in his will or on his deathbed. Nearly all states, by statute, allowed this appointment in some form. When the colonies, and later the states, first enacted testamentary guardianship statutes, they almost all copied the English statute of 1660 verbatim. The statute provided that a father might "by deed executed in his lifetime, or by last will and testament in writing dispose of the custody of his minor children," and that this disposition should be "good and effective against all and every person claiming the custody and tuition of such children."[80]

Originally, this law was interpreted as giving the guardian authority even against the widowed mother.[81] It extended the paramount rights of the father to the custody and control of his children beyond the grave. Theoretically, the mother, now a widow *femme sole*, had no more rights to her children then when she was *femme couvert*. In practice, the father's testamentary appointment was most often exercised upon the mother's death, or upon her remarriage, when she was considered, once again, civilly dead.

Two forms of guardianship existed during the nineteenth century: guardianship of the estate and guardianship of the person. Most frequently, the father used testamentary guardianship to appoint a male relative to control the child's estate until the child reached twenty-one or, in the case of a girl, until she married. In most states he could do this without the mother's consent.[82] Sometimes the father gave full guardianship rights over the person as well as the estate, merging the two as a single property issue over which he had testamentary control.

Over the course of the nineteenth century testamentary guardianships yielded to the same forces that transformed custody law following divorce and separation: the steady advance of married women's property rights and the growing cult of motherhood. By the end of the century the law did not eliminate a father's right to attempt to control his child's estate after his own death, but seriously curtailed this right in favor of mothers.

The struggle by women's rights advocates to secure legal rights for married women naturally included testamentary rights. Women were not only barred from appointing a testamentary guardian in their own right if their husband was alive but could also become the victim of their husband's will if he appointed someone other than themselves as guardian of their children.[83] An early women's rights state convention held in Rochester, New York, in 1853 firmly tied testamentary guardianship to the fundamental property rights sought by married women. The convention resolved to present the legislature with certain questions: "Why should not widows, equally with widowers, become by law the legal guardians . . . of their own children? On what just ground do the laws make a distinction between men and women in the regard to the ownership of property, inheritance and the administration of estates?"[84] Legislatures were more sympathetic to widows than they were to married women, since granting widows custody rights did not encourage the breakup of the family. By the end of the nineteenth century most states allowed the father to testamentarily appoint anyone to be the guardian of the estate of his minor children, but only Florida, Delaware, South Carolina, and Tennessee authorized such a guardian to take physical custody away from the mother without her consent. Several states also allowed the widow to appoint a testamentary guardian, but only if the father had not already chosen one in his will.[85]

Perhaps the most significant advance for the rights of widowed mothers was the judicial reexamination of their status following remarriage. At common law a mother lost the natural right to custody of her child upon remarriage. A wife living with her husband could neither be guardian of her own nor of other people's children because, having no individual legal existence, she could not give a valid bond.[86] A few states altered this impediment by statute in the nineteenth century, asserting that marriage did not extinguish her powers as guardian, but more often judges removed the impediment by applying the new best interest of the child standard.[87] A Louisiana court, for example, declared that a ten-year-old daughter should remain with the mother following her remarriage because the ancient Spanish law requiring a widow to give up the rights to her children upon her remarriage was outmoded and "of sinister spirit."[88] The court then went on to say that the maternal bond and natural affection between mother and child cannot be replaced by a guardian.[89]

An Alabama court in 1860 also applied the best interest standard, though in a peculiar way, to favor the mother. The court denied the plea of three children under fourteen who petitioned to have their mother removed as their guardian upon her remarriage. The children claimed their stepfather used profanity and had adulterous relations with slaves. The court responded that the best interests of the children rule prevails, but only the gross misconduct of a parent justifies court interference. The courts found no evidence that the mother was incapable of taking care of her children, and asserted that placing the children in the home of a third person would lead to alienation of maternal affection.[90]

But courts did not always apply the best interest standard. In some custody disputes following the death of a father, a few courts interpreted the father's testamentary powers very strictly. A New Hampshire court in 1850 awarded an infant daughter, Elizabeth Adelaide Copp, to the father's brother to raise until age twenty-one, as specified by the father's will, against the protest of the widow. The court claimed it was obliged to follow the statute allowing the father to appoint a guardian to have control and custody of Elizabeth until age twenty-one. The judge stated, "The power thus given was so ample, that whenever it was exerted it wholly superseded the claims of various persons entitled by the common law to any participation in the control of the person or estate of the infant, and was in fact regarded as almost coextensive with that of the parent himself."[91] Similarly, a few poor widows found that they lost the guardianship of their children as well as the rest of their legal identity when they remarried.[92]

Overall, however, mothers were increasingly recognized as the natural guardians of their children following the death of their husbands. Even when statutory support blatantly supported the father's last will, judges were likely to endorse mothers, with their special qualities, as the appropriate caretakers for their children.

Bastardy Law

Perhaps the greatest legal advance for children and their mothers (or at least for mothers with means of support) occurred with the transformation of bastardy laws. The common law definition of an illegitimate child as *filius nullius* gave way to firm legal recognition of the bond between mother and child. Although illegitimate children frequently were raised by their mothers, that social fact had not been supported by the law. However, by the end of the nineteenth century almost every state had passed legislation declaring that the child was a member of its mother's family, with a right to inherit from the mother, the same as a legitimate child.[93] The mother, in turn, was given the parental prerogatives normally given to the father in a family where the parents were married. Beyond that, the criminal punishment for producing the illegitimate child (e.g., whippings, fines, etc.) that took up so much of the courts' time and energy in the colonial period, virtually disappeared, leaving only a civil procedure for determining paternity and enforcing support.

The women's movement was not responsible for these drastic legal changes. The early years of the women's movement were almost entirely dedicated to securing legal and political rights that were largely the concern of middle-class women, as in the campaigns to win property rights for married women and to promote female suffrage. The rights of middle-class women included the control and custody of children within marriage and following divorce or the death of the father, but did not include the rights of illegitimate children, whose mothers usually were members of the working class. Ironically, organized women viewed the new rights of unwed mothers with some envy. The New York State Women's Suffrage Society, in an address to women and voters in 1877, noted that laws treated married women "as criminals by taking from them all legal control of their children, while those born outside marriage belong absolutely to their mothers."[94]

The laws relating to bastards changed in response to two separate nineteenth-century phenomena: the evolution of inheritance laws and, once again, the growing cult of motherhood. Changes in inheritance law were related to changes in married women's property rights, since control of inherited property was one of the major rights that married women wished to gain; but who controlled property over generations was an even more fundamental issue in the developing republic, perhaps as fundamental as whether one person was allowed to own another.

Sweeping changes in the feudal inheritance laws accompanied the birth of the new republic; these changes were a major impetus in creating the legal relationship between unwed mother and child. Virginia led the way in 1785 by abolishing the rules of primogeniture and entail, which could make one sibling rich at the expense of all others and tie up large estates for generations. These new laws allowed for a more equitable division of property and put more emphasis on individual initiative rather than family continuity insured by property. At the same time Virginia passed a law declaring that bastards "shall be capable of inheriting or transmitting inheritance on the part of their mother, in like manner as if they had been lawfully begotten of such mother."[95]

Children were to be given, as much as possible, an equal start in life; this included bastards, who before were legally shunned—their misfortune serving as a warning to those who would engage in sexual activity outside of marriage. This new shift in inheritance law not only transformed property rights but also changed the communal rules of morality, no longer emphasizing harsh punishment as a form of sexual control by the community.[96] Legitimacy ceased to be a central social issue once it became disengaged from strict rules of inheritance.

Putative fathers were still expected to support their illegitimate children, and paternity proceedings were brought against putative fathers who tried to evade this obligation. These proceedings were initiated, somewhat irregularly, by the town poor law officials or by the mother. Paternity trials were largely civil in nature, with money rather than punishment as the focus of the proceedings. However, the accusatory nature of the proceedings and the kinds of evidence produced more closely resembled criminal trials. As legal treatise writer Tapping Reeve observed: "The object is wholly civil: but the proceedings are altogether in a criminal dress."[97]

Fathers retained their obligation to support their illegitimate children but they lost any claim to custody. This was a reversal of the colonial practice, where fathers could choose to raise the child rather than pay support to the mother. A New Hampshire court in 1836 recited the emerging rule in response to the father of a twenty-two-month-old "bastard," who offered to take the child rather than pay the Town of Hudson forty cents per week. "It is well settled that the mother of an illegitimate child has right to custody and control against putative father, and is bound to maintain it as its natural guardian. . . . The putative father has no right to the custody and control of the child, except, perhaps, as against a stranger; and his right to this extent is questionable."[98]

A father's claim to his illegitimate child became no stronger if the mother died or abandoned her child. In one New Jersey case, although the father and mother had married, it was discovered that the father, under a false name, had previously married and failed to divorce a woman in England. The mother died when her daughter was one-month old, and the court appointed the maternal grandfather rather than her husband as guardian. The court reasoned that the child was an orphaned bastard, and the most appropriate guardian would be one of the mother's closest relatives.[99] In another case the mother had remarried and abandoned the child to the charitable care of strangers. The father asked for custody of the child and relief from support payments to mother. A tough-minded Minnesota court refused, stating that although the mother may neglect to support the child, "this is no reason why the [father] should be relieved from the payment of the allowance, nor from the obligation of the bond." The court explained that the father "has, in law, no better title to its custody, and no more right to ask for it, than any other person."[100]

While virtually extinguishing fathers' rights, judges paid homage to the virtues of mothers. Often courts combined natural rights arguments with sheer sentiment. A court in Tennessee denied the right of a father who legitimated his son three years after the birth, stating, "Perhaps the strongest law in animated nature is the disposition of the female to protect and support her offspring. . . . The mother is the natural guardian of the child. . . . It was never intended, even by the marital relation of husband and wife, that the great law of nature should be violated by a separation of the mother from her infant."[101]

It is ironic that these mothers of illegitimate children were never taken to task by the courts for their immorality, as were married mothers accused of adultery. The cult of motherhood, based as it was on the moral superiority of women, remained apparently untarnished by the unwed mother's immoral acts. Perhaps the explanation is that mothers of illegitimate children enjoyed a special status as both mother and father to the child. Several courts reasoned that the mother is obliged to support and educate her child just as a father in a valid marriage. Also, with the changes in the inheritance laws the mother enjoyed the testamentary rights with regard to her child normally held by the father. For all these reasons courts adopted a tone of sympathy rather than disgust.

The special status of the mother and her bastard child was muddled if the mother married the father after the child's birth or if the child was legitimated in some other way. Under English common law a child could not be legitimated by the marriage of his parents after his birth, nor was the offspring of an annulled marriage considered legitimate.[102] All this changed in the nineteenth century, as the law tried to limit the boundaries of bastardy by making children legitimate whenever possible. Many states passed laws recognizing common law marriage and others allowed putative marriage, where parents wed unaware that there was a technical impediment—such as faulty divorce. Presumptions of legitimacy within a valid marriage were also strengthened.

While these legal reforms worked in favor of legitimizing the child, they sometimes worked against the mother's special claim to custody of a bastard, as she was treated like any other mother in a separation or divorce situation. In one convoluted California case the mother and father had been married for five years when the mother learned that the father actually was married to another woman in Tennessee. Upon learning that her marriage was fraudulent and void and that her two children were therefore illegitimate, she left her husband and went to Oregon with her children. One year later the father came to Oregon, brutally assaulted the mother, and abducted the two children. The mother then went in search of the children. In the appellate decision the judge, bent on recognizing the legitimacy of the children, took no notice of their best interests and awarded custody to the father. He reasoned that since marriage is a civil contract only intent is necessary to make it valid for purposes of making the children legitimate, although legally the marriage was null. The father, the court said, "has the unquestioned right to [the children's] custody, control and obedience to the same extent as if they were the issue of a valid marriage."[103]

While unwed mothers theoretically gained legal stature and powerful rights to claim the custody of their children, the harsh reality of their economic situation often defeated these new rights. In nineteenth-century America a mother who could not support her child could lose her child. Under English law, since the child was not legally part of the mother's family, a bastard's place of settlement was the town in which he or she was born. If an indigent mother gave birth in a town where she was not a resident, the poor law official could separate the mother from the child and send the mother back to her original town of residence.[104] Changes in bastardy law that recognized the child as part of its mother's family prevented poor officials from separating mother and child on the basis of the child's place of birth. These changes, however, did not protect a mother from losing her child because of poverty.[105] Divorced mothers and fathers, intact families, widows, widowers, and unwed mothers alike faced the stern mandates of poor laws in the nineteenth century. If the community was called upon to provide aid to an indigent parent, that community had the right to offset its expense by apprenticing the child, once he or she had passed the age of nurture.[106] Apprenticeships, or the later variation of "placing out," could begin as soon as the child was as young as four or five.

As we shall see later in this chapter, the softening of judicial proclivities toward the best interest of the child in custody disputes did not extend toward children who had become a financial burden upon the community. In spite of the toughened legal actions to wrest support from putative fathers, many unwed mothers found themselves dependent upon community support and therefore subject to the custodial decisions of poor law officials. As one court asserted, the illegitimate child "has the same rights as any pauper when its custody is shifted from one keeper to another."[107]

Adoption

Families had cared for children not their own throughout the colonial period and early republic in situations where the parents were dead, or incapable or unwilling to care for them. However, under common law these children could not attain the same legal status as natural born children. Beginning in the second half of the nineteenth century the American law of adoption diverted sharply from its common law origins and eventually allowed these children, through an appropriate legal procedure, to gain all the rights that they would have gained if born into that family. This was a major step; it freed property inheritance from its attachment to bloodlines. This common law emphasis on bloodlines connection had been the major barrier to legal adoption in England, while adoption had long been permitted in countries with civil codes and different attitudes toward inheritance.

The spirit of equal opportunity that prompted changes in the inheritance laws and rights of mothers of illegitimate children allowed for a new definition of family, based not on blood but on child nurture. Led by Massachusetts's landmark adoption law of 1851, virtually every state enacted modern adoption laws by the end of the century.[108] As with the changes in bastardy laws, women's rights advocates did not pursue the statutory enactment of adoption law since it did not fit into their legislative agenda of property and legal rights. Indeed, according to historian Jamail Zainaldin, who made a study of the origins of the landmark Massachussetts law, no group appeared to be pushing this theoretically radical law, which was easily enacted and quickly picked up by most other states.[109]

Perhaps the easy passage of these statutes reflected the increasing cultural sensitivity to the best interests of the child and an effort to provide a nurturing and stable environment for children who might already have been living in the home of a third party because of the death, poverty, or incompetence of their parents. Perhaps it also reflected an effort to permanently relieve the poor law officials of their continuing obligation to supervise the welfare of children, usually involuntarily apprenticed, whose parents could not support them.

One complex New York case illustrates the inadequacy of involuntary indentures and the increasing reluctance of courts to enforce them. The father, a widowed saloonkeeper, left his three very young children with a nearby family, allowing the family to adopt (unofficially at that date in New York) the daughter Anna, while agreeing to pay for the care of the boys. The father neglected to pay, and the family arranged for the poor officials to indenture the boys to the family. When the father sought to regain custody the court ignored the indentures, stating that the children's bests interests are of greatest importance, "not to be defeated by one having a mere legal title to the custody of the child."[110] However, using this standard, the court found the father "anything but a fit custodian," and returned the children to their master and his family.[111]

The new adoption statutes almost always included two elements: the adopting parents had to be deemed "fit" by the judge, to ensure, as required by the New York statute, "that the moral and temporal interests of the child will be promoted by the adoption," and the natural parents, if alive, had to consent to the act.[112] Courts made exceptions to the requirement of consent, however, and these normally included those stated in the 1873 New York statute—a father or mother "adjudged guilty of adultery or cruelty and who is, for either cause, divorced, or is adjudged to be an insane person or an habitual drunkard, or is judicially deprived of the custody of the child on account of cruelty or neglect."[113]

This rather broad list of exceptions included those for whom adultery or cruelty was the grounds for their divorce, thereby in effect including a large proportion of divorced parents. Most often the issue of consent appeared only in litigation following the death of an adoptive parent, where the natural heirs sought to invalidate the adoption. In these instances the courts tended to follow a strict construction of the statute. In one Oregon case a daughter had been adopted at age ten with the written consent of her mother and the verbal approval of her father. The court followed the technical requirement of the law and claimed that since the court never acquired jurisdiction without the father's written consent, the adoption was never consummated.[114] The court reached a contrary conclusion in another Oregon case, where the father's consent had not been obtained. However, in this case the mother had divorced the father on grounds of adultery.[115]

By far the greatest controversy confronting the new adoption laws focused on inheritance. Initially, there was strenuous resistance to severing the traditional English common law connection between blood lines and inheritance rights. Although few objected to the child-nurturing goal of adoption, state legislatures vigorously opposed allowing adopted children full inheritance rights. The above noted 1873 New York Statute excluded the adoptees' right of inheritance, declaring, "A child, when adopted, shall take the name of the person adopting, and the two thenceforth shall sustain toward each other the legal relation of parent and child, and have all the rights and be subject to all the duties of that relation, excepting the right of inheritance."[116] This exception was not removed until 1887.

When inheritance was not at issue, and the struggle was between the child's original parent and the adopting parents for the custody of the child, the courts tended not to follow a strict interpretation of the technical requirements but rather, as in other custody situations, looked to what they considered to be the best interests of the child. In an Iowa case a widow gave up her six-year-old daughter to a wealthy farmer and his family. The articles of adoption were executed but not filed. Two years later the widow remarried and sought to regain the custody of her daughter based on the legal deficiency of the adoption proceedings. The court ignored the technical defect of the adoption and instead decided it was in the child's best interests to remain with the farmer, "a man of substantial means," and his family, rather than return to the mother and her new husband, "a man of modest means—a day laborer."[117]

Apprenticeships

The indenturing of minors, a fifteenth-century English common law form of custody, was fast disappearing as the nineteenth century drew to a close. Indentured servitude, as we have seen, was a common experience for colonial children. Many children without parents emigrated to America, particularly the southern colonies, as indentured servants. Other children were placed with a skilled master by their father in order to learn a trade. In a voluntary apprenticeship the father, having complete control and custody of his children and benefit of the child's services, could assign these rights to another, by an indenture agreement, in return for the maintenance and training of the child. In most states the child had to consent to his or her indenture if older than fourteen. The normal termination of a voluntary apprenticeship for a boy was twenty-one, and eighteen for a girl. In an involuntary apprenticeship the poor officials assumed this right from nonconsenting parents, who may be dead, absent, or simply indigent, and indentured the child in order to relieve the obligation of the town to support the child. In an involuntary apprenticeship the child's consent was not required at any age.[118] While the indenture contracts for voluntary and involuntary apprenticeships looked similar with regard to training and education, without the presence of parents masters often avoided teaching their involuntary apprentices a trade and simply used them for any manual labor.

In the interdependent world of the colonial household this exchange of labor for education, skill, and a place in the family was both functional and socially acceptable. In the nineteenth century apprenticeships gradually lost their value and their acceptability. The reasons for this were somewhat different for voluntary and involuntary apprenticeships, but both were affected by the newly developing concept of child nurture.

When deciding disputes regarding voluntary apprenticeships judges began applying reasoning from other forms of custody disputes, releasing minors from their apprentice contracts and returning them to their families if they considered it in the best interests of the child, particularly when the mother was the petitioner. Taking a young child of ten or eleven—sometimes younger—away from his or her family and sending the child to live in the home of a stranger was no longer looked upon with judicial approval.[119] In addition, courts increasingly failed to enforce laws that mandated the capture and return of runaway apprentices.[120]

In a somewhat contradictory trend mothers gained more rights to consent to their child's apprenticeship and to receive their wages. Consistent with their campaign for greater property rights, women's rights advocates did not seek to abolish apprenticeships but rather to gain powers of equal consent while the father was alive and the exclusive right to bind out and receive the wages of their children if the father were dead. As Elizabeth Cady Stanton fumed, "The father may apprentice his child, bind him out to a trade without the mother's consent—yea, in direct opposition to her earnest entreaties, prayers and tears. He may apprentice his son to a gangster or rum-seller, and thus cancel his debts of `honor.' "[121]

While the father was alive the consent of the mother was a question of equal custodial rights, and, as noted earlier, women activists made only slight legislative gains in this arena. They were blocked by male legislators who feared for the survival of the family.[122] When the father was dead, however, widows received much better treatment from the courts. In addition to granting mothers new rights as testamentary guardians, courts increasingly recognized the widow as the natural guardian with full contractual rights in apprenticeship situations. In 1857 a New Jersey court ruled in favor of a mother receiving the wages of her nineteen-year-old son after the husband was presumed dead. The court reasoned that "by the well settled law of this state, a mother is not only authorized, but bound, the father being dead, to exercise authority over her children."[123] The court added that while she remains unmarried "the mother has a right to the services of a minor child . . . so long . . . as the child remains under her protection."[124]

The assertion of mothers' rights in the apprenticeships of the children reflects the fundamental conflict between the goal of child nurturing and the goal of women's property rights. The concept of nurture forced the court to reject the arrangement of apprenticeship in favor of child welfare. The women's rights movement did not seek to terminate apprenticeships, however, but rather to give mothers the right to consent to the contract and to receive the wages. Once again, as with all issues of child custody, the orientation of the women's rights movement was more in the conservative tradition of viewing children in terms of property rights rather the modern view of child nurture.

What broke the back of the voluntary apprentice system ultimately, however, was not simply the changing attitude of the courts—it was the changing nature of the demand for child labor. The tradition of artisans and small tradesmen was being replaced by factories and mass production. Child labor was particularly suited to routine and repetitive tasks. The southern textile industry, for instance, was based largely on the labor of children. Between 1880 and 1910 manufacturers reported that about one-quarter of their work force was under sixteen years of age, and many cases of child labor went unreported. Children of seven or eight commonly doffed spun cotton and performed many different sorts of casual labor.[125] By 1880 the U.S. Census Bureau estimated that 17 percent of all children, ages ten through fifteen years, were gainfully employed outside the home. This figure ignores all children under ten and children involved in home production or on consignment from manufacturers.[126]

Toward the end of the nineteenth century, therefore, children still worked, perhaps in greater numbers and in worse conditions than before, but they now remained in the custody and control of their own parents; their employer had only limited control over them at the workplace and no obligation for their welfare.

Involuntary Apprenticeships

While voluntary apprenticeships waned the majority of involuntary apprenticeships changed their legal form to "placing out" and became the primary custodial arrangement for tens of thousands of abandoned and indigent children in the second half of the nineteenth century. Most of the these children were placed in rural homes. "Placing out" retained much of the character of apprenticeships, in that labor was given in exchange for room, board, and education. However, since no indenture contract was signed and custody and control remained with the association that made the arrangement, it represented a significant legal departure. Theoretically, the association would continue to supervise the arrangement to ensure that the child was treated well.

The association could terminate the arrangement at any time.[127] The hope was that some of these children would gain the affection of their placement family and be legally adopted. In this sense "placing out" was an effort to straddle the line between the purely economic arrangement of involuntary apprenticeships and the child-nurturing focus of adoption.

Charles Loring Brace, the founder of the New York Children's Aid Society in 1853, is credited with introducing the "placing out" system in America. It was initially hailed as a positive and less expensive alternative to the asylum, almshouse, or house of correction. As Brace explained it,

> The demand here for children's labor is practically unlimited. A child's place at the table of the farmer is always open; his food and cost to the family is of little account. A widespread spirit of benevolence, too, has inspired all classes—perhaps one of the latest fruits of Christianity—such as opens thousands of homes to the children of the unfortunate. The chances, too, of ill treatment in a new country where children are petted and favored, and every man's affairs are known to all his neighbors, are far less than in an old.[128]

In its first twenty-five years the New York Children's Aid Society placed approximately forty thousand homeless or destitute children from New York City into farm homes.[129] Other associations placed untold thousands as well. After an initial screening to weed out "the mentally defective, diseased and incorrigibles," children between the ages of five and seventeen were sent with agents to rural communities along the East Coast and in western and southern states. Farm families quickly took the children, but the experience was not always as Brace had predicted, and many critics denounced the system.

Lyman P. Alden, the superintendent of the State Public School in Coldwater, Michigan, critically observed the results of placing out in farm families:

> It is well known by all who have had charge of the binding out of children that the great majority of those who are applying for children over nine years old are looking for cheap help; and while many, even of this class, treat their apprentices with fairness, and furnish them a comfortable home, a much larger number of applicants do not intend to pay a quid pro quo, but expect to make a handsome profit on the child's service . . . furnishing poor food, shod-

dy clothing, work the child beyond its strength, send it to school but a few months, and that irregularly, and sometimes treat it with personal cruelty.[130]

Since the "placing out " system required no formal indenture contract, the courts rarely got involved in disputes between the placement family and the agency. There was, in fact, no legal regulation of this custodial system until the end of the nineteenth century, when some states, alarmed by what they considered the dumping of juvenile delinquents in their states, passed laws either requiring the society to post a bond protecting the state from future support or prohibiting the placement of criminal, diseased, insane, or incorrigible children in their states.[131]

While "placing out" grew to be the most popular custodial arrangement for orphaned, abandoned, and indigent children, traditional indentures were still frequently employed by local poor officials and, as we shall see, applied to a whole generation of freed slave children.

Freed Slave Children

When President Lincoln signed the Proclamation of Emancipation in 1861 the generation of slave children less than twenty-one years old theoretically became part of their mother's family and, since slave marriages were never legally recognized, subject to the same laws governing illegitimacy as free children.[132] Technically, masters lost their absolute ownership rights of custody and control and their ability to freely sell slave children. Under the new laws and judicial attitudes regarding bastardy, mothers of slave children should have gained paramount custodial rights,

In the confusion and dislocation following the war, however, states passed laws permitting slave children to become involuntary apprentices, placing them legally, once again, under the control and custody of their master. As a Georgia court explained in 1866, the act enabling ordinaries (county officials) to bind out apprentices was designed to relieve the problem of black children, "who, by the results of the civil war, have been thrown upon society, helpless from want of parental protection, want of means of support, inability to earn their daily bread and from age and other causes."[133]

The involuntary apprenticing of slave children was, of course, an extension of the laws that allowed poor law officials in all states to take a free child from the custody of its indigent parents and indenture the child to a third party. In the case of slave children, this legal transformation, in effect, exchanged slavery for involuntary servitude. Several former slaveholding states passed laws that eliminated the educational requirement of apprenticeships.[134]

Within a decade after the end of the war, however, all the former slave states recognized the offspring of slave marriages as legitimate, primarily for the purposes of inheritance, since former slaves could now own property as they could not under slavery. Slave marriages were deemed to be legitimate, if they followed somewhat traditional patterns. An 1865 Mississippi law was typical: "All free persons of color, who were living together as husband and wife in this state while in a state of slavery are hereby declared to be man and wife and their children legitimately entitled to an inheritance as full an extent as the children of white citizens are now entitled."[135] Some judges were confused over what "traditional patterns" were, given the fact that slaves could not dictate the condition of their own lives and could be rented or sold away from the mother of their children. Generally, courts bent over backwards to legitimize the offspring, even when one of the parents died before being freed,[136] but stopped short of recognizing polygamous relationships.[137].

Conclusion

A complex interaction of political and social forces directed the evolution of child custody law during the nineteenth century. Fathers no longer enjoyed paramount common law rights to custody and control of their children. Instead, the law emphasized the best interests of the child, with a presumption in favor of mothers as the more nurturing parent. This evolution was characterized by a continuing tension between the traditional view of child custody as a parental right, and children as an economic asset, and the emerging legal emphasis, not on clearly defined children's rights, but on child nurture as a legitimate state concern that supercedes the rights of parents or the contract prerogatives of masters.

The fledgling women's rights movement, in its effort to gain the same custody rights for mothers as fathers enjoyed, looked backward, perpetuating the feudal view of custody and control of children as a right of a parent rather than adopting the emerging modern view of the best interests of the child. In some instances, as with their demand for the right to apprentice their children and receive the child's wages, women were not promoting the best interests of children but rather supporting an ancient system that often exploited child labor. While women had some success in lobbying legislatures regarding custody issues, particularly with regard to testamentary guardianships (asserting their rights as natural guardians where the father was dead), their demands for equal custodial rights in marriage and divorce were considered too disruptive of family stability by all-male legislatures.

It was principally the new middle-class judiciary, with its idealization of mothers and its tender attitude toward children, that guided the transformation toward the modern rule of the child's best interests. These judges were citizens of their culture. They believed, as they were told by mass circulation magazines and child-rearing manuals, that mothers were more nurturing and morally superior to fathers and that children were best raised under their gentle guidance. They were willing, on a case by case basis, to award custody to mothers of young children, not as a woman's right, but for the sake of the child's nurture. Courts also became reluctant to enforce voluntary indentures that separated children from their parents.

Child nurture became a central concern of judges in private law disputes, where the parents were challenging each other or a third party, such as a master to whom a child was apprenticed. This concern, however, was lacking for children who had no parents to fight for them. Poor law officials exercised nearly unchecked power in disposing of poor and orphaned children by early indentures or "placing out" in farm communities. Judges rarely saw these children, since their custodial arrangements were not governed by formal contracts. They were outside the circle of interests of the early women's rights movement as well, with its focus on the property and civil rights of middle-class women.

A few legislative initiatives, however, apparently not prompted by any organized group, hinted at an early concern for poor children that would mature in the beginning of the next century. The newly created right of adoption and the legal recognition of illegitimate children as belonging to their mother's family reflected, in part, a concern for the nurturance of poor and disadvantaged children. The judiciary enforced this trend when given the opportunity, defending the unwed mothers' rights to the custody of their children and overlooking defects in the adoption proceedings in favor of the best interests of the child.

As a transitional period in child custody law the first century of the new republic is filled with contradictions and inconsistencies. Women's rights are suspect, while mother love is idealized. In the same state, one court might uphold the primacy of father's rights while another would eloquently defend mothers as the natural guardians of young children. Children were viewed as little angels in need of protection and nurturing, yet children were regularly apprenticed at age ten or eleven or sent as day workers to factories.

In one respect the emerging judicial concern for child nurture in the new republic strikes us as the foundation for modern family law. The emphasis on maternal nurture, however, with the judicial presumption toward mothers, must be seen now as an old trend being dissolved by the contemporary insistence on the formal legal equality of mother and father. While fathers are regaining some of the ground they lost in the nineteenth-century, modern child custody law is still riddled with contradictions and still evolving.

3

The State as Superparent: The Progressive Era, 1890–1920

The rich cannot say to the lowly "You are poor and have many children. I am rich and have none. You are unlearned and live in a cabin. I am learned and live in a mansion. Let the State take one of your children and give it a better home with me. I will rear it better than you can." . . . The deepest, the tenderest, the most unswerving and unfaltering thing on earth is the love of a mother for her child. The love of a good mother is the holiest thing this side of heaven. The natural ties of motherhood are not to be destroyed or disregarded save for some sound reason. Even a sinning and erring woman still clings to the child of her shame, and though bartering her own honor, will rarely fail to fight for that of her daughter.[1]

With this reasoning the appellate court of Georgia reversed the trial court, which had awarded the custody of Mrs. Moore's three illegitimate children all under age twelve to an orphanage. The trial court had relied upon a Georgia statute that declared that any child under age twelve could be removed to an orphan asylum or other charitable institution if it "is being reared up under immoral obscene or indecent influences likely to degrade its moral character and devote it to a vicious life."[2] Without questioning the statute, the court of appeals determined that the trial court had failed to prove that Mrs. Moore was "of an immoral character, unsuitable and unable to rear the children."[3]

In this case the court struggled with two powerful, sometimes contradictory principles. One was a belief in the importance of preserving the family, no matter how poor.[4] The other was the conviction that the state must intervene into families in order to protect children from abusive, neglectful, or immoral parents. These two principles had a profound effect on child custody decisions in the first two decades of the twentieth century. They prompted state courts like Georgia's to abandon the common law doctrine allowing the exploitation of children. Instead, both courts and legislatures formulated new rules aimed at protecting children.

For example, the concept of the child's best interest was extended to poor children. Originally this concept was developed in the late nineteenth century by judges to determine private custody disputes between divorcing parents. Now, it was applied to poor children generally, not just to the children of divorcing parents. In a radical departure from traditional poor law principles, the state made a tentative commitment to allow poor but "worthy" mothers to maintain custody of their children. Poor children who would have been "bound out" to a master in return for labor in the colonial years, and "placed out" to labor on a midwestern farm or sent to an almshouse or orphan asylum in the nineteenth century, were now more frequently supported in their mothers' home. (Rarely was support provided if the father were present.) If that failed, or if they had no suitable parent, children were increasingly placed in a foster home, which was considered a substitute family rather than an orphanage, or put up for adoption by a new family.

State legislatures also acted to protect children in other important ways during this era, adopting a huge amount of child welfare legislation. The hours and the workplaces where children could labor were closely regulated; other laws dictated the establishment of public schools and required attendance of all children. A juvenile court system was put in place in many states.

State legislatures diluted judicial discretion in dealing with the welfare of children, confining it within an elaborate statutory scheme.

At the same time, the divorce rate was exploding, and both courts and legislatures were concerned about the impact that this social change might have on the future of the family. For reasons discussed later in this chapter, courts responded by pursuing a new trend in child custody following divorce. The decided trend favored mothers, who were seen as the more nurturing parent, even if the mother was not entirely above moral reproach. Legislatures, meanwhile, passed strict laws, often buttressed with severe criminal penalties, to compel child support from all fathers, including those who lost their children by judicial decree following divorce. Overall, both courts and legislators paid far less deference to fathers, virtually ignoring their common law rights to the custody and control of their children.

In effect, the state became the superparent, generous and nurturing, but judgmental. It made the final decisions on how children should be raised and with whom they should live. In assuming this role, the state finally shattered the common law relationship between parents and children. That relationship once had assumed that a father (and sometimes widowed mother) had complete custody and authority over his children, including absolute right to their services or wages if they worked for others, in return for maintenance and varying degrees of obligation for their education. Child labor legislation now severely restricted the right to the child's services. The right to custody, once absolute, could now be severed if the father or mother misused their authority in an abusive or neglectful manner. Furthermore, both legislators and judges decided that maintenance and custody were no longer mutually dependent rights. A father must support a child even if he lost custody. Finally, the obligation to educate passed from the parent to the state. The public school teacher, not the father or mother, would control the child's education and a good deal of the child's socialization.

Child saving and Childsavers

The new concern for the welfare of the children was part of the larger, broader reformist movement placed historically in the "Progressive" era. During this era states intruded into the privacy of families in a manner not seen since the selectmen of Massachusetts visited homes to determine whether children were behaving well and receiving religious and civic training.[5] "Childsavers," as they were called, were originally a large and very active coalition of volunteer philanthropists, Women's Club members, and assorted urban-based professionals who rallied against the mistreatment of poor and abused children toward the end of the nineteenth century. In the Progressive era the child-saving movement was increasingly dominated by the developing profession of social work. In contrast to the volunteer childsavers, social workers were trained, paid, and career minded. Social workers focused more on providing services to support a child within his or her family, rather than simply removing a child from a cruel environment.

While men still outnumbered women in early child welfare social work activity, a high proportion of women entered the field, and many reached the top of the profession. These were the women who had benefited from the efforts of the first wave of feminism and from the growing wealth of the middle class. They were college graduates who did not need to marry immediately in order to attain financial security. In ever larger numbers they gravitated to settlement houses, set up to help urban poor, mainly immigrants,[6] and began to train at the growing number of institutions, such as the University of Chicago, that offered training courses in conjunction with a social service agency.[7]

Julia Lathrop, the first chief of the Children's Bureau, created by President Howard Taft in 1912, is an example of this second wave of feminists. A child of middle-class abolitionist reformists, who provided encouragement and financial support, Lathrop rode on the victories of the first wave of feminists. Because of their efforts to open up education to women, she acquired a first-class education at Vassar and went on to read law. However, her career choices were severely limited; child saving was one of the few fields where she could use her talents and education on an equal footing with men. She was appointed as the first woman member of the Illinois Board of Public Charities in 1892, the organization responsible for orphaned, abandoned, and neglected children, and in 1899 helped found the Chicago Juvenile Court, the first in the country and the model for the nation. Thereafter, her career soared with the rapidly evolving child welfare movement. Her commitment to children was deeply felt. "Sooner or later,"she declared, "as we choose, by our interest, or its lack, the child will win."[8]

Referred to as social feminists (as opposed to pure women's rights advocates), this dedicated group, led by such remarkable women as Jane Addams, Florence Kelley, Lillian Wald, and Julia Lathrop, forced a significant ideological shift in the women's movement.[9] The social feminists, in what might be called the second wave of feminism, turned away from the nineteenth-century feminists' focus on individual property and civil rights for middle-class women, as expressed in the seminal feminist manifesto, the 1848 Seneca Falls Declaration of Rights and Sentiments, and instead focused their attention on poor children and their families. In so doing the social feminists conformed to the nineteenth-century stereotype of the family as women's sphere and the world as men's sphere. For this reason, historians and modern-day feminists have criticized social feminists as backsliders who relinquished the goal of equality with men and retreated into family concerns. Historian William O'Neill claims that "their benevolent enterprises met women's desire for useful and satisfying work without touching the sources of their inequality."[10]

Still, by supporting rather than challenging the family and the role of women within it, social feminists achieved important political gains, including suffrage and equal custodial rights for mothers—goals that had eluded their more individualistic nineteenth-century predecessors. Most of the leading social feminists of the early twentieth century supported women's suffrage but based their argument on family welfare rather than individual rights. Jane Addams, in a speech entitled "Why Women Should Vote," argued that women "bring the cultural forces to bear upon our materialistic civilization; and if she would do it all with the dignity and directness fitting one who carries on her immemorial duties, then she must bring herself to the use of the ballot—that latest implement for self government. May we not fairly say that American women need this implement in order to preserve the home?"[11] The nonthreatening argument that the vote was a means for mothers to promote the family, not their own political interests, proved to be the winning strategy in persuading all-male legislatures to grant female suffrage.

This same argument in favor of mothers promoting their children's interests permitted the passage of legislation giving mothers equal custody rights to fathers—a victory not attainable by the first wave of feminists, who fought for equal rights for married women. The arguments of earlier feminists, focusing on the individual rights of women, not those of children or the family, threatened the all-male legislators who feared that equal custody rights would encourage women to leave their husbands.[12] Social feminists, on the other hand, allied with philanthropists, juvenile court advocates, and other reform-minded groups, pushed for a broad program of child protection and support legislation that often benefited their mothers as well. Legislative emphasis on children's rights rather than those of their parents was a winning approach. As Florence Kelley remarked in regard to the common law as interpreted by Blackstone, "Nowhere in the Commentaries is there a hint that the common law regarded the child as an individual with a distinctive legal status." However, she believed that the Progressive era began by recognizing "the child's welfare as a direct object of legislation."[13]

Social feminists promoted family interests while redefining the relationship between children, parents, and the state. They abandoned the nineteenth-century policy of family privacy, which effectively gave parents or, most often, fathers, the right to complete control of their children, as long as they supported them. Instead, the social work profession recognized the role of the state as parent as well. In fact, the state, as represented by its agents, child welfare workers, became the superparent, determining the conditions under which natural parents could raise their children. Critics of the newly developing "helping profession" of social work claim that social workers set out to undermine the family culture of poor immigrants and replace it with their own middle-class values. Historian Christopher Lasch maintains that social workers, through children's aid societies, juvenile courts, and family visits, "sought to counteract the widespread `lack of wisdom and understanding on the part of parents, teachers, and others,' while reassuring the mother who feared, with good reason, that the social worker meant to take her place in the home."[14]

Still, the new social work philosophy emphasized maintaining poor children in their families, if fit. This commitment represented a major shift in American poor law philosophy regarding the custody of children, probably the most significant change since the Elizabethan Poor Laws of 1601 mandated the apprenticing of poor, idle, or vagrant children.[15] Propelling this ideological shift was the emerging belief that poverty did not necessarily reflect moral weakness; social conditions could force otherwise worthy people into a state of poverty. A good part of the child-saving debate during the Progressive era focused on when and how to support parents so that they would not be forced to give up their children. The first White House Conference on the Care of Dependent Children, called by President Theodore Roosevelt in 1909, offered this agenda:

> Should children of parents of worthy character, but suffering from temporary misfortune, and the children of widows of worthy character and reasonable efficiency, be kept with their parents—aid being given to parents to enable them to maintain suitable homes for the rearing of the children? Should the breaking of a home be permitted for reasons of poverty, or only for reasons of inefficiency or immorality?[16]

Reformers at the conference quickly adopted the position that poverty alone should not justify the removal of a child from his or her parents; only severe physical abuse or neglect or lack of moral fitness would provide sufficient grounds. Far more divisive was the question of how to support a family in poverty. The majority leaned toward private charity rather than government relief as a means of accomplishing this goal. There was widespread concern within the social welfare community that public aid would produce a "dependent" personality and would discourage relatives and charities from carrying their share of the burden. Social feminists, who uniformly agreed upon the family as the best institution for child raising, reflected this split within their own ranks. Jane Addams, Florence Kelley, Julia Lathrop, and Grace and Edith Abbot, all prominent leaders of the settlement house movement, concurred that private charity could not reach far enough to solve the problems of poor families, while others, particularly those associated with well-established charities, including Josephine Lowell Shaw, of the New York Charity Organization Society, and Mary Richmond, who headed the Philadelphia Society for Organizing Charity, strongly opposed the demoralizing factor of state aid. As one Mary Wilcox Glenn of the Brooklyn Bureau of State Charities characterized it, it would encourage "pathological parasitism"[17]

Mothers' Aid

In spite of strong opposition, the shift to state support occurred rapidly at the end of the Progressive era; public law mandating the juvenile court to order support for "worthy" parents unable to maintain their children passed the Illinois legislature in 1911. This law was officially known as the "Funds to Parents," and used gender-neutral language in describing parents.

> If the parent or parents of such dependent or neglected child are poor and unable to properly care for the said child, but are otherwise proper guardians and it is for the welfare of such child to remain at home, the court may enter an order finding such facts and fixing the amount of money necessary to enable the parent or parents to properly care for such child[18]

By 1919 funds for dependent children in their own homes had been provided by thirty-nine states and the territories of Alaska and Hawaii.[19]

The gender-neutral posture was soon discarded and subsequent state acts were called "Mothers' Pensions," for, in fact, mothers, not fathers, were almost always the beneficiaries of public support. Not all needy mothers received these pensions, however, for not all mothers were considered to be worthy. In the hierarchy of worthy mothers, widows stood supreme.[20] Eventually, these support acts came to be popularly known as "widows pensions." Indeed, as late as 1931 82 percent of mothers receiving aid were widows.[21] Less than half the states allowed pensions for women whose husbands were feebleminded or incapacitated, and most states refused to grant aid to divorced women whose husbands were still alive or to wives whose husbands had deserted. Massachusetts, for example, insisted that no deserted wife's application would be considered until one year had passed and she had shown her willingness to prosecute her husband for desertion and nonsupport.[22]

A mother's sexual morality also became an important consideration in her receiving and maintaining public aid. Support was generally restricted to mothers of good moral character, in an extension of the nineteenth-century distinction in private custody disputes following divorce between good mothers, who were the fount of all nurturing, and bad, adulterous mothers, who tainted their children's moral development. By definition unmarried mothers were considered to be of bad moral character. Hawaii, Michigan, and Nebraska specifically allowed unmarried mothers to receive assistance, but most states considered them ineligible. Massachusetts law declared that giving support to mothers of illegitimate children would "offend the moral feeling of respectable mothers and would do violence to a traditional sentiment that is inseparable from a respect for virtue."[23]

All single mothers were in the same bind, whether their single parenthood was the result of the death or desertion of their husbands, or the fact that they had never married. A "worthy" mother was one who devoted full time to her children, did not work outside the home, and led a conspicuously virtuous life with no male companionship. The reality of life for most single mothers was that, even if they were fortunate enough to warrant mothers' aid, they could not make ends meet. Their choices were limited: if they worked outside the home, they would not meet the conditions for aid, and ran the danger of being considered "neglectful," especially if they had to leave their children unattended for any period of time. This could be grounds for removal. If they sent their older children out to work so that they could remain in the home with younger children, that was also considered neglect. If they took in male boarders so that they could remain in the home, it was considered highly inappropriate, if not downright immoral. If they received help from males not their relatives, prostitution would be surmised.[24]

The story of Cora Simpson, deserted mother of two small daughters, who came to the Massachusetts Society for the Prevention of Cruelty to Children (MSPCC), for help in 1917 illustrates this bind. According to the records of the society, as reported by historian Linda Gordon, "The ch. [children] were about half-starved during the winter: the mothers was about ready to give the ch. up but she reconsidered this when Mrs. W offered to take her into her home to board but the expense was too great." Rather than give Cora Thompson any aid, the MSPCC attempted to get $17.50 every two weeks from her husband. This was not forthcoming, and Mrs. Simpson returned for help with a third child, apparently illegitimate. Once again the agency refused help, and the record indicates that "Miss B. [the Associated Charities worker] seemed to think the mother was an immoral woman." The last record of her case indicates that she disappeared, and her three children became wards of the state and were placed in an orphanage. Immediately before her disappearance she had been working as a seamstress for fifteen dollars a week. She paid half of that salary for child care, keeping the baby with her in the shop where she worked. In July 1919 her landlord evicted her, accusing her of earning by "illeg. means."[25]

Deserted mothers had custody of their children by default, but, like Cora Simpson, they had great difficulty supporting these children and were often forced to relinquish them to the custody of the state. According to one prominent social worker, about one-quarter of the juvenile commitments to New York institutions at the turn of the century were the result of abandonment and failure to support.[26] While deserting fathers (and much less frequently, mothers) were by no means a novelty in the American experience, the state laws forcing their compliance had been weak and poorly enforced. Perhaps only in the watchful Puritan colonies, most prominently the Massachusetts Bay colony, were fathers regularly taken to task and sometimes imprisoned for shirking their family support obligations.[27] Other colonies and, ultimately, states in the new republic had been far more lax about pursuing deserters. The common law tradition was not very helpful in this regard either. James Kent, the much-cited nineteenth-century treatise writer on family law, observed, in 1826, "The obligation of parental duty is so well secured by the strength of natural affection that it seldom requires to be enforced by human laws."[28]

Social workers, philanthropists, and other reformers of the Progressive era rallied against this laissez faire attitude. They believed that nonsupporting fathers should be dealt with quickly and harshly. Within individual states they launched campaigns for tough legislation that would criminalize nonsupport and offer the resources of the police and courts to pursue and convict fathers who had abandoned their children without support. The motivation for this initiative was twofold. First, large numbers of destitute families were seeking relief from charitable organizations; agencies reported that up to 20 percent of the families they supported were the products of desertion. Second, in the scenario of the ideal family that the reformers promoted, deserting fathers were true villains. While some recognition was given to the stress of unemployment and financial difficulties, most studies of desertion undertaken during this era concluded that the deserters were morally unfit. Intemperance, promiscuity, gambling, and laziness were most frequently cited as the cause of desertion, not economic problems or marital incompatibility.[29]

Social reformers convinced state legislatures that these morally unfit deserters deserved serious punishment. More in the spirit of revenge and deterrence than rehabilitation, all states toughened their desertion and nonsupport laws. Forty-six states passed separate laws for the crimes of desertion and nonsupport, allowing the state to prosecute fathers who did not leave home but were not supporting their family. Twenty states declared failure to support was a misdemeanor, fourteen deemed it a felony, punishable by a year or more in state prison, the other states simply labeled nonsupport a crime.[30] Penalties for the separate crime of desertion were similar.

The courts enthusiastically supported the spirit of the newly toughened laws, often adding moralistic messages to the convictions they affirmed. One Oklahoma court claimed the new law

> is not only the law of the land, but the plain dictate of humanity and justice. It is also in strict harmony with the Divine Law. In the eighth verse, fifth chapter I Timothy, we are told: "But if any provide not for his own, and specifically for those of his own house, he hath denied the faith and is worse than an infidel."[31]

In practice, the law left a good deal of discretion to individual judges. Forty-five jurisdictions made provision for suspension of sentence and probation of the defendant if he undertook, under court supervision, a plan to support the child.[32]

How did these tough new laws work for the destitute family? Although it is difficult to obtain accurate data, available information indicates that they did little to help families, and few nondeserting fathers were sent to jail. A study of 899 trials held in 1909 in the District of Columbia reveals that sentences were suspended in three-quarters of the cases, and only 11 percent of the fathers were committed to the local workhouse, where their small earnings of fifty cents per day were given to the families.[33] In another study where orders for support were given in 69 cases, only 40 fathers paid anything at all, and these irregularly. The amount they were asked to pay, three to five dollars per week, would have been insufficient to support a family under any circumstance.[34] If fathers could not or would not contribute, most courts, hampered by the lack of enforcement, did little to carry out the tough laws.

Ironically, the deserted wives with children to support probably would have been better off without the laws. As noted, mother's pensions were given out almost exclusively to widows, in the belief that the law should force deserting husbands to support their families. In the 1931 survey of mother's pensions only 3,296 out of a total of 60,119 pensions went to families where the father had deserted.[35] Private agencies, as illustrated by the treatment given Cora by the Massachusetts Society for the Prevention of Cruelty to Children, often refused to aid the deserted wife and instead fruitlessly pursued the elusive husband. This attitude reflected less concern with the interests of the children than with the punishment of the father.

Unwed mothers posed still other problems for child protection workers. By definition, the mother had engaged in illicit and immoral behavior before the child was born. In the colonial era these mothers were whipped, and their child, *filius nulius,* became the responsibility of the town in which it was born.[36] In the nineteenth century the law adopted a kinder attitude toward "fallen" women, and most states passed laws that made the child part of his or her mother's family, not the father's. This recognition provided a legal nod in the direction of motherhood, and gave the child at least half a legal identity, but it did little to ensure that mothers could keep their illegitimate children. Unwed mothers who could not support their children invariably lost their children.[37]

The all-embracing concern for children displayed by child welfare reformers of the Progressive era eventually focused on illegitimate children. In fact, there was little precise information about these children. How many were they? Who were their mothers? What happened to them? When the Children's Bureau attempted to gather statistics on illegitimate children in 1915, it found that most states did not keep accurate records on these children. The bureau nonetheless estimated that approximately 32,400 illegitimate children were born that year, representing 1.8 percent of all live births.[38] Local children's protective agencies also undertook surveys that yielded unsurprising results. The great majority of unwed mothers were young and working class. The Juvenile Protection Association of Chicago found that the largest number, almost half (43 percent), were domestic servants or hotel workers, trailed by factory workers, seamstresses, and stenographers. [39]

Concern for illegitimate children appeared on the agenda of several child welfare conferences and became an important issue for the newly developing social sciences. Articles devoted to the topic appeared in the *American Journal of Sociology* and the *National Humane Review*.[40] The discussions focused on the stigma of illegitimacy suffered by innocent children. This widespread attention pressured state legislatures to change their laws in order to wipe out the legal discrimination experienced by children born out of wedlock. The more progressive reformers wanted to erase the distinction between legitimate and illegitimate children. Children born out of wedlock, once paternity was established, would be able to inherit from their father, as well as their mother, and to take his name. Opposition to this sweeping approach came from other reformers who feared that this recognition would denigrate marriage. Surely, they insisted, society must promote legal marriage over a nonmarried status.

Given the confusion within the ranks of those dedicated to helping illegitimate children, it is not surprising that only a handful of states actually changed their laws significantly before 1920.[41] North Dakota offered the most radical model; its 1917 legislation declared, "Every child is legitimate and is entitled to support and education to the same extent as if born in lawful wedlock, and inherits from natural parents and from their kindred heirs, lineal and collateral."

While radical in its pronouncement of legitimacy, this statute maintained the nineteenth-century judicial sentiment that gave mothers absolute right to custody of their children, and putative fathers nothing, simply stating, "Mother of illegitimate child entitled to custody." The North Dakota law also restricted children from receiving full status as a natural child if the father were married. "Child does not have the right to dwelling or residence with family of its father if father is married to another than mother of child."[42] In effect North Dakota was willing to give fathers responsibility for support but allow mothers to retain the right of custody. The law goes even further by protecting the families of a married father from the imposition of custody, indicating that, for custodial purposes, the child was still indeed the child of its mother.

Other states were less clear about the issue of custody. Only eleven states specifically mentioned custody of an illegitimate child. In nine of these states the legislatures asserted the mothers' right to custody of illegitimate children. Meanwhile, Illinois, which was one of the few states to rewrite its legitimacy laws, gave the right to the mother only to age ten and to the father if the mother is unfit. Georgia gave the mother custodial rights unless the child is legitimated.[43]

While fathers were not given significantly more custodial rights, their obligations to support were more firmly enforced, sometimes with the teeth of criminal penalties, including prison. The English common law rule that gave fathers of illegitimate children neither the right to custody nor the obligation of support had not been followed in most states or in the colonies before them, where it was usually possible for an unwed mother to charge the father for support.[44] These proceedings, however, varied from state to state, and some states had adhered to common law and imposed no obligation of support on fathers. All this changed during the Progressive era, where the concern for children and the general trend toward pursuing nonsupporting fathers, wed or unwed, prompted almost all states (with the exception of Alaska, Texas, and Virginia) to enact or strengthen what were still called bastardy proceedings.[45] Many of these new laws provided for criminal rather than civil proceedings.

California is a good example of this rapid evolution in bastardy proceedings. In 1915 putative father Gambetta (first name unstated), was convicted of child neglect under California Penal Code 270 for failure to support. His conviction was reversed by the appellate court, which stated that "Penal code 270 has no application to the father of illegitimate children."[46] The legislature promptly remedied this situation, making the section applicable to a parent "of either a legitimate or illegitimate minor child." In 1923 the legislature further amended the law, adding a prison sentence to the monetary penalty for committing the crime of neglect.

A father of either a legitimate or illegitimate minor child who willfully omits without lawful excuse to furnish necessary food, clothing, shelter or medical attendance for his child is guilty of a misdemeanor and punishable by imprisonment in the county jail not exceeding two years or by a fine not exceeding one thousand dollars ($1000) or by both.[47]

Most states left the initiation of the bastardy proceedings to the mother and deferred the nature and amount of support to judicial discretion. However, Minnesota, in a model statute much admired by child advocates, allowed the State Board of Control to instigate action when necessary. It also removed as a defense evidence that the mother had sexual contact with other men in the period when the baby might have been conceived. Most important, if a man were found guilty he was "subject to all the obligations for the care, maintenance and education of such child and to all the penalties for failure to perform the same, which are or shall be imposed by law upon the father of a legitimate child."[48]

While legislatures may have been moving toward treating illegitimate children as natural children, the reality was that their mothers were not treated as other single mothers by the social service agencies. In a national survey of mother's pensions dispensed by thirty-eight states and the District of Columbia in 1931, only 55 unwed mothers were given pensions out of a total of 49,477 mothers.[49] Private charitable organizations were sometimes more sympathetic, but these also distinguished between what they considered redeemable and unredeemable unwed mothers. The Florence Crittendon Missions, the most famous of the maternity homes for unwed mothers, aspired to teach mothers-to-be "the beauty and necessity of perfect obedience, the requisite of a perfect character." They turned away mothers who did not intend to keep their children or whom they considered "unfit." Often they refused to take in women who previously had illegitimate children.[50]

Lack of support from social services combined with the difficulty of securing support from the father through the legal system produced grim custody statistics. Of illegitimate children born in Boston in 1914, more than three-fifths would become wards of welfare agencies in the first year of their lives. In a Boston survey that same year only 13 percent of identifiable fathers were taken to court and only 7 percent were actually ordered to pay anything at all.[51] Minnesota, the state with the shining model of legislation designed to legally coerce unwed fathers, reported only 35 percent of unwed mothers studied in 1921 still had their children at two years of age.[52] While judges and reformers officially recognized that poverty alone was not a reason for removing a child from its parents, little real economic help was offered to support these sentiments when the children were illegitimate.

These sad statistics for the first two years of a child's life tell only part of the story. Unwed mothers who managed to hold onto their children were more vulnerable than other mothers to being declared unfit and losing them at a later date. Sexual immorality or intemperance by the mother could lead to child-neglect charges. A father suffered no penalty for such behavior. A mother of illegitimate children already had a track record for immorality and was therefore suspect. For instance, a twelve-year-old girl in Boston, one of nine children—at least six of whom were born out of wedlock—was accused of shoplifting and other larceny and taken into custody of the juvenile court. The psychiatric social workers in this case determined that her difficulty was maternal neglect, even though the agency records offered no evidence of poor parenting.[53]

Mrs. Moore, the mother of three illegitimate children introduced at the beginning of this chapter, was able to retrieve her children from Orphan's Home of the South Georgia Conference of the Methodist Episcopal Church South, yet the prognosis for keeping them in her custody would not be good. Unless she had support from relatives or other sources, she had to work outside the home in order to support these children, since, as an unwed mother, she probably would not be eligible for a publicly funded mother's pension, if offered in her state of Georgia.[54] Her fitness as a mother would be suspect because she both worked outside the home and her children were illegitimate. Most likely, she would receive little or no aid from private charities, and would be watched more carefully than other single mothers for signs of unfitness or neglect that could lead to removal once again.

Removal of Children

Social reformers affirmed the family as the appropriate vehicle for raising children and assisted some mothers in retaining custody of their children. Yet, child welfare workers, acting as agents of the state, also intervened in families and took away children from parents they considered unfit. It is here that the middle-class American-born orientation of the social reformers was most apparent. There was little tolerance of cultural, ethnic, or class differences, particularly when it came to alcohol or what was considered immoral sexual behavior. Single mothers were the main beneficiaries of social and economic support, but they were also the disproportionate target of social worker intervention and removal of children. In part this was because single mothers, as in previous eras, were still more vulnerable to losing their children because of their inability to support them. But it was also because mothers were held to a high standard of sexual morality and the lives of poor single mothers were clearly exposed to social workers.[55]

Categories defining child abuse and neglect were developed during the Progressive era. For the first time the state took seriously its role as child protector. All states wrote legislation defining abuse and neglect and sanctioning child removal. Theoretically the state had been permitted to intervene to protect children under the English common law doctrine of *parens patriae* as defined in the seventeenth-century Blisset's Case; in reality family privacy and parental autonomy had held sway.[56] "The state" was represented by local poor law officials who were ill-equipped to handle even the abandoned and orphaned children they were forced to take charge of. They had little energy left for children in more or less intact families.

The stirrings of organization for the protection of children began as an outgrowth of humane work for the protection of animals. Beginning with the founding of the New York Society for the Prevention of Cruelty to Children in 1874, large numbers of societies sprang up about the country. These societies, popularly referred to as the "Cruelty," were originally staffed by volunteers, who, following the turn of the century, were regularly replaced by the new professional social workers. At first their mission was narrowly conceived. As the first annual report of the New York Society related:

> We have agents about the city to look after poor children in the streets. In cases where we find children are hired to beg, we arrest the parties who hire them out. This is frequently done by Italian organ-grinders. . . . If a complaint is made to us of any child being ill-used, we send an officer to investigate the

case and see what can be done. . . . The society in all its transactions in reference to children, brings them before the court having jurisdiction in the matter.[57]

Later, most Cruelties, staffed with paid social workers, supervised troubled
families and provided them with a variety of services. Some Cruelties continued to provide for animals as well as children, in part because they received
most of their funding from this function. The Ohio Humane Society, for
instance, was unhappily forced to protect both children and animals because
it was supported by the "Sheep Fund," financed by dog registrations, which,
according the president, were "originally intended to reimburse sheep owners
whose flocks had been attacked by the wild dogs which used to infest the state
many years ago."[58]

Once abuse or neglect were identified by the Cruelty, the police, or another child welfare organization, the protective society investigated, sometimes
working with the police, and the case was brought before a juvenile court, if
there was one. With the initiation of the first juvenile court in 1899, jurisdiction over dependent, neglected, and delinquent children up to the age of sixteen was fairly rapidly transferred out of the regular court system to the juvenile courts, with the theory that the causes of delinquency were closely tied to
those of neglect. Laws giving these courts the power to remove children from
their parents and to make them wards of the state were loosely written in these
states, giving a great deal of judicial discretion to the juvenile court judge as a
protector of children. While the bulk of the juvenile court caseload dealt with
delinquent children, a significant portion was devoted to dependency, which
included parental neglect and abuse and abandonment. For instance, the
Cook County Juvenile Court in 1915 handled 1,886 cases of dependency as
compared with 3,202 charges of delinquency.[59] Criminal complaints against
parents arising from abuse complaints were handled separately in adult criminal courts.

Ironically, while the societies for the protection of children developed in
reaction to the cruel treatment children were receiving from their parents,
children were rarely removed because of physical cruelty. Nor were their parents punished. Social acceptance of corporal punishment in the name, at least,

of child discipline was so established that the laws were more likely to protect parents than to punish them.

Judicial decisions also reflected the wide latitude given to parents in cases of physical punishment. Reciting the facts of the case, a North Carolina appellate court stated:

> Mary C. Jones, aged 16 claimed that her father frequently whipped her without cause and on one occasion he whipped her 25 times before witnesses at the front gate with a switch or small limb, about the size of a thumb which produced welts on her back. He then went into the house, quickly returned, whipped her five more times then choked her and threw her to the ground, causing a dislocation of her thumb. Her stepmother testified that she was habitually disobedient, had several times stolen money, and was chastised on that occasion for stealing some cents from her father. No permanent injury was sustained.[60]

The jury in this case convicted Mr. Jones for criminal assault and battery, but the appeal court reversed the decision, claiming that in a situation where a parent is correcting a child the standard is the infliction of permanent injury, or that the action proceeded from pure malice. The judge explained, "We do not propose to palliate or excuse the conduct of the defendant in the present case. The punishment seems to have been needlessly severe, but we refuse to take cognizance of it as a criminal act, because it belongs to the domestic rather than legal power, to a domain into which the penal law is reluctant to enter, unless induced by an imperious necessity.[61]

Child protection was the major focus of hundreds of societies to prevent cruelty to children. Even so, prevention of physical cruelty by parents made astonishingly little progress during the Progressive era, and relatively few children were removed from their homes because of their parents' physical abuse. According to historian Elizabeth Pleck, most of the work of anticruelty societies consisted, not in the rescue of physically abused children, but in the investigation of complaints against drunken and neglectful parents. In Pleck's investigation of the Pennsylvania Society to Protect Children from Cruelty, she found that between 1878 and 1935, only 12 percent of this agency's cases concerned child cruelty. The society intervened, she claims, primarily in immigrant poor and working-class homes. The occasional investigation into a middle-class home was handled gently, incurring slight risk of removal.[62]

By the end of the era only five western states (California, Montana, North Dakota, Oklahoma, and South Dakota) specifically created excessive use of parental authority as a reason for removing a child from the home. By contrast, eighteen states defended in various ways the rights of parents to use physical discipline, and nine specifically excused them from murder if death occurred while lawfully correcting the child. (If excess force was used, manslaughter could be charged.) South Carolina apparently even defended the use of knives in discipline. "Provisions on killing by stabbing do not apply to person, who in chastising or correcting a child chances to commit manslaughter without intending to do so."[63] South Dakota presented a curious hybrid of these two positions, stating,

> Abuse of parental authority subject to judicial cognizance in civil action brought by child, relative, or office of poor. Child may be freed from dominion of parent. Homicide excusable when committed by accident or misfortune in lawfully correcting child, with usual and ordinary caution, and without unlawful intent.[64]

More often, the passive behavior of neglect rather than the action of physical abuse prompted intervention and sometimes removal of children during the Progressive era. There were two types of neglect: the first concerned parental *incompetence*, not properly caring for the everyday needs of a child, and the second focused on parental *unfitness*, usually immoral behavior on the part of the mother or drunkenness on the part of either mother or father.

Neglect based on parental incompetence, the most common ground for removing children from their home, was most problematic for Progressive social reformers and for the courts. The basic contradiction was that parents who could not properly clothe and feed their children were most often victims of poverty, yet the new enlightened view of child nurture was that poverty alone should not be the basis for the removal of a child from his or her parents. In the colonial era children whose parents could not support them would automatically become wards of the town poor law officials. Later in the nineteenth century custody, particularly in large cities, would be assumed by the appropriate charitable board or institution. The emerging environmentalist doctrine put forth the belief that the poor were not inherently unfit but victims of their environment. Therefore it was unfair to take away their children. Yet, as we have seen, public and private support of poor parents was often inadequate to guarantee the basic obligations of parenting. Women were disproportionately victims of this contradiction since single mothers had great difficulty combining work and parental duties, but were rarely provided adequate support. Courts struggled with reconciling this new doctrine rejecting poverty as the ground for removal with the plain fact that children were indeed neglected when their parents were extremely poor.

The decisions reached by courts during this era clearly illustrate the gap between reformist thinking and harsh reality. A Massachusetts court was forced to ponder the definition of neglect in determining the legal custody of a seven-year-old boy, William Dee, who had been put in an almshouse at age three by his widowed mother, who could no longer support both him and his younger sibling. The court found that before coming to the almshouse, the boy "was properly clothed and fed by the mother, and affectionately cared for, and there was nothing in the case to indicate that the child suffered from any failure on the part of the mother to do what a mother should." Nevertheless, the Central District Court of Worcester found that the defendant was a neglected child and ordered that he be committed to the custody of the state. The high court reversed, reasoning that there was a distinction between pauper or dependent children, on the one hand, and neglected children, on the other.

> Whether considered from the standpoint of the dependent child or of the parent entitled to its custody and care, but temporarily and unavoidably disabled from providing for its support, a grave injustice would be done to such innocent victims of poverty by bringing them into court with its stigma of criminality.

However, the end result for William Dee and his mother was that William remained in the almshouse. The appeals court was not empowered to order support but could only suggest that "the facts here disclosed present a case for relief by public agencies."[65]

In other cases the court had less difficulty in considering poverty as justification for the state assuming permanent custody, particularly if the mothers were foreign born and the children illegitimate. The same Massachusetts court eight years earlier, composed of two out of five of the same judges, had looked quite differently at Mary Jamrock, a Polish Catholic immigrant. Her children were committed to the custody of the state board of charity because they were "dependent upon public charity." The issue before the court was a subsequent attempt at adoption by a non-Catholic couple. Mary refused her permission, but the court ruled that permission is not necessary since Massachusetts law does not require a mother's consent in the case of an illegitimate child "if she suffered such child to be supported for more than two years as a pauper by the commonwealth." As evidence that Mary "suffered" this support, the court noted that she never made any real effort to furnish support and made only three or four inquiries as to her children's whereabouts. The court rejected Mary's plea that when she made these inquiries she could not speak English and that the only person who could understand her was the Polish priest.[66]

Another form of neglect engendered by poverty was the refusal of many parents to send their children to school regularly. It was not easy or even economically feasible for many poor parents to accept the new concept of a parent-child relationship no longer based on the mutuality of economic obligations. The wages and services of children over which the parents had previously held complete control in exchange for maintenance were now being denied. Instead, parents were obliged to support their children. From the point of view of many parents, their children enjoyed the luxury of attending school while providing nothing for their parents. Often girls were kept out of school to take care of younger siblings while their mother worked and boys were sent to work in factories for wages or organized into urban begging brigades. The public was particularly incensed by the sight of children playing the violin or engaged in other forms of street entertainment for pennies. Neglect laws often singled out this form of child labor. The New York neglect law prohibited the employment of children "in peddling, singing or playing upon a musical instrument, or in a theatrical exhibition, or in any wandering occupation."[67] In a study of cases investigated by the Massachusetts Society for the Prevention of Cruelty, 9 percent listed children's overwork as a problem, and 5 percent noted that children were prevented from attending school.

Parental unfitness also contributed to a large proportion of neglect cases. The prevailing philosophy was that lack of moral fitness was worse than neglect. As Charles E. Faulkner, superintendent of the Soldier's Orphan's home in Atchison, Kansas, explained,

> If a mother is very poor and unable to care for her child, and in consequence has temporarily given up her child, when she gets to her feet again it should be returned to her: but if the mother is unworthy and on that account the child has been taken away from her, and she comes and seeks to recover it, then refuse to return the child to her custody and control.[68]

This philosophy was widely shared by social reformers, adopted by state legislatures, and enforced by courts. Lack of moral fitness on the part of a parent, most often a mother, was taken more seriously than ordinary incompetence in failing to provide proper care and supervision of children. There also was a hierarchy of unfit behavior. Although fathers could be considered unfit through their drunk and dissolute behavior, it was more often the extramarital sexual activity of the mother that was considered to create "an unfit place for a child." Moral neglect counted for a high percentage of child protection cases, about 24 percent in Boston. Of those reports claiming child neglect due to moral neglect, more than three-quarters of the offenders were mothers.[69] Usually moral neglect was combined with other forms of physical neglect. The immorality claim was far more likely to turn into a criminal charge than was simple physical neglect.

As noted earlier, unwed mothers were by definition considered morally suspect. Other single mothers, usually deserted wives or widows, were forced to earn a living for themselves and their children as best they could; this sometimes meant taking on a live-in lover or turning to prostitution. Agency workers did not always distinguish between the two and broadly defined prostitution to cover any sexual arrangement outside of marriage. Such a case was that of Anola Green, an African-American mother of three who migrated from Washington, D.C., to Boston in 1920, fleeing an abusive husband. She came to Boston with her lover; both, however, were still legally married. Her brother-in-law, for reasons unknown, sought revenge on Mrs. Green and reported her living arrangement to the police, who arrested her for lewd and lascivious conduct. Her children were seized and placed in the Massachusetts Society for the Prevention of Cruelty to Children's temporary home. The social worker assigned to the case reported that they lived in a three-room tenement that was "fairly well furnished. . . . The chn. [children] are attending sch. [school] and are properly clothed; have enough to eat." The children were examined to determine the effects of her lascivious conduct. The social worker reported that "medical examination proved that [older girl] had not been tampered with, but [younger] was a masterbater [*sic*]." This story ended relatively happily. Mrs. Green fought for her children, even convincing a friend to steal them from the court at one point, and finally was allowed to regain their custody under the condition she move back to Washington and never see her lover again. The MSPCC agent wrote ahead to Washington to ensure that the Washington Board of Children's Guardians maintained supervision over her.[70]

Child Placement

What happened to children when they were removed from their families because of abuse or neglect or abandoned by their parents through death or inability to support? Children were often removed temporarily and then returned to their parent or parents. For many children this became a familiar pattern. Temporarily shelters were often sponsored by the local "Cruelty," while more permanent arrangements, such as orphan asylums, were sponsored by charitable organizations, particularly churches. There was, however, a steady move toward placement of children in homes. In keeping with the Progressive focus on the family as the best institution for raising children, the tradition of placing out initiated by Charles Loring Brace and the Children's Aid Society before the Civil War was widely adopted and modified by the rapidly proliferating children's home societies.

Placing out had evolved in the nineteenth century from child apprenticeship or *binding out*. Binding out was basically an employment contract that gave the master complete custody and control as well as benefit of the child's services in exchange for maintenance, moral supervision, and sometimes a limited educational requirement. The only restriction of the master's authority was in the local courts, who could only enforce the terms of the contract. Placing out, on the other hand, did not give the master complete custody and control of the child, since the child was still under the authority of the agency that had placed him or her, and the placement could be rescinded at will by the agency that theoretically supervised the placement. Although labor was still the major attraction for prospective families in the early days of placing out, there was genuine concern for child welfare on the part of the agencies and a belief that a family situation, particularly in the country, was healthier than an asylum for dependent children.

Adoption was the hoped-for goal of a child placed out. The new legal form of adoption gave the child virtually all the rights of a natural child, and was supposedly based on familial sentiment rather than child labor. With adoption the rights of the natural parents, if alive, were decisively terminated. In contrast, under binding out and placing out, living parents did not totally relinquish their parental rights but were rarely in a position to assert them.[71]

By the Progressive era it became clear that only a small percentage of the orphaned and now increasingly neglected children removed from their parents would be adopted. Most would-be parents preferred children three years old or younger in healthy condition. Moreover, the adoption laws themselves were strict. In most states parents would not lose their parental rights unless convicted of physical abuse or neglect (a rare event), and the consent of both parents was required before the child could be adopted. Some states had different rules for illegitimate or abandoned children, as noted earlier in the case of Polish-speaking Mary Jamrock, who lost her parental right to consent since the court determined she had "suffered" her children to be placed in an almshouse for more than two years, even though it was shown that her inability to speak English had thwarted her several attempts to locate her children.[72] In some states the parent who lost custody in a divorce was not required to consent, in others this was limited to divorces on the grounds of adultery, cruelty, abandonment and desertion.[73] Most courts tended to guard parental rights and treat the consent issue seriously. A California court returned eight-year-old Linda Cozza from a good adopting home to her mother, even though she had been forced out of the house by her mother's new husband and her mother had been at fault in her parents' divorce. The court claimed that the cruelty for which the mother was found at fault in the divorce action was directed against her husband, not children, and "it is a matter of no consequence in the proceeding for adoption what may be the conduct of parents toward their children, their environment or home surroundings or the moral or material advantage that the children might receive by being taken from the custody of their parents and placed elsewhere."[74] Courts also exercised wide discretionary powers in considering the race, sex, age, wealth, and religion of the adopting parent.[75]

For most dependent or neglected children a family situation could only be achieved by placing out. Early placing out customs were oriented to farm labor. Children's aid societies often sent the children far out of their urban environments to rural areas in western states. The child welfare community increasingly criticized these practices. While reformers were successfully passing child labor laws that limited work in factories and peddling on city streets, agencies were still sending children to hard labor on farms. It was not clear that city children were suited to this labor, and in fact few stayed on farms once they were old enough to leave. Moreover, these children were seldom well-supervised, and agency records revealed that contact with placement parents was frequently lost. Newly organized children's home societies sought to eliminate the labor exploitation, using "placing out" to fulfill families' emotional rather than economic needs. These homes came over time to be known as foster homes. A national campaign to promote home placement was initiated by Theodore Dreiser in the popular women's fashion magazine, the *Delineator*, from 1907 to 1911. Each month the stories of several homeless children were offered by agencies in the pages of the *Delineator*. Prospective families were given several choices. A family could receive a child through placing out, with no written instrument, "but those responsible for placing it reserve the privilege of visiting your home from time to time to see that all is well with the child." A family could also receive a child through indenture, by which the family signed a contract binding them to provide a home, clothes, and schools (no mention of labor or services), without visits. Finally, for some children, a family could choose adoption. Explaining adoption, the magazine stated that "the child becomes legally yours to be brought up as your own, and, if it is desired, arrangements may be made that the world shall not know otherwise."[76]

Despite these campaigns, "free" placements could not be found for many children, compelling children's home societies to consider the alternative of "paid" placements. Homer Folks, a major figure in child protection, recognized the problem and advocated payment for the board of children in families when necessary, the model for the contemporary foster care system. Assailing the myth of more applicants offering free placements than children available to fill them, Folks claimed,

> It is true as regards healthy infants, and in some seasons of the year, for children evidently able to work. It is not true with regard to ordinary boys from four to eight or ten years or age, it is not true as regards delicate or unattractive children, or children who may be reclaimed by parents.[77]

Initially paid home placements or "boarding out" were strongly opposed, both because they cost money and because they countered the spirit of charity that the children's home societies wished to promote. They claimed that paying families was soulless and commercial. In this period of slow and grudging acceptance of paid placements, the only alternative for children who were of the wrong age or sex, not attractive, or beset with physical or emotional disabilities were orphan asylums. These categories, in fact, included most children, and orphanages continued to provide for the majority of homeless children. According to the U.S. Bureau of the Census survey in 1923, the first accurate account of child placing, 64.3 percent of dependent and neglected children were still found in orphan asylums, while 23.4 percent were in free home placements and 10.2 percent in paid home placements. [78] The number of adopted children was not reported.

Divorce

In 1890 the arbitrary date often used to mark the beginning of the Progressive era, there were 33,461 divorces in the country. In the year 1920, the year considered to end of the reform era, there were 167,105 divorces. While these numbers may not be precise, as local records are often incomplete or missing, they do suggest that there was a remarkable increase in the numbers of couples who experienced divorce.[79] Not all of these couples had children: in fact, less than 50 percent of these divorces involved children. Still, for the first time, the number of children who lost a parent from divorce began to approach the number who lost a parent through death.[80] Moreover, countless parents simply deserted, with no divorce sought, and many couples lived apart without divorce.

For the courts and the legislatures the unusual event of divorce was now commonplace; child custody was no longer an arcane and rarely exercised area of the law and the lives of thousands of children and their parents were affected by custody decisions. This fact accelerated trends begun in the nineteenth century, such as the father's obligation to support without the benefit of custody, for which there previously had been little case precedent. The judiciary still took the lead in developing rules to resolve the private disputes between divorcing couples, but state legislatures increasingly codified these rules, often narrowing the margin of judicial discretion.

The case of Mr. and Mrs. Harmon provides a glimpse of an era known as the "roaring twenties" but it also reveals that a woman's sexual conduct was no longer a complete bar to custody. Two married couples in Kansas, Mr and Mrs. Harmon and an unnamed husband and wife, associated in the same social circles and became good friends, going on late-night rides and spending much of their free time together. One day Mr. Harmon found Mrs. Harmon engaged in an act of adultery with the other husband. He insisted that she must go to live with her parents and renounce the custody of their five-year-old daughter. Both men made her sign a written agreement admitting her guilt and agreeing to the custody arrangement. Mr. Harmon then sued for divorce on the ground of adultery and sought custody of their daughter. The trial court found that adultery was committed with "the knowledge, connivance and consent of the plaintiff," and denied the appeal. The court was silent on the custody issue.

On appeal a higher court agreed that adultery was encouraged by the husband. "He must have known the absurd lengths to which extraordinary intimacy, informality, and unconventionality [with the other couple] had grown was bound to culminate as it did." The court affirmed the denial of a divorce to the Harmons, but granted temporary custody of the daughter to the mother, reasoning that "except for defendant's temporary infatuation for her paramour, she was a good mother."[81]

Other courts concurred with this assessment, gradually turning away from the double standard of moral fitness that viewed a mother's sexual misconduct as damning and a father's as forgivable.[82] The leading family law treatise of the 1920s, *Keezer on the Law of Marriage and Divorce*, states the "new" rule.

> Where the children are of tender years, other things being equal, the mother is preferred as their custodian, and this more especially in the case of female children, and this though she may have been guilty of delinquencies in the past but there is no evidence that she was delinquent at the time of determining the matter by the court.[83]

In Crabtree v. Crabtree the court even overlooked the fact that the Mrs. Crabtree had almost murdered Mr. Crabree, cutting his throat with a razor blade, slicing through his fingers, and stabbing him in the back. The court explained: "It does not follow that because the wife tried to kill him in a fit of anger, she did not have any parental affection for the children. On the contrary the record discloses that she loved them and was properly caring for them."[84]

Some courts went further, standing the nineteenth-century double standard on its head and declaring the a father's adultery gave all custodial rights to mother. In New York state Mrs. McNeil won a divorce from Mr. McNeil on the based on his adultery. She was granted the two girls, aged two and four, but Mr. McNeil claimed she was incapable of taking care of them properly and took away the older girl to live with his parents. The court sternly rebuked the father, declaring, "When the wife is entitled to a divorce for the adultery of the husband, she has an absolute right to the custody of the children, unless their good requires some other disposition."[85] Not all courts were so forgiving of mothers' transgressions, however. Individual judges still retained ultimate decision-making power, and many of them staunchly maintained the old punitive standards regarding the sexual transgressions of mothers. While acknowledging the prevailing maternal preference, a Washington court gave

Mr. Frates the custody of his three daughters, aged twelve, ten, and eight, because the mother, now remarried, had affairs both with her husband's brother and with an employee of her husband whom she later married. "Such influences would be prejudicial to the best interests the children, who should not be further denied their natural right simply out of respect for the holy institution of a mother's love, which in this case is proven to be dishonored by maternal instinct more fancied than real."[86]

Overall, the courts in this era appear to be less concerned about a mother's irregular sexual behavior than were the child protection workers. Perhaps it was the fact that child welfare workers were working with women of a different social class, where inappropriate sexual behavior was frequently combined with intemperance or unacceptable child-raising and housekeeping customs. In addition, these women sometimes displayed parental inadequacies spawned by poverty. Judges, on the other hand, often shared a middle-class culture with their divorcing couple, which may have included a more tolerant attitude toward changing sexual mores.

Flowery prose regarding the inimitable nature of mother love abounds in court decisions in this era, but the most important support for mothers came from legislatures. The legislation that had eluded the campaigns of nineteenth-century women's rights crusaders, granting mothers equal rights to custody and control of their children, swept through the state legislatures in the first third of the twentieth century. By 1936 forty-two state legislatures granted mothers equal rights to their minor children.[87] Only four states, Georgia, Hawaii, Oklahoma, and Texas, expressed common law language regarding father's rights, and then asserted only in reference to testamentary guardianships, not custody following divorce.[88] While most of these statutes did not incorporate maternal preference, they abolished the old common law advantage of fathers and allowed the courts to create clear presumptions in favor of mothers under the general rule dictating the best interests of the child.[89] In effect, the legislatures were ratifying rules that the courts had created on their own initiative. New Mexico's statute is representative: "Parents of minor children have equal powers, rights and duties concerning minor. Mother as fully entitled to custody and control as father."[90]

Following the same trend toward equality, parents' equal rights to the guardianship of their child upon the death of a spouse were now legislatively asserted in all forty-seven states. Likewise, in most states mothers and fathers were given equal rights to their children's services and earnings and in twenty-two states the law gave exclusive rights to the parent who received custody of the child following the abandonment, desertion, or death of a spouse, or upon a court decree.[91] In only four states could the father appoint a testamentary guardian following his own death and that of his wife.

Why were legislatures now willing to pass laws giving mothers equal rights to custody and control when they had strongly opposed this form of legislation in the nineteenth century, claiming that if mothers were granted custody they would leave their husbands?[92] The reasons for this varied. In part it was deference to judicial reality, since courts regularly sidestepped fathers' paramount rights in favor of mothers. It was also a response to the new legislative efforts, discussed earlier, by social workers, philanthropists, and other child welfare reformers. This legislation was not put forward as part of a package for women's rights by organized feminists as it had been in the nineteenth century. Instead, custody reform was presented as a child welfare and support package. Gone was the fearful specter of wives walking out on their husbands, children in tow, that had deterred nineteenth-century legislators from considering equal custody rights.

Most of the new nonsupport legislation did not specifically mention parents who no longer had custody following separation or divorce.[93] This left the determination of child support obligations to the courts. Judges were very willing to throw deserting, nonsupporting fathers in jail. They were, however, very unsure what to require of fathers who simply lost custody of their children by judicial decree. This increasingly common situation forced courts to reexamine the mutuality of obligations that were the foundation of the common law rules governing child custody. At common law fathers enjoyed complete custody and control, including the services and wages of their children in return for maintenance, support, and education. If fathers no longer were allowed custody and control, why should they be forced to provide support? According to some courts they were not, especially if the divorce decree were silent as to support.[94] California courts stood firm on mutuality: "When a parent is deprived of the custody of his child, and therefore, of its services and earnings, he is no longer liable for its support and education."[95] The majority of courts, however, ruled the opposite, employing a variety of reasons to require support. An Oklahoma court claimed it was decreed by divine law: "In the Eighth verse, Fifth Chapter I Timothy, we are told: `But if any provide not for his own, and specially for those of his own house, he hath denied the faith, and is worst than an infidel.' " In a different line of reasoning a Texas court insisted that Mr. Milburn, an elderly father who could no longer lift heavy objects or perform continuous labor, was nonetheless obliged to support his daughter, now in the custody of her middle-aged mother, because "the primary duty to support rests on the father since human experience demonstrates that he is best able to perform the duty."[96]

Courts employed the same reasoning to require fathers to support their children even when one of the divorcing spouses remarried. The ever ambiguous role of stepfathers did not include the mandatory support of children not their own. However, if evidence could show that they acted in loco parentis, and voluntarily supported the child, some obligation might incur.[97] In State v. Langford an Oregon mother was awarded custody of her six-year-old son, Wendell Langford, in a divorce action. Subsequently she told the father (falsely) that the child had gone to South America and was not available for visitation. The father, George Langford, paid no child support. Both mother and father remarried. Five years after the divorce the mother brought criminal charges for nonsupport under a new law that no longer exempted a noncustodial parent from child support following a divorce. The father pleaded that he had injured his arm, and that as an injured barber he could barely make enough to support himself and his new wife, for whom he had not purchased any new clothes since their marriage. He was nonetheless convicted of the crime of nonsupport, a felony punishable in Oregon by as much as one year in state prison. On appeal the court held that the father's remarriage and his lack of access to the child were no defense to failure to pay child support. In addition, the fact that the mother could adequately support the child on her own salary was not relevant. Since Mr. Langford had offered no evidence that the mother's new husband was serving in loco parentis, this also was deemed irrelevant. Mr. Langford was saved from a possible prison sentence only by the fact that the strict nonsupport laws had only recently passe, and did not apply retroactively to Mr. Langford.

Finally, while mothers and fathers dominated custody disputes, in a bow to the best interests of the children over the rights of the parents, courts were willing to look beyond natural parents and consider third parties, particularly when it involved the continuity of the child's lifestyle.[98] My own study of appellate court decisions in the 1920s indicates that mothers were awarded custody in 41 percent of the cases, fathers gained custody in 31 percent of the cases, siblings were split between their parents in 13 percent of the cases, and in 15 percent a third party was given custody. A grandmother was the most likely recipient as third party (5 percent of cases).[99] Although legislation almost always mandated the mother or the father as custodian, unless unfit, the courts seemed willing to stretch this rule and allow children to remain with grandparents or other parties if they had been living with them for a period of time. In one such Utah case, when Mrs. Jacques sought to regain custody of her two children from their paternal grandmother, the appellate court made no mention of the mother's competence, and simply stated that "the grandmother is properly rearing and educating children and they are attached to her."[100] Another common situation was the placement of a child with a friend, neighbor, or relative for several years while the parents were having either personal or financial problems. When the parents wanted their children back a custody battle sometimes ensued. In Buseman v. Buseman the mother agreed with the father, following their divorce, to place the child in a family who agreed to raise her.[101] Seven years later, when the parents tried to reestablish their parental rights, the court, with no other finding of unfitness, interpreted their agreement to relinquish their daughter as a confession as to unfitness and held that the best interests of the child did not require that she be removed from her new family.[102] It may be, however, that these decisions do not demonstrate that judges gave less respect to natural parents over third parties than they do today but rather that parents had fewer support systems and were forced by poor circumstances to leave their children in the care of others for years at a time.

Conclusion

The organized effort on behalf of children during the Progressive era had not been seen before nor matched since. Legislators enacted many bills protecting and supporting children at home, at work, and at school; laying the foundation and raising most of the structure of modern child welfare. The newly developed juvenile courts set a model for dealing with abused, neglected, and delinquent children. But beyond that, the enormous amount of personal time and effort put into child welfare on the part of thousands of individuals, largely unpaid, has no modern-day equivalent. Social feminists, in particular, focused on children and families in direct contrast to their nineteenth century precursors, who often viewed the family as the major barrier to the achievement of women's rights.

Aggressive state actions designed to protect and promote children in this era finally demolished the fundamental common law relationship between parents and children, which had been only chipped at by nineteenth century courts. Never again would a father command absolute custody and control of his children, including their wages and services, in exchange for maintenance and education. The state now severely limited the child's ability to deliver wages or services while assuming the obligation to educate children. The state also set minimum standards for child raising that a parent had to meet in order to retain custody of a child.

This rearrangement of the child-parent relationship gave mothers further rights at the expense of fathers. The nurturing ideal of mothers, which had captured the imagination of nineteenth-century judges in custody actions following divorce, now pervaded all areas of public and private policy. Legislatures finally granted equal custodial rights to mothers. Most judges treated the tender years presumption in custody disputes following divorce as if it were long established in common law; often blinking at mothers' sexual discrepancies as long as the mothers were now "reformed." Fathers, on the other hand not only lost the paramount right to the custody of their children, they were forced to support children even when judges determined that the mother was the more fit custodial parent or when the father had no custodial rights, as when the child was born out of wedlock. In fact, this era may be considered the historical nadir for fathers, who were disfavored in custody disputes and vulnerable to criminal prosecution if they fail to support their children.

Perhaps the greatest advance for mothers, and, it may be argued, for their children as well, was the pervasive belief on the part of child welfare reformers that children were best nurtured by their own parents, if fit, and that poverty alone should not deprive parents of the custody of their children. This belief led to the new and tentative commitment on the part of the state to support "worthy" mothers who could not support their children. Families where the father was present rarely received state aid, since fathers were always expected to support their families, but were often helped by private charities and settlement houses. Mothers' pensions laid the ground for our current system of family support. Limited by the middle-class mores of the era, "worthy mothers" were fairly narrowly defined; widows usually qualified, as long as they led sexually respectable lives, but unwed mothers did not. Deserted or divorced mothers had to look first to the fathers for support. Even otherwise worthy mothers, particularly if foreign born, were deemed neglectful if they insisted that their children work to help support the family rather than go to school. Still, for the first time in America's history, children of poverty were not automatically "bound out" or "placed out" to provide work in return for maintenance. Adoption for children whose parents were dead or retained no custodial rights was promoted and, increasingly, free foster home care and paid home care replaced orphan asylums.

In the Best Interests of the Child? 1960–1990

By the last third of the twentieth century law relating to child custody had permeated the casual discourse of everyday life; indeed, few households were untouched by a custody matter. A child born in 1990 had about a 50 percent chance of falling under the jurisdiction of a court in a case involving where and with whom the child would live.[1] Unlike previous eras, where child custody issues ordinarily involved orphans or children of parents who could not care for them, the great majority of child custody matters in the modern era were the product of an exploding divorce rate.[2] In addition, the state increasingly intervened and sometimes removed children from their families, as the number of single parent families below the poverty line swelled.[3]

The event of divorce and the increase of poverty once again rearranged the tentative symmetry between mother, father, and the state with regard to the custody of children. In the wake of the divorce explosion the balance of power between mothers and fathers was rearranged. State legislatures and courts weakened mothers' legal claims to the custody of their children following divorce actions, systematically wiping out the maternal preference, or tender years doctrine, leaving only the vague "best interests of the child" standard. Some lawmakers replaced the maternal preference with new gender-neutral preferences, such as joint custody and primary caretaker, hoping to provide consistency in decision making where there was no longer an easy choice. Procedural changes were initiated as well; mothers, fathers, and the court called upon expert witnesses, usually mental health professionals, to assist the court in making the difficult selection between legally equal adults and mediation was increasingly considered as an alternative to litigation.[4] Children remained the silent party in custody disputes, rarely given voice until adolescence.[5]

The state took an ever more active role as superparent, providing more economic support while dictating stricter standards of behavior to mostly poor families. The number of single parent poor families grew rapidly, largely as a consequence of the rising divorce rate and a startling upsurge in the incidence of illegitimacy. The state no longer distinguished between worthy mothers and unworthy mothers as a criteria of support; however, its social service arm vigilantly supervised the behavior of those it supported, with the threat of removal and ultimately termination of parental rights.

In addition, new custodial issues forced a redefinition of parenthood during this volatile era. Large numbers of nonbiological parents with no legal rights to custody and control played central nurturing roles in the lives of the children who lived in their homes. Stepparents, inheritors of a problematical legal status from common law, grew in numbers as divorce, remarriage, and redivorce became more common. Foster homes became the state's preferred choice for its dependent children, but foster parents, who sometimes raised the children until adulthood, held the legal status of a vendor under contract. And finally, a complex set of custodial issues emerged from the new reproductive technology, testing the law's limit in defining who is a mother and who is a father.

Custody Following Divorce

The simple fact of being a mother does not, by itself, indicate a capacity or willingness to render a quality of care different from that which the father can provide.

With this simple statement a New York court challenged nearly a century of a judicial presumption in favor of mothers.[6] The court rejected the notion that mothers and their children shared a special bond, invoking the authority of social scientist Margaret Meade, who charged, "This is a mere and subtle form of anti-feminism by which men—under the guise of exalting the importance of maternity—are tying women more tightly to their children than has been thought necessary since the invention of bottle feeding and baby carriages."[7]

Not all courts were as outspoken in reducing the importance of mothers or in suggesting that maternal presumption was a male conspiracy. Nevertheless, the presumption that the interests of a child of tender years is best served in the custody of the mother was legally abolished or demoted to a "factor to be considered" in nearly all states between 1960 and 1990.[8] In the vacuum created by the retreat of a maternal presumption, state legislatures drafted specific statutes to direct judges left with the task of applying the elusive best interests standard.[9] Most legislatures also suggested joint custody as an alternative. This solution gave fathers equal time with mothers; thereby avoiding the problem of having to choose between legally equal parents and at the same time displaying deference to equal treatment. Some states adopted a primary caretaker preference, a quantitative standard of time spent with the child, which facilitated the decision-making process.[10] While custody determinations following divorce were most often settled between the parents and merely ratified by the courts, these negotiations took place in the shadow of the changing custody laws. If parents could not agree, they were aware that the court would make the determination according to the new legislative standards.

Child custody law was only one manifestation of the rearrangemet of roles between men and women in this era, and followed directly in the wake of radical divorce reforms. Drastic changes in divorce law rendered divorce a unilateral decision not based on fault. This fact made divorce far easier to obtain and in most states created a fundamentally different framework for the distribution of property and the allocation of support following divorce. Following the lead of California's revolutionary Family Law Act of 1969, all states by 1985 offered some form of no-fault divorce.[11] In some states one disgruntled party was required simply to complain that the marriage had reached a point of "irretrievable breakdown" with no requirement of proof; in other states "incompabibity" or "irreconcilable differences" had to be demonstrated if one party objected, but it was considered sufficient proof if one partner chose to live separately for a period of time. Moreover, the removal of fault as the basis for divorce diluted the moral stigma from the act, contributing to a sharply rising divorce rate. By the 1980s demographers were predicting that one-half of new marriages would end in divorce.[12]

The basic assumption underlying the radical changes in divorce and custody law was that men and women should be treated equally before the law. This was a sharp departure from the established beliefs in the era of fault-based divorce. Family law had then favored women (and children) by making divorce hard to obtain and by requiring extended support for the wife and children in the event of divorce, in the belief that wives were less able to take care of themselves economically than were husbands. A maternal presumption in custody disputes, well-established by the Progressive era, likewise favored mothers, reflecting society's belief that they were more nurturing than fathers. The push for equal treatment between men and women in divorce and custody reflected, in part, the larger societal campaign for the rights of the oppressed, especially minority groups, but it but it was particularly impelled by the newly formed movement to obtain equal rights for women.[13]

Taking form in the late 1960s, the third wave of feminists were willing to move away from the protected sphere of the family to an extent not conceivable to the early nineteenth-century women's rights advocates and not acceptable to the second wave of feminists, the social feminists of the Progressive era who had focused their energies on troubled families and children.[14] The third wave embraced a wide range of sometimes incompatible groups and ideologies, held together for more than a decade by an ultimately unsuccessful campaign for an equal rights amendment. The Equal Rights Amendment was first introduced in Congress in 1923. Most social feminists then opposed it, fearing it would repeal their hard-won legislation for improving working conditions of women factory workers. Sporadically revived over the years, it was not until 1970 that the ERA was seriously rejuvenated by the National Organization for Women (NOW). The long, hard-fought, but failed campaign that ensued represented not only a bid for equal treatment before the law but for equal participation with men in all spheres of life, especially the marketplace.[15]

The impact of the campaign for the ERA on divorce and custody law was not direct. NOW's founding statement in 1967 decried the "half equality" in the marriage relationship and called for a reexamination of laws governing marriage.

> We reject . . . that home and family are primarily woman's world and responsibility—hers, to dominate—his to support. We believe that a true partnership between the sexes demands a different concept of marriage, an equitable sharing of the responsibilities of home and children.[16]

Yet, in spite of the forceful language of the NOW platform, feminists were rarely prominent actors in the legal revolution that transformed divorce and custody law over the next twenty years. The California no-fault divorce law was passed in 1969 by a nearly all-male legislature before the modern ERA crusade was launched. And when California, the pioneer no-fault state, once again led the nation in 1980 by legislating a preference for joint custody, a newly formed fathers' rights group pushed the bill over the legislative hurdles.[17]

Although organized feminists were not often direct participants in the revolution transforming divorce and custody law, their crusade for the ERA and for other gender discrimination issues strongly contributed to the legal climate that fostered the revolution in family law. A critical example is the manner in which feminists dealt with motherhood. Seeking to eradicate gender discrimination in the workplace, feminists faced the reality of pregnancy and childbirth, physical conditions not shared equally by men and women. Feminists successfully cut new legal ground in promoting the federal Pregnancy

Discrimination Act of 1978, which mandated that pregnancy must be considered a disability, like any other, and must receive equal treatment with other disabilities under the individual states' disability laws. This position was a step forward in many states; however, it put into question some state laws, like California's maternity leave act, that gave a childbirth a significantly *longer* leave than it gave to all other other disabilities.

Faced with an employee who demanded the longer leave following childbirth, the California Federal Savings and Loan Association filed a suit in federal court claiming that in California pregnant women were given *greater* rather than equal consideration, thereby violating the federal Pregnancy Discrimination Act. Feminists were divided by this legal and strategic dilemma. Still, NOW and the National Women's Political Caucas joined forces with others to write an amicus (friend of the court) brief *opposing* the longer maternity leave. This brief stated in part: "Distinctions based on pregnancy tend to perpetuate the stereotype of women's primary role and function as childbearer."[18]

While the U.S. Supreme Court did not agree with this analysis and allowed California's maternity leave law to stand, state legislators and judges took seriously the feminist message that mothers should not be given special consideration.[19] Maternal presumption was largely eliminated as an explicit reason for determining custody. By 1990 thirty-six states had followed California's lead, suggesting some form of joint custody arrangement, although rarely elevating it to a rebuttable presumption.[20] A comparison of one hundred appellate court decisions in 1960 with one hundred decisions in 1990 reveals that while judges cited a preference for mothers as a reason for their decision in twenty-one of the one hundred cases in 1960, there was not a single mention of mothers in their 1990 reasoning.[21]

It was not only feminist rhetoric promoting equal treatment that persuaded legislators and judges to abandon the maternal presumption; equal treatment arguments were combined with the reality that great numbers of women had abandoned full-time housekeeping for the workplace, moreover, most of these new workers were mothers. In 1970 only 27 percent of women with children under the age of three were in the workforce; in 1985 this figure was more than 50 percent.[22] While many, if not most, of these women were driven to work by economic necessity in a downward-drifting economy, legislators and judges were confused by the new roles that mothers were playing. An Illinois court declared, "the `tender years' doctrine has no application if the mother is working and not in the home full time."[23]

While mothers mostly lost ground, there was one area in which changing cultural mores seemed to work in their favor. The venerable doctrine of maternal moral fitness made a retreat, if not a complete exit, from the courtroom. The tender years doctrine was usually expressed as: "Children of tender years are awarded to the mother unless the mother is unfit."[24] Lack of fitness could include physical neglect or abuse or mental illness, but in most cases it was applied to the mother's sexual behavior. As we have seen, nineteenth-century judges condemned adulterous women, considering them unfit to have any contact with their children. They were somewhat more forgiving of fathers. Progressive-era judges viewed mothers' extramarital sexual activities more leniently, provided they had clearly mended their ways and their transgressions had occurred in the more or less distant past. The decade of the 1960s promoted individual rights in many venues, including sexual expression. Sexual activity outside the institution of marriage became so commonplace that the law gradually reflected the more tolerant attitude expressed by large numbers of Americans. The establishment of no-fault divorce eliminated the need for alleging adultery as one of the most common grounds for divorce, and in most states the transformation of custody law that followed in the wake of no-fault divorce excluded a specific reference to moral fitness as a factor in custody decision.[25] Homosexual acitvity on the part of the one of the parents, which in previous eras would have undoubtedly been a deciding factor against that parent, also was increasingly tolerated. A few states still viewed homosexuality as evidence of parental unfitness per se,[26] but most states required proof that the homosexual activity (or extramarital heterosexual activity) was having an adverse affect upon the child.[27]

Still, changes in law do not necessarily force changes in judicial attitudes. With sexual mores, as with the maternal presumption, judges frequently found other reasons within their powers of discretion that allowed them to reach the same decision they would have reached under the old laws. In the 1985 Indiana case D. H. v. J. H. there were three children, ages eleven, nine, and eight. Much of the testimony at the trial involved the alleged homosexual relationship of the wife and two young women, K. B. and K. R. Both of these young women testified at trial that they had engaged in homosexual activity with the wife. The husband testified that he observed his wife and one of the "young ladies" swimming nude in the parties' pool. These were late at night when the children were in bed. The husband presented photographs that he took of his wife and K. R. The husband also introduced other evidence indicating that the wife left dirty dishes around and that the husband frequently had to prepare meals for the children because their mother was running around. The wife presented evidence of her active involvement with all of the children's needs and actitivities and conversely of the father's lack of concern for his children.

The trial court awarded all three children to the father. The mother appealed, claiming the court had not followed the statutory guidelines in Indiana, which listed six factors to be considered in deciding between parents, none of which mentioned homosexuality or moral fitness. The appellate court responded that although sexual behavior was not specifically mentioned, the statute also enjoined the court to consider "all relevant factors," and that the mother's homosexuality must be considered relevant. At a loss to find precedent regarding lesbian mothers, the court decided to treat a lesbian mother as it would an adulterous mother. In that case "we believe the proper rule to be that homosexuality standing alone without evidence of any adverse effect upon the welfare of the child does not render the homosexual parent unfit as a matter of law to have custody of the child."[28] The appellate court then found that no such evidence had been presented in this case. Nonetheless, the court approved the award of all three children to the father on the grounds that "the evidence concerning wife's lack of proper housekeeping standards, that the husband fixed meals for the children because wife was out running around, and that husband assisted children with lessons are all relevant factors which the court could consider and which would support the decision."[29] This result might have been reached by a nineteenth-century judge as well.

What actual effect did virtual elimination of the maternal preference have on custody determinations? Early studies indicated that there was very little difference in result; mothers gained custody of the children about 90 percent of the time before and after the changes in the law.[30] Later, more extensive research questioned this figure and looked behind the statistics. A comparative study of appellate court decisions indicates a sharp rise in the awards to fathers, from 36.7 percent in 1960 to 45 percent in 1990, slightly more often than custody was awarded to mothers.[31] A consistent result was found by the American Bar Association survey of judges in 1989, which revealed that the fact of motherhood was rated as a fairly insignificant in the decision-making process—only 10.6 percent, compared with greater economic stability (46.5 percent) or primary disciplinarian (33.3 percent).[32] These studies indicate that fathers who took their case to trial (admittedly a small percentage of all custody matters) had at least as favorable odds as mothers in gaining custody. Mothers also steadily lost sole custody in favor of the new concept of joint custody, which was the most frequent outcome of the increasingly popular mediated settlements.

Moreover, while only a small percentage of custody disputes reached trial and were decided by a judge rather than the parties, the fact that judges were more willing to look favorably upon fathers' appeals for custody influenced the private bargaining process. Some fathers who may have had no real desire for custody, threatened mothers with the possible loss of custody under the new rules in order to secure advantages in property division, spousal support, and child support.[33] On the other hand, fathers who did want more time with the children could use the law to bargain for greater access.

Joint Custody and Primary Caretaker Solutions

A direct consequence of the demise of the maternal presumption was the rush to new standards. Legislatures strived to achieve greater predictability in decision making and to offer more precise guidance to judges in difficult cases where neither motherhood nor moral fitness were controlling factors any longer. Most legislatures turned to two contrasting solutions: joint custody[34] or a primary caretaker preference,[35] sometimes embracing both as possible alternatives. As will be discussed in the following chapter, each concept was based upon a fundamentally different notion of parenting and of gender roles, each supported by opposing social science camps. In short, joint custody presumed both that parenting roles are relatively interchangeable and that the best interests of the child are best advanced if the child has substantial contact with both parents. On the other hand, a primary caretaker preference focused on granting custody to the parent who has attended to the basic needs of the child, with the underlying rationale that a child needs the continuity and the stability of one parent rather than the divisive experience of time spent in two households.

California led the way in custody initiatives, as it had in no-fault divorce, by introducing a preference for joint custody in 1980.[36] By 1988 thirty-six states had followed California's lead.[37] As New York judge Felicia K. Shea observed: "Joint Custody is an appealing concept. It permits the court to escape an agonising choice, to keep from wounding the self-esteem of either parent and to avoid the appearance of discrimination between the sexes."[38] Legislatures, and sometimes courts, produced several variations on the joint custody theme. Joint physical custody dictated that parents should share their time with the child as equally as possible. This might entail a schedule in which the child spent half the week with each parent or every other month. In a few cases the child remained in the home and the parents moved back and forth. Many state legislatures endorsed this arrangement, but only a few went as far as California in imposing it upon unwilling parents. Joint legal custody, on the other hand, allowed a more traditional sole custody arrangement with visitation for the noncustodial parent. Both parents, however, retained equal input into decisions affecting the child such as choosing medical treatment and schools.

Taylor v. Taylor, a Maryland case, provides some idea of how the courts struggled with this newly popular concept.[39] Maryland had no legislation specifying joint custody, and the issue before the court was whether a trial court could impose it—in this case against the wishes of the mother, who maintained that the joint custody arrangement she and her husband had originally agreed upon was unworkable. While noting that the only precedent in Maryland was a 1934 case in which the court denounced joint custody as an arrangement "to be avoided, whenever possible as an evil fruitful in the destruction of discipline, in the creation of distrust, and in the production of mental distress in the child," the Taylor court nevertheless endorsed the concept of forced joint custody.[40] The court explained that the earlier view on joint custody required reexamination in light of the "significant changes that have occurred over the ensuing half century." The court did not specify the nature of these changes.

The court reviewed the trial court's "visitation schedule" regarding the parents' responsibilites to the two children, Christina, age four, and Neil, age three at the time of trial..

> Both parents teach school. The father's work day is from about 8:30 A.M. to 4:15 P.M. and the mother's 12:30 P.M. to 4:15 P.M. . . . In November 1982 the parties agreed upon a sort of joint custody of the children. Their base is in the father's home but the mother probably sees them more of their waking hours. The mother is in the home with the children Monday to Friday from 7:30 A.M. to 12:30 P.M. The mother has the children in her home from 4:15 P.M. to 8:00 P.M. Tuesday and on alternate [weekends] from 10:00 A.M. Saturday until 8:00 P.M. Sunday. The paternal grandmother babysits Monday to Friday from 12:30 to 4:15 P.M. i.e., from the time the mother leaves the children until the father gets home. The father pays his mother $29.00 weekly. The mother contributes no money for child support.[41]

Maintaining that the trial court had the right to impose joint custody when it was in the "best interests" of the child, and avoiding mention of the convoluted schedule, the appellate court set out several criteria for the trial court to consider before imposing joint custody. The most prominent criterion was the parents' ability to communicate and reach shared decisions. Noting evidence of considerable hostility between the Taylors affecting their ability to communicate, the court remanded the case for a new trial.

California's experiment with joint custody quickly revealed unanticipated problems. The most extensive study on child custody, the Stanford Child Custody Study, which examined 908 families, found that joint physical custody was elected by nearly a fifth of all divorcing couples, however, a large number of these cases involved "intense" parental conflict, suggesting that the parents could agree on no other arrangement. Nearly all were were negotiated through a mediator or attorneys not determined by the courts.[42] Other researchers suggested that mediators under California's mandatory mediation

scheme were highly motivated to reach a settlement and joint physical custody, favored by the law, became the compromise position, not an arrangement actively sought by the parents.[43] The inappropriateness of this choice
for many parents was exemplified by the fact that in the high-conflict families in the Stanford study, a majority of the children in fact resided with the
mother and spent three or fewer overnights with the father in a typical two-
week period.[44]

On the other hand, the great majority of parents in the Stanford study,
including those who decided upon joint physical custody, voluntarily chose
joint *legal* custody, where one parent has custody but both parents share in decision making. As the researchers explained it, "The fact that joint legal custody
carries with it so little by way of actual consequences proabably explains why it
has become so popular. Lawyers for mothers no doubt tell their clients that
they are giving up nothing of importance in agreeing to joint legal custody."[45]
Other states embraced this relatively noncontroversial approach, which served
to provide at least the appearance of an egalitarian standard.

Primary Caretaker

If parents refused to agree to joint custody, or any other custody arrangement,
many legal scholars advocated a "primary cartaker" presumption as a means of
breaking the impasse.[46] As legal scholar David Chambers, a noted proponent
of the theory, explained it, "They should define the primary caretaker as the
parent if there is one, who has performed a substantial majority of the care-
giving tasks for the child that involve intimate interaction with the child."[47]
This attractive gender-neutral presumption was adopted by at least two states,
Minnesota and West Virginia, and included as a factor to be considered in
many others.[48]

While many commentators considered this merely a reenactment of the
maternal presumption in a new guise, this result was not always reached in the
postno-fault divorce era. Kennedy v. Kennedy, a Minnesota case, reveals the
complexity of parenting roles following divorce.[49] When Carole and Duane
Kennedy divorced they had four children, ages eleven, six, four, and five and
a half months. Duane was a lawyer and Carole had worked only occasionally

since their second child was born. At the time of separation the three older children were awarded to the father, who kept the family home, situated on several acres with ponies. There was extensive testimony describing the property as an ideal place to raise children. Carole moved twice in order to find a job, and at the time of the hearing she was caring for an aging parent in another town. The trial court awarded the three older children to the father and the youngest to the mother stating, "I feel that the children have a total adjustment of their rural home and their school. . . . Respondent's position appears reasonably secure, and permanence of the family unit seems assured. I have considered also the uncertainty of the petitioner's future plans."[50]

On appeal the majority reversed the decision, emphasizing that Minnesota supported a primary caretaker preference, and remanded it for a new trial to determine "which parent was the primary caretaker *at the time the dissolution proceeding was commenced.*"[51] The dissenting judge, however, insisted that there had been substantial evidence regarding which parent was the primary caretaker at the trial, including two court-appointed custody investigations. The weight of this evidence was that both parents were active in their upbringing and had a warm and affectionate relationship with the children.

This case illustrates the difficulty in determining who is the primary caretaker between two involved parents. It also suggests that the result may have been different under earlier divorce and custody laws. Carole, as a fit mother, likely would have been awarded custody of all the children. (Although if the eleven-year-old were a boy—the gender not in testimony—the father might have had a chance.) While the details of this divorce settlement are not revealed in the opinion, in the preno-fault era Carole most probably would have retained the family home and also received spousal support. While seemingly unfair to the father, the new divorce laws arguably discriminated against a homemaker like Carole who did not have a steady income to maintain a stable home for herself and the children.[52]

Rights of Nonparents Following Divorce

The near epidemic of divorces, frequently followed by remarriage and sometimes a second (or more) divorce, created a huge class of nonparents, such as stepparents and grandparents, who had intimate ties with the children, yet whose access to them could be summarily cut off. Included in this group of nonparents was a small but growing contingent of nonmarried partners. For the most part nonparents did not enjoy custodial rights. Except in extreme circumstances the best interests of the child framework did not allow for custody award to a nonbiological parent. In fact the rights of biological parents were strengthened overall during this era, perhaps in reaction to the instability of the traditional family. The comparative study of appellate court decisions reveals that custody was awarded to a nonparent following divorce in about 15 percent of the cases on appeal in 1920 but to only 3.8 percent in 1990.[53] English common law and its American derivation had always placed the highest value on blood relationships between parent and child, particularly with regard to inheritance; however, this consideration was limited to unions sanctified by marriage. In this modern era biology itself—with or without marriage—became the bond recognized by law as the custodial rights were extended to unwed fathers.

The U.S. Supreme Court did not specifically deal with custody disputes between natural parents and nonparents following divorce. However, in Santosky v. Kramer the Court emphatically stated that rights of natural parental rights could only be terminated upon clear and convincing evidence of parental neglect. Writing for the majority, Justice Blackmun emphasized that the fundamental liberty interest of natural parents in the care, custody, and management of their child does not disappear simply because they have not been model parents or have temporarily lost custody of their child to the state.[54] Since the standard applied only to those cases where states intervened to terminate parental right—the states were not required to apply this standard to custody decisions following divorce—many pursued the spirit of the law, if not the exact standard, in considering the possible choice of stepparents or relatives over natural fathers and mothers as custodians. The standard in California, similar to those in many states, went well beyond a best interests test and required a finding that a custody award to the parent would be detrimental to a child before a third party could be considered.[55] Other states required clear and convincing evidence that the natural parent was unfit.[56]

It was a rare and therefore a sometimes noteworthy event when a nonparent, even if a relative, was chosen in place of a competent parent. In such a celebrated case the Iowa Supreme Court awarded a young child whose mother had died to the maternal grandparents, farmers praised by the court as "stable, dependable conventional, middle class, middle west." The court granted custody to them rather than to the father, a "political liberal" whose home "would be unstable, unconventional, arty, bohemian and probably intellectually stimulating."[57] The case received national publicity and did not end there.[58] The father was finally granted visitation rights and took advantage of his son's visit to obtain a decision in his favor from a California court. California apparently viewed the matter of fathers' rights, or perhaps fathers' competence, differently than Iowa.[59]

Grandparents, as blood relatives with presumably close affectional ties, did receive special consideration for visitation following divorce, if not for custody, under the new laws. Common law had not recognized grandparents' rights in this regard; however, while revising their custody codes, most legislatures gave a sympathetic nod toward visitation rights for grandparents if it were deemed in the child's best interests. The U.S. House of Representatives, in an unusual intrusion into family law, also called on the states to be generous to grandparents.[60]

When a conflict arose between a new adoptive steppparent and the grandparents, the law usually favored the stepparent, on the theory that the parental rights of the biological parent were aborted upon adoption, and with them the rights of the biological grandparents, no matter how close their affectional bond and support. For example, Alabama's highest court disagreed that the trial court had the discretion to decide whether it was in the best interests of the two Bronstein grandchildren to continue to visit their grandparents, John and Nancy Murphy, following their adoption by their stepfather, Alvin Bronstein. Conceding that there had been a close and continuing relationship between the children and their grandparents, the high court determined that the best interests of the children was not the overriding rule. "We hold that because there is a societal importance in the establishment of a permanent and stable family unit, an adoption of a child must necessarily sever all former family bonds and relationships."[61]

The rights of stepparents, meanwhile, grew more muddled.[62] The revolution in divorce and custody laws that swept through the states in the late twentieth century almost totally ignored the growing presence of stepparents. Family law continued to view stepparents through common law lenses, giving them no legal rights over their stepchildren and imposing few obligations. At common law a stepfather could choose to support a child in his household, but was not obliged to do so. If a stepfather died intestate his stepchildren would not inherit from him. The position of stepmothers at common law was of course significantly different due to their married status as *femme covert*. In the rare case of divorce as well as the far more common occasion of the death of the natural parent, stepparents, unless they had adopted their stepchildren (an option not available until the nineteenth century), were considered in the lowly ranks of all other nonparents as contenders in custody disputes. This fact was largely untouched by the late twentieth-century divorce and custody reforms. Stepparents were not mentioned in the Uniform Marriage and Divorce Act, and only one state, Oregon, appeared to have specified stepparents as potential custodians in their new statutory scheme.[63] The state laws were silent also regarding their right to visitation following divorce. Visitation, if not granted willingly by the natural parent, would not likely be enforced by a court .

Appellate court decisions varied widely in their treatment of stepparents who contended with a natural parent for custody following the death of the custodial parent. Although few in number, these cases reveal the law's ambivalence about the rights of stepparents. Some courts employed the Santosky standard requiring clear and convincing evidence of parental unfitness while others subsumed biological parenthood under a best interests of the child standard. A Michigan case, Henrikson v. Gable, involved a stepfather, Gable, who had raised two children from infancy, ages nine and ten at the death of their mother.[64] The biological father, Henrickson, had rarely visited the children but sought custody. The trial court awarded custody to the stepfather. The appellate court, struggling with the difficulty of a situation where the best interests of the children seemed on the side of remaining with their stepfather, nevertheless applied the letter of Michigan law, which required the tough clear and convincing standard of proof. Under this standard the court found for the biological father, stating that the trial judge made "a clear legal error on a major issue." The appellate court said,

> It was not enough that the factors in favor of Gable outweighed those in favor of Henrikson. In order to give full effect to the natural parent presumption, the trial judge was required to find by clear and convincing evidence that the best interests of the children required maintaining custody with defendant. Defendant failed to meet this burden.[65]

On the other hand, in a similar situation in Wisconsin the court reached the opposite conclusion when Duane Biseck sought custody of his nine-year-old stepdaughter following the death of her mother in a car accident. The girl's natural father wanted her as well. Duane Biseck stated that the girl never lived with her natural father, Odell Olson, and that Olson never visited his daughter during the first three years of the girl's life. Moreover, in the last six years visitation had been sporadic and rare. Appellant also presented numerous affidavits from Mary Biseck's family and friends indicating that Odell Olson had little interest in a relationship during the early years of the child's life. These observers also said that Olson repeatedly physically abused Mary and that the marriage also suffered from problems related to Olson's alcohol use. The higher court overturned the trial court's granting of the daughter to her natural father, stating,

> In sum, the lower court recognized only one of two principles to be considered. The rule of law it overlooked is the superior one: "The principle that the custody of young children is ordinarily best vested in the [parent] . . . is distinctly subordinate to the controlling principle that the custody proceedings is in the child's welfare."[65]

The only protection offered stepparents was adoption, which would afford them the same status as natural parents. Some states did extend somewhat more favorable adoption terms to stepparents than had been customary. States that adopted the Uniform Adoption Act permitted adoption by a stepparent without the noncustodial parent's consent when the parent "for a period of at least a year has failed significantly without justifiable cause to communicate with the child or to provide for the [child's] support."[67] In this instance a father who did not pay child support for a year could have his parental rights terminated. Other states set a higher threshold, requiring both failure to communicate *and* failure to support.[68] On the other hand, as we shall see, the greater rights afforded to unwed fathers posed a new barrier to the adoption efforts of stepfathers.

It was with child support, rather than custody, that the law looked anew at stepparents. As part of a national effort, directed by Congress, to wrest child support from fathers of children who were receiving some form of public support, states were required to consider the income of stepparents who were living with their stepchildren in determining the child's eligibility and benefits. This action forced states to consider the obligations they imposed on stepparents. In the Slochowsky decision, for example, the issue was a New York state law that imposed an obligation on stepparents to support stepchildren only if they were "recipients of or in need of public assistance." The Slochowsky family's economic situation was typical of many "blended" families. Mr. Slochowsky had three children by a previous marriage for whom he was paying child support to their natural mother plus their medical, dental, and life insurance. Mrs. Slochowsky had two children by her first marriage for whom she received Aid to Families with Dependent Children (AFDC). Officials discontinued Mrs. Slochowsky's support, counting the whole of Mr. Slochowsky's income as being available to the chlidren. While the Slochowskys only questioned the computation of his income, the court took the opportunity to overthrow New York's stepparent law, declaring it only applied to children on public assistance and was not a statute of "general applicability" to all stepparents as was required by the federal law. Justice Harnett claimed that the intention of the "general applicability" requirement "is that a duty of automatic support only as to welfare stepchildren places upon them an added burden inhibiting remarriage of their natural custodial parent, not equitably imposed upon the rest of society's stepchildren."[69] The result of this case and subsequent federal legislation was that AFDC still required calculation of the stepfathers' income in order to confer a benefit, but states could only impose an obligation to support on all stepparents or none.[70]

The obligation of stepparents, however, was sharply divided from that of biological parents upon divorce. In no state were they obliged to pay child support, regardless of the length of residence with the child or the neediness of the child. This was in contrast to the laws of England and Wales, which held that if a stepchild were treated as a member of the family before separation the stepparent would be liable for support upon divorce.[71]

Nonmarital partners who were not the biological parents received even less legal consideration than stepparents in custody disputes. Traditionally, nonmarital partners were punished with regard to property settlement and support following their break-up; presumably because as unwed cohabitors they voluntarily flaunted the social and legal institution of marriage. Moreover, in terms of moral fitness to be custodians, cohabitation per se put both partners, including the natural parent, at a disadvantage. While the law was gradually changing to recognize the right of nonmarried cohabitors to establish property claims, the law did not recognize this category of partners in custody law.[72] While stepparents received little consideration over any other unrelated third parties, nonmarital partners received none.

Reproductive Technology and Parenthood

During the last half of the twentieth century advancing technology permitted adults to circumvent each stage of the normal procedure of insemination, conception, pregnancy, and childbirth. These technological interventions, often involving a test tube at some juncture, raised basic questions regarding the essence of motherhood and fatherhood; they also elicited new custodial issues regarding the custody rights over the product of each discrete stage in the cycle of reproduction: ova, semen, preembryo, embryo, and finally, baby. These complex issues were further confounded by the separate but extremely volatile legal controversy regarding women's rights to abortion. The law in this rapidly evolving area began to address a few of the custodial issues, usually only after the technological invervention had been well launched; these technologies included artifical insemination, surrogate mothers, and frozen embryos.

Artificial insemination—the process by which a woman is artifically inseminated by a donor other than her husband—was the first and most widely established form of reproductive intervention. Most legal wrinkles were ironed out in cases and statutes in the course of the 1960s and 1970s. The earliest case came before the California Supreme Court in 1968. Mr. Sorenson was diagnosed to be sterile, and after fifteen years of marriage reluctantly agreed in writing to his wife's artificial insemination from an unknown donor provided by the doctor. A male child was born to Mrs. Sorenson and the three lived together as a family for four years. When they divorced in 1964, Mrs. Sorenson did not request child support. Two years later, however, she fell ill and requested public assistance under the Aid to Needy Children program. The district attorney then sought support from Mr. Sorenson, who objected on the ground that the child was not legitimate. The Supreme Court refused to deal with the concept of legitimacy but insisted that for purposes of support Sorenson was clearly the father. The court stated,

> A child conceived through heterologous artificial insemination does not have a "natural father," as that term is commonly used. The anonymous donor of the sperm cannot be considered the "natural father" as he is not more responsible or the use of his sperm than is the donor of blood or a kidney. Moreover, he could not dispute the presumption that the child is the legitimate issue of Mr. and Mrs. Sorensen, as that presumption may be disputed only by the people of the State of California.[73]

This line of reasoning was soon adopted by the Uniform Parentage Act, which provided that a child born of artificial insemination, if the insemination was performed by a licensed physician with the written consent of husband and wife, is legally the husband's child. The donor is specficially "treated in law as if he were not the natural father."[74] While this act solved the problem in states that adopted it or enacted similar legislation, in many cases it did not settle the matter in those states that did not. In addition, in many cases the husband did not consent in writing, or the insemination was not performed by a licensed physician, and perhaps there was no husband, leaving in doubt the rights and obligations of the donor.

Donor mothers raised far more legal controversy than donor fathers. Women, of course, had far more biological options available to them: women could donate eggs or embryos, they could serve as the nurturing womb for someone else's embryo or they could carry their own baby, conceived by artifical insemination and under contract to relinquish the baby at birth to the father. The last scenario caused the most legal difficulty. Popularly known as "surrogate mothers" (although, in fact, they were the real biological mothers), these women, in growing numbers, agreed to bear a child for a couple in which the wife was not capable of doing so. Normally the surrogate mother was articially inseminated with the husband's sperm, carried the baby to term, and was given some payment for her service.

While the California Supreme Court could consider the donor of sperm the same as the donor of a kidney in the Sorenson case, the law was unable to treat surrogate mothers in the same fashion. In a struggle for custody, In the Matter of Baby M., that was highly publicized, Mr. Stern entered into a surrogacy contract with Mary Beth Whitehead and her husband. Mrs. Whitehead agreed to become impregnated by artificial insemination with Mr. Stern's sperm, carry the child to term, deliver it to the Sterns, and then do what was necessary to terminate her parental rights. Mary Beth Whitehead did deliver the baby upon birth, but was overcome by an "unbearable sadness" and, threatening suicide, pleaded to have the baby returned to her for only a week. The Sterns complied, but when Mrs. Whitehead failed to return the baby as promised they began a legal action to enforce the contract. Mrs. Whitehead and her husband fled to Florida where they evaded the police and the media by staying in roughly twenty different hotels and homes. Police found the child and turned her over to the Sterns. A thirty-two day trial ensued in which the trial court found the surrogate contract valid, ordered that Mrs. Whitehead's parental rights be terminated, and granted sole custody of the child to Mr. Stern.

The New Jersey appellate court rejected the trial court's decison to uphold the contract, declaring that under public policy surrogacy contracts were void. The court said these contracts skirted protections afforded by adoption proceedures, and were akin to baby selling.

> The evils inherent in baby bartering are loathsome for a myriad of reasons. The child is sold without regard to whether the purchasers will be suitable parents. The natural mother does not receive the benefit of counseling and guidance to assist her in making a decision that may affect her for a lifetime. In fact, the

monetary incentive to sell her child may, depending on her financial circumstance, make her decision less voluntary.[75]

Still, the appeals court decided that the thirty-two-day trial had extensively reviewed testimony regarding the best interests of Baby M. Treating the surrogacy contract as nonexistent, it deemed the legal issue to be custody between a natural mother and a natural father. Under the Uniform Parentage Act the claims of natural mother and natural father (whether wed or unwed) are given equal weight. Therefore, the court determined that the best interests of the child were shown at the trial to reside with the more stable and wholesome father, with some visitation available to Mrs. Whitehead.[76]

Several states did not share the New Jersey court's clear-cut contempt for surrogacy contracts, and enacted statutes that would allow the practice so long as it complied with the state's statutory scheme for adoption.[77] No state, however, considered treating surrogacy as it did seminal donation. It was the process of pregnancy and birth that clearly separated surrogate mothers from semen donors in the eyes of the law. The New Jersey court struggled with the analogy but did not provide a reasoned distinction. The court stated,

> It is quite obvious that the situations are not parallel. A sperm donor simply cannot be equated with a surrogate mother. The state has more than a sufficient basis to distinguish the two situations—even if the only difference is between the time it takes to provide sperm for articial insemination and time invested in a nine month pregnancy—so as to justify automatically divesting the sperm donor of his parental rights without authmatically divesting a surrogate mother.[78]

Finally, parental rights involved in in vitro fertiliztion reached the courts and the legislatures. In vitro reproduction, translated literally as "in glass," covered many possible combinations. The ova and sperm could come from the married couple themselves or from another male or female or any combinaiton therein. The embryo thus conceived in glass could be implanted in the womb of the wife or the womb of another woman, who could be likened to a surrogate mother, except for the fact that, unlike a surrogate mother, she had no biological connection to the fetus. In another variation the embryos could remain unplanted, but frozen for future use.

Among these many possibilites a custody dispute relating to the last variation, frozen embryos, caught the public's attention and created new law in
Tennessee. In March 1989 a Tennessee resident, Junior Lewis Davis, sued his
wife in a divorce action to restrain her from having any of their seven fertilized eggs implanted. During their ten years of marriage Mrs. Davis had experienced five tubal preganacies, which led to her infertility. At an in vitro fertility clinic the doctors harvested her ova and twice unsuccessfully attempted
to implant the eggs fertilized with her husband's sperm in her uterus. When
the couple divorced there were still seven frozen preembryos awaiting implantation.

The court actions which ensued reveal a painful confusion about the
respective legal rights of mother, father, and frozen embryo. The trial court
awarded custody to Mary Sue Davis, that she "be permitted the opportunity
to bring these children to term through implantation." The court of appeals
reversed, finding that Junior Davis has a "constituionally protected right not
to beget a child where no pregnancy has taken place," and awarded them
"joint control . . . and equal voice over their disposition," effectively granting
each former spouse veto power.[79]

While the case dragged through the courts, each of the parties remarried,
and Mary Sue decided she did not want to use the embryos for herself, but
rather to donate them to another needy couple. When the case finally came
before the Supreme Court of Tennessee, it was carefully watched by lawmakers across the nation. The court entertained extensive scientific testimony
before definitively labeling the frozen embryos as preembryos, thereby avoiding the growing body of law that gave some rights to the fetus. As preembryos, the frozen matter had no rights, and the test was not a "best interests"
of the child test but rather a contest between the rights of the adults. The
court determined that the rights at stake were the right to procreate and the
right not to procreate. Upon carefully weighing the interests of each party, the
court decided in favor of Junior Davis:

> We can only conclude that Mary Sue Davis's interest in donation is not as sig-
> nificant as the interest Junior Davis has in avoiding parenthood. If she were
> allowed to donate these preembryos, he would face a lifetime of either won-
> dering about his parental status or knowing about his parental status but hav-

ing no control over it. He testified quite clearly that if these preembryos were brought to term he would fight for custody of his child or children. Donation, if a child came of it, would rob him twice—his procreational autonomy would be defeated and his relationship with his offspring would be prohibited. The case would be closer if Mary Sue Davis were seeking to use the preembryos herself, but only if she could not achieve parenthood by any other reasonable means.[80]

Avoiding a presumptive rule, the court determined that, absent an agreement or a contract, the party wishing to avoid procreation should prevail, assuming that the other party has a reasonable possibility of achieving parenthood by means other than the use of preembryos; if not, that party's argument should be considered. This reasoning was not likely to convince all states, however. As state legislatures struggled with the issues, Louisiana, the only state to pass a law, declared that disputes between parties should be resolved in the "best interest of the embryo," and that interest would be "adoptive implantation."[81]

Illegitimacy

Until very recently the law controlled sex outside of marriage by punishing the doers. During the colonial era fornicators were whipped publicly. Later the law punished unmarried fathers by refusing to allow them the right to custody while maintaining their obligation to support. Until the second half of the nineteenth century mothers, also, had no legal right to custody but always had the obligation of support. Even through the Progressive era unwed mothers were considered unworthy mothers and were given little help in supporting their children. This put them them at risk of losing their children. In the second half of the twentieth century, however, the state quit punishing sexual behavior outside of marriage. This trend mirrored the no-fault revolution in divorce; if the state was not going to consider adultery or other sexual misconduct in divorce and custody actions, then it could no longer legitimately punish illegitimacy.

The numbers of children born out of wedlock grew dramatically between 1960 and 1990. In 1960 one in every forty white children was born to an unmarried mother; in 1990 it was one in five. There was a pronounced racial differential; among African-Americans the figure rose from one in five to two out of three.[82] The reasons for this sharp rise were many; they included not only the long history of racism and the demotion of the traditional family model but also changes in law and policy that moved toward removing the stigma of illegitimacy, and also provided at least minimal economic support for the unwed mother and her child. The custodial implications of these changes in law and policy were twofold: under certain circumstances the unwed father, for the first time, had a decisive right to the custody of his child and the unwed mother could not lose custody of her child by reason of poverty alone.

Unwed Fathers

The long but sporadically fought campaign to treat illegitimate children as natural children before the law greatly advanced in the last part of the twentieth century through a combination of Supreme Court decisions and statutory law. In truth, this crusade was more concerned with insuring that at least one parent supported the child than consideration for the child's best interests; it also reflected the shifting balance toward fathers and the emphasis on biological parenthood that characterized other aspects of custody law reform.

The new thrust of the law considered the rights and obligations of all biological fathers the same, no matter their marital status, and extinguished the term illegitimate in legal reference to children. This change extended to custody following the death of the mother (but not usually when she was still alive), visitation rights, consent to adoption, inheritance, and, of course, child support. Theoretically an unwed father received the same right to custody following the death of the mother and the same right to visitation as that afforded to the natural father who was legally married to the mother. This policy was a great departure from previous eras where an unwed father may have been assigned the obligation of support, and, in more recent times, the status of a natural father in terms of inheritance, but was rarely given the right to custody or visitation, nor was his consent necessary for adoption.

In 1971 the U.S. Supreme Court in Stanley v. Illinois considered the custodial rights of unwed fathers; specifically the right of an unwed father to retain custody of his children upon the death of their mother.[83] Joan and Peter Stanley had lived together intermittently for eighteen years, during which they had three children. Upon Joan Stanley's death, the children were declared wards of the court under an Illinois statute mandating that children of unwed fathers become wards of court on the death of the mother. Peter Stanley objected, claiming that equal protection under the Constitution required that he be treated like married fathers, who are presumed fit custodians under Illinois law whether they are divorced, separated, or widowed. The Supreme Court agreed, and determined that there must be a fitness hearing to determine custody, as there would be for all natural parents in this circumstance. Justice White declared: "The private interest here: that of a man in the children he has sired and raised, undeniably warrants deference and, absent a powerful countervailing interest, protection."[84]

Most unwed fathers were not like Stanley, however; they did not live with their offspring and often had little or no contact with them. In a series of consent to adoption cases the U.S. Supreme Court struggled to determine the limits of the rights held by biological fathers.[85] Did biology alone create a father's right or was fatherhood a more complex phenomenon? In Lehr v. Robertson Jonathan Lehr and Lorraine Robertson had never lived together, and when their daughter, Jessica, was eight months old, Lorraine married Richard Robertson. When Jessica was over two years old Robertson filed a petition to adopt Jessica. There was a factual dispute concerning Lehr's attempts to see his daughter; Lehr claiming that Lorraine tried to hide their whereabouts and that at one point he hired a private detective to find his daughter.

Lehr insisted that he was denied equal protection under the Constitution, since he received no notice and opportunity to protest termination of his parental rights. The majority of the Supreme Court disagreed. Justice Stevens stated:

> The significance of the biological connection is that it offers the natural father an oppportunity that no other male posesses to develop a relationship with his offspring. If he grasps that opportunity and accepts some measure of responsibility for the child's future, he may enjoy the blessings of the parent-child

relationship and make uniquely valuable contributions to the child's development. If he fails to do so, the Federal constitution will not automatically compel a State to listen to his opinion of where the child's best interests lie.[86]

This Supreme Court ruling did not inhibit the states from going further in
treating unwed fathers the same as natural fathers, nor did it deal with the
common event of mothers giving up their children for adoption at birth, when
there was no opportunity for the unwed father to have established a relationship. The California Supreme Court wrestled with this second issue in the
case of Michael U. v. Jamie B.[87] When their son Eric was conceived Jamie was
twelve years old and Michael was sixteen. Jamie placed their son up for adoption at birth and Eric had been living with the couple who planned to adopt
him, the Whites, for five months when Michael sought temporary custody. In
California a grant of temporary custody would have allowed Michael to prevent the adoption of his child and to sue for permanent custody.

The trial court was obliged to apply the same standard as for natural parents, which mandated that a child will be awarded to a natural parent unless
there is a finding that it would be detrimental to the child. The trial court
found in favor of Michael and awarded him temporary custody. A divided
court reviewed the evidence regarding Michael's fitness as a parent, leaning
heavily on the high school dean's report regarding his frequent fighting
episodes, his poor academic and attendance record, and the dean's description
of Michael as "very defiant. I would say very immature, disruptive, lack of
respect for authority."[88] The court did not question the application of the
same standard for unwed fathers who had no contact with their child as for
married fathers. Instead, the majority determined that the trial court had
abused its discretion in not finding that an award of custody to the father
would be detrimental to the child. While concurring with the majority decision as the only one possible on the facts, Justice Kaus insisted that the law
was wrongheaded: "We should return to the traditional rule: When there is
an unmarried mother who proposes to place her child for adoption and a biological, but not presumed father, the trial court should consider only the best
interest of the child."[89]

Unfortunately, the most common legal disputes involved, not fathers seeking to retain custodial rights, but rather fathers who were not voluntarily sup-

porting their children. In this instance the law did not require an actual involvement with the child but simply the fact of biological paternity. Beginning in 1975 the federally funded AFDC program required all states who participated to locate the fathers of the recipient children, married or unmarried. Up until this time social service agencies had attempted only spotty and desultory efforts at collecting child support from absent fathers (and occasionally mothers). In large part to clarify who would qualify as a father for purposes of support, the Uniform Parentage Act was adopted in many states and adapted in many others. This act changed the focus of child support, shifting the right from the mother to the child. The act created presumptions regarding fatherhood, ranging from the standard one, in which the parents are married, to the circumstance where the father acknowledges his paternity in writing without objection from the mother.[90] The process of judicially determining paternity included a new rule, which allowed evidence regarding another man's sexual relationship with the mother only if blood tests did not exclude the other man and if he could be made a party to the litigation.[91]

Unwed Mothers

As unwed fathers' rights expanded unwed mothers relinquished a portion of the absolute right to the custody of their children that they had gained during the Progressive era. This loss was more than compensated for, however, by the aggressive efforts undertaken by law enforcement agencies to wrest child support payments from reluctant fathers. As we have seen, support laws had been on the statute books in all states since colonial times. At last, spurred by the federal government, states firmly asserted that it was the father's obligation, not the state's, to support a child born out of wedlock.

By no means did all unwed fathers support their children. Many fathers were unemployed, or not to be found. The state still provided support to a substantial portion of unwed mothers who alone could not support their children. Aid to Families with Dependent Children, or AFDC, the principle vehicle of support, differed in character from its Progressive-era precursor, Mother's Pensions. AFDC, first enacted in 1935 as part of the Social Security System, was federally administered, providing matching funds for individual states. Unlike Mother's Pensions, where each state determined its own criteria, with many states excluding unwed mothers, AFDC set uniform criteria that distinguished eligibility solely on income, not marital status or lack of marital status. Social welfare officials were concerned not with the moral character of the mother, as demonstated by her unwed status or perhaps by cohabitation without benefit of marriage, but rather with her other sources of support. Two Supreme Court decisions and several congressional amendments led to the rule that the income of stepfathers[92] must be considered but not that of unmarried cohabitants.[93]

Benefits under AFDC were by no means lavish; the average family receiving benefits experienced a standard of living at about 67 percent of the nation's poverty level, with dollar amounts varying widely from state to state. Still, for the first time in American history poverty alone was not an accepted condition for removing children from their parents, no matter what their marital status or with whom they chose to live.

Removal of Children and Termination of Parental Rights

By the second half of the twentieth century the child protection organizations initiated by nearly all volunteer childsavers in the Progressive era had evolved into large publicly funded bureaucracies staffed by professional social workers. In contrast to the social feminists the third wave of feminists manifested little interest in child welfare, focusing instead on equal opportunity for women in the world outside the family. In all fairness, there was little room for volunteer activity in the well-organized world of child protection. The state in its role as parens patriae had almost completely taken over the role of child protector from private citizens, actively intervening in families to supervise their conduct toward their children and, often, to remove their children temporarily or permanently. Following an adjudication of abuse or neglect or dependency (parents unable or unwilling to care for the child), the court appointed a temporary or permanent guardian who could be an individual, a state agency, or a private insitution. The guardian was responsible for the child's well-being, but guardianship did not involve termination of all parental rights or necessarily a transfer of custody. Sometimes the state would claim custody of the child and place it in a foster home. More often the child would be returned to its family under the supervision of the guardian. Under both circumstances the natural parents still claimed "residual" parental rights and obligations, including the right to visitation, the right to refuse consent to adoption, and the duty of rendering support. Ultimately, if the child was removed from the family for a period of time the state determined whether or not to terminate parental rights.

The delicate balance between the state as child protector and the privacy rights of parents to the custody and control of their children definitely tilted toward the authority of the state. The state intervened in families at a rate unknown in history, providing a wide variety of support and sometimes removing the children when the support could not, in the state's opinion, cure the families' problems. The publicly supported child protection agencies still enjoyed some state and even local autonomy, but the trend favored ever more federal government control. Federal control was exacted by U.S. Supreme Court decisions governing procedure in the removal of children from their homes and termination of parental rights, and by federal statutes exacting uniform requirements in exchange for federal funds.

Mandatory reporting laws, perhaps the most significant federal contribution to the child protection arena, were introduced in 1974 with the passage of the Child Abuse Prevention and Treatment Act.[94] This act offered funds to states that developed laws requiring medical, education, social work, child care and law enforcement professionals to report suspected physical abuse, sexual abuse and exploitation, physical neglect, and emotional maltreatment. Failure to report triggered civil or criminal penalties. The general public was encouraged, but not required, to report suspicion of child abuse as well. Many states had such laws already in place and nearly all the others followed suit.

These reporting acts produced immediate and dramatic effects. In 1963 approximately 150 thousand children were brought to the the attention of public authorities, in 1982 the number had soared to 1.3 million. Social service organizations intervened into custodial matters with increasing frequency; the removal and children from their homes and the termination of parental rights also became more common. Following thorough screening of reports by child protective agencies, more than 400 thousand American families were placed under home supervision.[95]

Responding to this rapid rise of state intervention into private homes, advocates for parents' rights and critics of child protection philosophy questioned several aspects of the state's procedures. How were protective agencies defining abuse and neglect? Were their definitions based on an ethnocentric vision of middle-class family life? Was the postremoval solution of foster care placement in the best interests of the children?[96] Were mothers on AFDC, who were under continual supervision in order to receive benefits, placed under unfair scrutiny while richer families never came to the attention of child protection agencies? And, finally, was the basic right of parenthood being terminated without due process?

At the core of these disputes was the fundamental question of what constituted neglect and abuse. Severe physical abuse certainly existed when displayed in broken bones and serious bruises, but other manifestations of abuse and neglect were more difficult to measure. A California appellate court dealt with the issue of when a home is an "unfit place" in the Matter of Deborah G. California law then authorized intervention and possible removal a child when "his home has become and is an unkempt and unsanitary place of living." George and Patricia G. were the parents of five children, ages two through fifteen. The family had been supervised by social workers for two years, but child protective workers declared that

> the house was "very filthy," and a strong odor emanated therefrom: the floors were "sticky" with food particles and dog hairs; the children were dirty and had body odors, lice were removed from the head of one child; garbage and litter were in the backyard; trash was in the living room; the bathroom was "terribly dirty" and "full of flies"; the kitchen floor was encrusted with food and dirt.[97]

Based on testimony of witnesses that the condition did not seem to improve, the social service agency moved to remove all the children except the oldest.

The parents spoke in their own defense, claiming that they were both overweight and in poor health, making it difficult for them to keep the house clean. They said they loved their children and the children were not dirtier than other children. A social worker testified that there was mutual affection between the parents and children, and that the children were in good health except for minor ailments, that the children were happy, and that there was no evidence of unkindness or cruelty.[98] Nevertheless, the trial court removed all four younger children and placed them in foster homes for one year, allowing parental visitation. The appellate court upheld the decision, claiming the evidence was sufficient to remove the minors.[99]

Meanwhile, a new category of abuse rarely mentioned in the Progressive era made a powerful entrance in the 1980s. Child sexual abuse, a category unknown in previous abuse and neglect statutes, became a prominent feature in child removal allegations, and virtually all states rewrote their abuse and neglect statutes to include this category. The number of reports rose dramatically. It was unknown whether these allegations were a result of the imposition of reporting requirements uncovering abuse that had always been there, or whether they reflected a real upsurge in the prevalence of abuse. Child sexual abuse allegations were a different matter than neglect, or even many of the physical abuse complaints, in that criminal convictions of the offenders were actively sought, even when the offender was a parent. Even if a jury could not sustain a criminal conviction beyond a reasonable doubt, a civil action could mandate removal of the child for the child's safety. Both criminal and civil trials relating to child sexual abuse were notoriously difficulty to pursue because most often the child was the only witness, and was frequently under age five, with limited language skills. Physical evidence of abuse was often ambiguous or nonexistent, and therefore courts commonly relied upon sexual abuse experts who had interviewed the child. Expert testimony of this nature was viewed skeptically by the court. Nevertheless an allegation of sexual abuse almost always triggered the removal of a child, at least temporarily, from the custody of the suspected adult. Sometimes this meant removing a child from the home and placing him or her in the custody of social services, the protective arm of the state.

In a much-cited California case, In re Amber B., a county department of social services brought a petition alleging that the father, Ron, had sexually molested his three-year-old daughter and that his one-year-old daughter was at risk of sexual abuse.[100] This case illustrates the difficulty of proving sexual abuse when the victim is a small child and the conflict experienced by judges, who must adhere to established evidentiary rules regarding expert testimony and yet feel obliged to protect a child.

Initially the judge in In re Amber declared the daughters to be dependent children of the juvenile court. The father appealed. At the hearing on the petition the department presented testimony by a psychologist, Dr. Henry Raming, who had seen Amber on three occasions. Over Ron's objection the court permitted Dr. Raming to testify that, in his opinion, Amber had been sexually molested, and she believed she had been molested by her father. Dr. Raming's opinion was based on two factors. The first was the nature of Amber's reports of abuse, in which she described instances of abuse in various ways. Dr. Raming that testified that it is "fairly well documented in the literature . . . that children who have been molested will talk about being abused, but they will do this by consistently giving the . . . same facts or the essence in different words such that they have an event or an experience in their minds and are not merely repeating . . . rote by rote, someone else's words." The second factor was the nature of Amber's behavior with an anatomically correct female doll in Dr. Raming's office. During two of Dr. Raming's examinations Amber placed her index finger in the vaginal and anal openings of the doll and pushed and twisted her finger vigorously. According to Dr. Raming, Amber's behavior with the doll "is fairly consistent with molested children. This is not the usual type of behavior one would see in children who are in a stage of age-appropriate sex exploration."[101] The only other witnesses presented by the department, a police detective and a social worker, also testified regarding the nature of Amber's reports of abuse and her behavior with an anatomically correct doll. Amber did not testify. Ron testified in his own behalf and denied the abuse.[102] Custody was granted to their mother with supervised visitation for Ron.

The court of appeals reversed the trial court's decision, asserting that the use of anatomical dolls to assess sexual abuse was a new scientific method of proof that was not accepted as reliable in the scientific community. Some states followed the reasoning in this California case; most other courts, however, accepted expert testimony regarding the occurrence of sexual abuse.[103]

Without dispute, children of poor parents were more likely to be removed from their parents' home for reasons of abuse and neglect than other children.

The law no longer recognized poverty alone as a ground for removal of children, as it had through most of American history. However, at least three factors made poor parents more vulnerable to state intervention and removal. First, immigrant and minority parents were more likely to be poor than native-born white parents, and, just as in the Progressive era, these groups sometimes exhibited cultural styles that were unacceptable to the white middle class. Many Asian immigrant families, for example, refused to take their children to the doctor for routine care, claiming it violated their spiritual practices. This practice was as unacceptable to social workers as the insistence of the Italian mother at the turn of the century that her children must work for organ grinders, rather than go to school, in order to support the family.[104] Second, poor parents who were dependent upon public assistance were scrutinized by social workers in a manner that other parents were not. Third, poverty was frequently associated with other lifestyle patterns, such as drug or alcohol abuse that could provoke child neglect or abuse.

When parents or parent advocates complained about bias regarding cultural syle, the court almost always held up the state's action on the basis of the "best interests of the child." A New York court, for example, rejected the argument that "impossible barriers" were created for poor black parents by requiring that they comply with the customs of "bourgeois urban existence" in maintaining a visitation schedule. The court stated, "To accept [this argument] would constitute regression to the period when the rights of parents were treated as absolute, and would negate the rights of children as developed by the legislature and courts of the State of New York."[105]

The U.S. Supreme Court addressed the issue of social service intrusiveness into the privacy of families receiving public assitance. The 1971 case involved a plaintiff, Barbara James, who refused to allow a scheduled home visit by a caseworker as a condition of continuing AFDC payments for her son Maurice, age two. The mother refused the visit on the ground that it consitututed unreasonsable search and seizure as defined by the Fourth Amendment.[106] At trial James introduced the affadavits of fifteen other AFDC recipients who complained about intrusive and frequently unannounced visits by social workers. Justice Blackmun, writing for the majority, noted, as an aside, that all was not well with Maurice, who exhibited evidence of a skull fracture, a dent in the head, and a possible rat bite. He stated that even if the home visit possessed some of characteristics of a search in traditional criminal law sense, the visit did not fall within Fourth Amendment's proscription against unreasonable searches and seizures, so long as the visit was made by a caseworker, did not occur outside working hours, and no forcible entry and/or snooping occurred. Blackmun claimed, "The caseworker is not a sleuth but rather, we trust, is a friend to one in need."

The final and most dramatic step taken by the state in its role as parens patriae was the termination of parental rights. With this step, the state, in the person of the social service agency, could retain guardianship and place the child in long-term foster care, or, when possible, the state could assign full custody and control to new adoptive parents. Natural parents became legal nonentities, foregoing even the right of visitation. Government agencies were required to make reasonable efforts to restore children to the family after removal. Nevertheless, there were many families, in the judgment of the social workers, for whom reunification was not possible.

What right did parents have to protect against this type of agency decision? What kind of due process. Ultimately, the U.S. Supreme Court in Santosky v. Kramer considered the procedures affecting termination of parental rights.[107] Like many other termination of parental rights cases the Santosky family had appeared before the court several times. What is unusual is that the parents pursued the case through several appeals. Petitioners John Santosky II and Annie Santosky were the natural parents of Tina and John III. In November 1973, after incidents reflecting parental neglect, respondent Kramer, commissioner of the Ulster County Department of Social Services, initiated a neglect proceeding and removed Tina from her natural home. About ten months later he removed John III and placed him with foster parents. On the day John was taken Annie Santosky gave birth to a third child, Jed. When Jed was only three days old the commissioner transferred him to a foster home on the ground that immediate removal was necessary to avoid imminent danger to his life or health. Following the removal of Tina, John, and Jed two other children were born. These were not taken from their parents' custody.

In October 1978 Kramer petitioned the Ulster County Family Court to terminate petitioners' parental rights in the three children. While acknowledging that the Santoskys had maintained contact with their children, the judge found those visits "at best superficial and devoid of any real emotional content." After deciding that the agency had made " `diligent efforts' to encourage and strengthen the parental relationship," he concluded that the Santoskys were incapable, even with public assistance, of planning for the future of their children. Termination of parental rights was granted, and this decision was affirmed on appeal.

The Santoskys appealed again, contesting the constitutionality of the preponderance of the evidence standard in terminating their fundamental rights as parents. The New York appellate court upheld the standard, claiming the standard balanced the children's rights against the parents, but the U.S. Supreme Court disagreed:

> Even when blood relationships are strained, parents retain a vital interest in preventing the irretrievable destruction of their family life. If anything, persons faced with forced dissolution of their parental rights have a more critical need for procedural protections than do those resisting state intervention into ongoing family affairs. When the State moves to destroy weakened familial bonds, it must provide the parents with fundamentally fair procedures.[108]

The court insisted upon a standard of clear and convincing evidence, demanding more than a preponderance of evidence but less than the "beyond reasonable" doubt required in criminal matters. In another case involving termination of parental rights, however, a divided court decided that parents do *not* have right to counsel in termination hearings since their physical liberty is not at stake.[109]

Foster Care and Adoption

When a child was voluntarily relinquished by his or her parents, or removed temporarily or permanently through state intervention, the child was likely to be placed in one of three custodial situations: guardianship, usually with a relative, short-term or long-term foster care, or adoption. Until the end of the nineteenth century guardianship by a relative or a person designated by will would have been the only alternative to binding out or placing in orphan asylums children whose parents were dead or incapable of caring for them. Unless the child owned property, however, the guardianship probably would have been informal, with no court involvement. Adoption and foster care were two new custodial arrangements that evolved in the second half of the nineteenth century, reflecting an effort to replace the work model of apprenticeships and the institutional model of orphanages with a family model.

Adoption, the nineteenth-century invention by which the full rights and obligations of natural parents are abrogated in favor of adoptive parents, suffered from success in the late twentieth century. The number of children available diminished for many reasons, including the state support of unwed mothers, yet the demand for children remained high. The lack of babies encouraged unregulated black markets and contributed to the growing popularity of new reproductive technologies, eliciting charges of baby selling as in the Matter of Baby M. In response, agencies tightened enforcement of statutory regulations designed to protect birth mothers from exploitation and to prevent adoptive parents from evading the scrutiny and supervision of state agencies.[110]

Adoption, however, was not an option for all children. As early twentieth-century child rights advocate Homer Folks had commented on the public's belief in the unlimited number of "free" placements: "It is not true as regards delicate or unattractive children, or children who may be reclaimed by parents."[111] Older children were particularly difficult to place in adoptive homes in the late twentieth century since there was no longer a demand for their labor. Adopted children were now seen entirely as an emotional outlet for parenting needs rather than as an economic asset. Minority children and children of mixed race were more difficult to place, as were children with emotional or physical handicaps.

At the beginning of the twentieth century most unplaceable children would have been put in an institution run by a private, voluntary agency. By the second half of the twentieth century, however, the state had nearly usurped the role of private voluntary (usually religious) agencies, and the familial model of foster homes replaced the institutional model of orphanages. In addition to sheltering orphans or abandoned children, foster homes provided short-term care for those children who came under the protective jurisdiction of the state but were returned to their parents when the home situation improved. Many parents also "voluntarily" placed their children in foster homes, without court intervention. It was not always clear how "voluntary" these placements were, in the face of social worker persuasion.[112] In theory foster homes served as a temporary respite between return to family or adoption. In fact many children spent nearly all of their childhood in the twilight zone of "temporary" foster care.

Foster care families usually were licensed by the state and subject to regulations regarding size of home, number of children, and age of parents. Their contract with the social service agency provided them with a monthly fee for each child in their care. Under the terms of the contract they acknowledged that the legal responsitibility for the child remained with the agency, and that the agency had the right to terminate the foster relationship. In many ways this put the foster parents in the same situation as stepparents, they had physical custody of the children but no legal claim. For many foster families this was extremely frustrating; they had developed familial ties to their foster children—sometimes over a period of many years—and yet these children could be removed from their foster homes at will.

Foster parents filed a class action suit to correct his inequity. The group representing the foster parents claimed that foster parents had a constitutionally protected liberty interest in the children they cared for, which demanded a full hearing before children were removed from their care. The suit eventually reached the U.S. Supreme Court.

One of the foster care parents who brought the suit, Madeline Smith, cared for two children, Eric and Danielle Gandy, for seven years, since they were five and two years old. The foster care agency sought to remove the children from her home because the supervising social worker believed that Smith's arthritis made it difficult to provide adequate care. The Supreme Court offered some solace to all those who stood in the role of parents but were not biologically connected:

> The importance of the familial relationship, to the individuals involved and to the society, stems from the emotional attachments that derive from the inti-

macy of daily association, and from the role it plays in "promoting a way of life" through the instruction of children, as well from the fact of blood relationship. . . . For this reason we cannot dismiss the foster family as a mere collection of unrelated individuals.[113]

Nevertheless, in this instance the Supreme Court deemed New York's existing procedures adequate and did not provide the relief the foster parents sought, nor did the court specify that foster parents had a constitutionally protected right in the continued custody of their foster children.

Conclusion

It is difficult to say that the best interests of the child were served during this era. Increased divorce and the rise of illegitimacy, among other factors, contributed to the breakdown of traditional families, but the law, perhaps overwhelmed by the sheer volume of custody matters, made little effort to rethink family relationships with a focus on children. Strictly biological ties, as with unwed fathers and surrogate mothers, received far more consideration than the ties of stepparents, nonmarried partners, or foster parents who had parented children over a number of years. In choosing between mothers and fathers political considerations regarding gender-neutral treatment took precedence over any thoughtful reformulation of what was in the best interests of the child.

Under strict new reporting laws far more children were removed from their homes, temporarily or permanently, for reasons of parental abuse and neglect. In part, because they were under social service supervision, the event of removal was more likely to occur in poor families dependent upon the state for support. Whether or not this trend was, in fact, serving the best interests of the child remained an unresolved controversy.

Theoretically in the best interests of the child, fathers' legal rights to the custody of their children rebounded in this era as mothers' rights waned. Fathers were given equal rights to the custody of children following divorce, and, for the first time, the rights of unwed fathers to the custody of their children were fully recognized, as was their obligation to support. Nonetheless, increasing legal rights for fathers did not mean that, overall, more fathers had custody and control of their children. As a result of the high rate of divorce and the growth in illegtimacy, mother-headed households grew dramatically. More children were in the sole custody of their mothers than at any other time in American history, and these children were at great risk of becoming poor.

The Ascendancy of the Social Sciences

5

In the changing world of twentieth-century child custody law lawmakers and state officials increasingly relied upon social and behavioral science concepts and applications. Beginning in the Progressive era the new social science theory that poverty was not a symptom of a corrupt or criminal character encouraged the state to provide financial support to poor parents to maintain their children rather then removing them. At the same time scientific concepts of proper child raising provided the state with authority to remove children from their homes when parental behavior fell below acceptable standards. The new profession of social work grew up to carry out these scientific principles.

Dependence upon the social sciences accelerated late in the century. The abolition of fault-based divorce and the maternal presumption, both of which fostered vague standards for judicial decision making, promoted this dependence. The use of social sciences in the late twentieth century expanded in three ways. First, social science scholarship, usually in the form of psychological theories to support the primacy of mother, father, or both parents, influenced both legislators and judges in custody disputes following divorce. Second, expert witnesses, most often mental health professionals trained in the social and behavioral sciences, were called upon to testify as to the capabilities of a particular parent and social workers were asked to evaluate the larger parent-child living situation and to intervene in cases of abuse or neglect. Third, the courts moved toward using a therapeutic model of mediation in place of the adversarial mode of litigation in all matters of family law.

From Divine Law to Social Science

Before the advent of the social sciences judges sometimes felt obliged to invoke a higher moral authority than man-made law. For the whole of the colonial period and the greater part of the nineteenth century, courts justified the primacy of fathers' rights to the custody and control of their children by relying on divine right, natural law, or both. In the colonial era divine right granted the father superior right over the mother to the custody and control of his natural (but not illegitimate) children and child servants and apprentices. As Puritan minister Samuel Willard explained: "If God in his Providence hath bestowed on them Children or Servants, they have each of them a share in the government of them: tho' there is an inequality in the degree of this Authority over them by God: and the Husband is to be acknowledged to hold a Superiority, which the Wife is to allow.[1]

The divine plan granted paternal authority, including the authority to utilize the children's labor, but also required heavy paternal obligations of support, vocational, moral, and religious training. This concept was, in fact, well suited to the struggling colonial experience, where survival required the labor of every member of the household, including children. As head of the household, the ever-present father supervised all economic and social aspects of its operation.[2]

After the founding of the new republic the concept of divine plan was steadily replaced by the Enlightenment concept of natural law. Here also there were clear rules that human beings need only apply to specific fact situations, but God was no longer actively involved in presenting the rules and could not be called upon as authority. Adherents of natural law believed that a single, correct legal solution could be reached in every case by the application of rules of logic to a set of natural and self-evident principles. This classical jurisprudence was formal and mechanical, since the process of deciding cases was understood to be purely rational and undoubtedly correct.[3]

During the nineteenth century courts increasingly relied upon natural law rather than divine law to bolster their decisions. Natural law was a very flexible concept, and its flexibility was particularly tested in dealing with custody issues, where it was used to support two opposing concepts: the primacy of fathers and of mothers. The court in one of the two primary English common law precedents, Blisset's Case, declared, "The natural right is with the father, unless the father is somehow unfit."[4] In this instance evidence of the father's acts of physical brutality rendered him unfit. Nonetheless, American courts often quoted the natural law language of Blisset throughout the century to support fathers' rights.[5]

Fathers' rights, however, became disfavored near the end of the century as a rapidly urbanizing culture and the burgeoning women's rights movement changed the role of the family. This trend saw the paramount rights of the father give way to the mother, who was increasingly seen as the more nurturing and, in a reversal of seventeenth-century beliefs, the more moral parent. Natural law was now turned on its head and used to block the application of common law with regard to fathers' rights. The court would state the common law right of the father to the care and custody of his children and then employ natural law—a higher law—to decide in favor of the mother. As the New York court asserted in 1840, "By the law of nature, the father has no paramount right of the custody of his child." But, the court declared that

> the law of nature has given to her an attachment for her infant offspring which no other relative will be likely to possess in an equal degree, and where no sufficient reasons exist for depriving her of the care and nurture of her child, it would not be proper exercise of discretion in any court to violate the law of nature in this respect.[6]

The trend toward natural law, however, was short-lived. Criticism of decision making based on allegedly immutable principles began to evolve in the 1880s, and dissatisfaction and loss of confidence in natural law theories spread. The law, instead, began to be viewed as a means of establishing social policy. Judges grudgingly acknowledged that legal problems vary according to the social context. The erosion of confidence in natural law was especially affected by the emergence of the social sciences. The new developing social sciences, first sociology, and later psychology and anthropology, suggested that social organizations, human personality, and even nations or cultures could be studied empirically. One could no longer depend upon self-evident or revealed truths, but must study the human condition as it was to determine norms of human behavior.[7] This approach put into serious doubt the concept of a moral universe, spreading uncertainty to the family unit as well. What was the role of the family? What rights or duties did each parent have in this new, functional view of human behavior?

The impact of the new social sciences on custody law was twofold: it ratified the superiority of mothers, based not on natural law but rather on empirical observations of the importance of the mother-child bond, and it focused on the overall importance of the (good) family to child development, extending this to poor children as well. These observations strengthened the initiative of the state in its developing role as superparent. State intervention into the parent-child relationship could be justified by scientific evidence regarding child development.

The official debut of the social sciences into the legal world usually is credited to the influential brief that Louis Brandeis (later Supreme Court justice) first presented to the U.S. Supreme Court in a 1908 case challenging an Oregon law that gave special protection to women workers by regulating their hours of work. In his brief Brandeis, representing several women's organizations, offered specific empirical evidence and statistics relating to the effect of unhealthy work conditions on women. Brandeis argued that as mothers, or potential mothers, women needed special consideration in the workplace. The Supreme Court agreed, claiming that "as healthy mothers are essential to vigorous offspring, the physical well-being of woman becomes an object of public interest and care in order to preserve the strength and vigor of the race."[8]

While this case did not deal with child custody, it did deal with motherhood, promoting the special relationship between mothers and children as the justification for the special treatment for women. The basis for this special treatment was no longer natural law, but empirical evidence. The legal climate created by this case promoted a flood of protective laws favoring women workers on both the state and federal level. This same legal climate promoted the confirmation of the tender years doctrine in judicial opinions, eliminating almost all reference to the father's common law right.

This is not to say that social science explicitly invaded judicial reasoning in custody disputes. An investigation of appellate court decisions between 1920 and 1924 reveals that judges, in custody matters of the era, did not specifically invoke social science authorities, nor did they use statistical or any other form of empirical evidence to bolster their preference for mothers.[9] On the contrary, judges no longer seemed compelled to provide any justification for their bias; the primacy of mothers as custodians for small children had become a given.

Social feminists played an important role in utilizing the new social sciences to establish special legal consideration for mothers. Prominent social feminists headed many of the women's organizations who hired Louis Brandeis to present his brief based on social scientific evidence. Social feminist Florence Kelley, founder of the National Consumer's League, was the source of much of the empirical evidence presented by Brandeis.[10] Many of these same women's organizations promoted settlement houses and supported other child-saving activities as well. Through their efforts in obtaining mother's pensions and other forms of support, at least some mothers were allowed to retain the custody of their children. Eager to advance any argument that would help poor women, especially mothers, the empirical approach of the social sciences offered them a powerful advocacy tool.

The most direct link between the social feminists and the newly developing social sciences, however, was in the evolving profession of social work. Social work grew up with the new science of society, sociology. Lester Frank Ward, one of the founding fathers of sociology, promoted a science of society for the purpose of understanding, and then improving, society through the abolition of poverty and ignorance. According to social welfare historian Walter Trattner, during the 1890s sociology was considered the theoretical study of human societies while social work the practical application of these theories for the amelioration of society.[11] Although the union of sociology and social work experienced a rocky and inconsistent development throughout the twentieth century, the concept gave credence to the interventionary role of the state as superparent. Poverty and its consequences were not immutable, the state could change the course of a child's life by providing mandatory education and family support, while setting standards for parental behavior, which, if violated, could lead to the removal of a child from its home. Even the criminal class could be reduced or eliminated by proper child raising. Early sociologists, such as Charles Cooley, rejected the traditional notion of criminal behavior as a largely inherited characteristic and claimed, "The criminal [or delinquent] class is largely the result of society's bad workmanship upon fairly good material."[12]

The union of sociology and social work was perhaps most clearly expressed in the Chicago school, the center of urban sociology and social work cultivated at the University of Chicago. For two generations the University of Chicago, led by Ernest Burgess and Albion Small and carried on by E. Franklin Frazier, Louis Wirth, and colleagues, was at the center of the developing discipline of sociology. In this fertile ground the Hull House settlement workers Julia Lathrop and Jane Addams initiated training courses for social work, which eventually became the Chicago School of Social Work. The unique philosophy of this school was to produce a true continuum between scholarship and practice by offering a curriculum in which the students were well grounded in both sociological and psychological theory, and in case management.[13]

The sociological theory that poverty was not a symptom of a corrupt or criminal character also influenced the view that poverty alone should not be the cause of the removal of a child from his or her family. This view was advanced in the statement of child welfare particpants at the first White House Conference on the Care of Dependent Children in 1909. In the spirit of scientific inquiry the conference called for "the establishment of a federal children's bureau to collect and disseminate information affecting the welfare of children."[14] The conference concluded with the goal that child welfare would no longer be an intuitive response to an individual child's problem; national patterns would be scientifically identified, and solutions rationally implemented by trained social workers.

The White House conference had a profound effect on child custody attitudes. During the twentieth century trained social workers, publicly supported, almost completely subsumed the work of child welfare. This work, for the most part, focused on poor children and their families. The state's increased support nearly eliminated poverty as a ground for removal of children from their parents. Consequently, abuse, neglect, or desertion became the primary grounds for removal of children.

Social Science Ascends in Divorce Procedings: 1960–1990

Outside the framework of social work, which dealt mainly with custodial issues of neglect and abuse in poor families, social science played a peripheral role in custody disputes until the last part of the twentieth century. In divorce trials judges almost never specifically mentioned social science theories, although they undoubtedly absorbed some of these theories through the popular culture, and social scientists themselves were rarely major players in custody matters. The only exception to the firmly held legal model was the gradual acceptance of social work evaluators, who were sometimes asked by the court in disputed custody cases to provide an evaluation, usually written, of the home situation. The legal model was shaken irrevocably, however, in the early 1970s, as social science theories, particularly psychological theories, began to be discussed by legislators and cited by judges. At the same time mental health professionals, trained in psychological theory, began to appear regularly in the courtroom as expert witnesses to testify on which parent was more fit. Finally, in the 1980s, social science threatened to remove custody issues from the courtroom entirely as the social science paradigm of mediation began to challenge the judicial model of litigation as the preferred mode for handling custody disputes.

The revolution in custody law that followed no-fault divorce confounded legislatures and judges. Divorce reform swept through all states, removing fault as a factor for consideration in divorce and custody disputes. At the same time gender-based biases were removed, primarily as a result of the organized campaign for gender equality before the law. With the old rules gone state legislators and judges turned to social science to develop new guidelines to aid judges in making these most difficult decisions. Psychological theories were enlisted to support two opposing models of custody. The first model assumed that one parent should take primary responsibility, but that parent need not be the mother. This model embraced sole custody (with visitation) and a primary caretaker preference. The second model stressed the importance of both parents in the child's development and promoted some form of joint or shared custody. Neither model gave any preference to mothers and neither model considered the age or developmental stage of the child, as was the case in the tender years doctrine.

The psychological authorities most frequently cited by the appellate courts were law professor Joseph Goldstein, child analysts Anna Freud, and psychiatrist Albert Solnit.[15] Their work was most often enlisted to support the sole custody model, but was applied to nonparent conflicts as well. In their 1973 book, *Beyond the Best Interests of the Child*, the authors created the concept of the "psychological parent": the one individual, not necessarily the biological parent, with whom the child was most closely attached. In their opinion this person should have total and, if necessary, exclusive custodial rights, including refusing visitation to noncustodial parents. This work became the centerpiece for those who objected to joint custody and advocated instead a model favoring a primarily responsible parent.

In criticizing a shared parenting model, Goldstein, Freud, and Solnit focused on the impact that the model had on the child:

> Children have difficulty in relating positively to, profiting from, and maintaining the contact with two psychological parents who are not in positive contact with each other. Loyalty conflicts are common and normal under such conditions and may have devastating consequences by destroying the child's positive relationships to both parents. A "visiting" or visited parent has little chance to serve as a true object for love, trust and identification since this role is based on his being available on an uninterrupted day-to-day basis. Once it is determined who will be the custodial parent, it is that parent, not the court who must decide under what conditions he or she wishes to raise the child. Thus, the non custodial parent should have no legally enforceable right to visit the child, and the custodial parent should have the right to decide whether it is desirable to have such visits.[16]

Ironically, this influential work was used by courts to justify many decisions, but almost never to give the custodial parent the right to determine visitation. A New York court granted visitation rights to Franklin Pierce, who had lived with his illegitimate five-year-old daughter for more than two years before he separated from the mother. The court apparently had found Goldstein, Freud, and Solnit's theory on the psychological parent persuasive, yet the advice on visitation unacceptable.

> The court totally rejects the specious notion so ingenuously urged by Professor Solnit and his co-authors that the custodial parent should have the sole right to determine in the name of the best interests of the child whether the non custodial parent should be permitted or denied association with his own child. Experience and common sense teach that given the imperfections of human nature from which flow the bitterness and resentment which all too often accompany a marital or illicit love affair breakup, no one parent can, under such circumstances be safely entrusted so susceptible of abuse.[17]

The concept of the psychological parent was also applied to disputes between a nonparent, who clearly had raised the child, and the natural parent. These cases involved foster parents, relatives, stepparents, and other nonrelated parties. As we have seen in the previous chapter, the rights of biological parents were almost always upheld against all others unless there was clear evidence that it would be detrimental to the child. However, courts occasionally were persuaded in favor of the nonbiological party. In Stell v. Stell Nathan had been raised by his Aunt Bonny, while his father had difficulty remaining employed and providing a home. When the father, Tom, finally gained employment, he sought custody of Nathan. The trial court granted him custody, in spite of the testimony of two psychologists that Bonnie had become the "psychological parent." The appellate court disagreed. Citing Goldstein, Freud, and Solnit, the court explained:

> Tom (the father) urges us to reject the "psychological parent" theory. We refuse the invitation to do so. . . . It was formerly thought that blood ties between parent and child were extremely important. Now it is learned that kinship is not as important as stability of environment and care and attention to the child's needs.[18]

Most often the concept of "psychological parent" was used by courts to choose between parents, to defeat a joint custody arrangement, or, more indirectly, to promote a primary caretaker preference.

In a North Dakota case the trial court imposed the joint custody of a preschool child on unmarried parents, against the wishes of the mother. The court ordered that the child was to spend six months sequentially with each of the parents until he reached school age. On appeal the higher court relied primarily on case law from several states to reject the concept of joint custody, but it also cited one scientific authority: the work of Goldstein, Freud, and Solnit. Cautiously, the court did not mention the concept of "psychological parent," but rather stated that "the adverse effects suffered by children from divided custody as well as experts' continued opposition to divided custody because of the instability and discontinuity, make the concept [of joint custody] extremely problematic."[19]

The use of Goldstein, Freud, and Solnit's work as a justification for a primary caretaker preference is somewhat dubious, as the concept of primary caretaker emphasizes care-giving tasks. This concept differs from the notion of a psychological parent, to whom the child was attached emotionally but upon whom the child was not necessarily dependent for everyday care. West Virginia, which adopted a preference in favor of a primary caretaker parent, defined the primary caretaker as the parent who: 1. prepares the meals, 2. changes the diapers and bathes the child, 3. chauffeurs the child to school, church, friends' homes and the like, 4. provides medical attention, monitors the child's health, and is responsible for taking the child to the doctor, and 5. interacts with the child's friends, school authorities, and other parents engaged in activities that involve the child.[20] Nonetheless, a West Virginia court cited Goldstein, Freud, and Solnit, and suggested the primary caretaker was synonymous with the psychological parent. The court stated: "Substantial research has confirmed that young children, as a result of intimate interaction, form a unique bond with their primary caretaker. This unique attachment to a primary caretaker is an essential cornerstone of a child's sense of security and healthy emotional development."[21] In other cases, however, the primary caretaker and psychological parent concepts are treated as separate roles. A mother in a North Dakota case argued that her husband should not have been awarded custody of their four children because she filled both roles. "Carmen contends that the court erred in its consideration of her role as homemaker, psychological parent, and primary caretaker of the children."[22]

The primary caretaker concept was further aided by an upsurge in father studies. Beginning in the 1970s, these studies occurred as a gender-neutral standard for custody was promoted by both feminists and fathers" rights groups. Until this date the literature on fatherhood had been scant. According to Milton Kotelchuck, the Harvard researcher who performed the first laboratory observations of father-child interactions in the early seventies, it took only one-half hour to review the literature, and he read, as he noted, "the full articles, not the abstracts!"[23] Most father researchers studied father-infant relationships in a laboratory setting where fathers were assigned tasks usually performed by mothers. Occasionally fathers were studied in a real-life situation, with the mother present. The findings from the many studies were ambiguous,[24] and produced a heated debate among legal scholars regarding their appropriate application to custody standards.[25] Few, if any, researchers claimed there were no differences between the responses of mothers and fathers to children, but they disagreed on the significance of these differences. Nonetheless, the message heard by lawmakers was that fathers were, on balance, interchangeable with mothers.[26] This message both supported a gender-neutral custody standard and also a primary caretaker preference, since fathers could fill this role as well as mothers. As the New York family court concluded in Watts v. Watts, "The simple fact of being a mother does not, by itself, indicate a willingness or capacity to render a quality of care different from that which the father can provide." The court further explained that scientific studies show that "the essential experience for the child is that of mothering, —the warmth, consistency and continuity of the relationship rather than the sex of the individual who is performing the mothering."[27]

Social science theories, like natural law in the preceding era, were sometimes used to support contradictory models. While father studies promoted a gender-neutral primary caretaker preference that supported the model of a single custodial parent, these same studies were also relied upon by advocates of shared or joint parenting. These advocates argued that if mothers and fathers both can serve as nurturers, the child will benefit by having two, rather than one nurturing parent. By the 1980s father studies were complemented with the findings of long-term studies of shared parenting. This research, like the father studies, yielded ambiguous findings. One of the most respected of these researchers, Frank Furstenberg, conducted a five-year study of children with a variety of parental arrangements, including two-parent families. Reviewing his own study and the longitudinal research of others, Furstenberg concluded,

> The policy implications of findings reported here are unsettling because they clash with the prevailing practice that attempts to invent policies which increase parental involvement. On the basis of our study we see little strong evidence that children will benefit psychologically from the judicial or legislative interventions that have been designed to promote paternal participation.[28]

Yet inconclusive findings did not dampen the ardor of those convinced that shared parenting was the best custodial arrangement. By the late 1980s courts could choose from a number of studies that supported shared parenting. In Zummo v. Zummo the court dealt with a shared custody arrangement that foundered over a conflict of religion between the two parents. The court chose this conflict to review the scientific literature regarding joint custody. Without individual analysis of each study, the Zummo court cited fifteen scientific studies[29] that it claimed justified joint custody, observing:

> The demise of gender stereotypes, and a wide and growing body of research indicating the importance of both parents to healthy child development have caused courts to reconsider the efficacy of the sole custody/visitation concept of post-divorce allocation of parental authority. . . . Current research indicates that, while it may not be appropriate for everyone, in appropriate cases shared custody options may significantly ameliorate the negative consequences of divorce for children, and for their parents.[30]

Focusing on father studies in the postmaternal preference era, lawmakers conspicuously avoided mother-infant research. This avoidance was criticized by a wide range of developmental psychologists, particularly Freudians. They claimed that nearly all psychological research and theory before the 1970s had focused on mothers, not fathers. For Freud and his followers the mother-infant attachment was the most important relationship in the infant's life. Freud claimed the relationship to be "unique, without parallel, established unalterably as the prototype of all later love relationships."[31] Latter-day Freudians continued the tradition; in her widely read work, *Every Child's Birthright: In Defense of Mothering,* Selma Fraiberg described the growth of this attachment.

Already at the end of the first year, the baby has gone through a sequence of phases in his human attachments: from simple recognition of the mother, to recognition of her as a special person, to the discovery that she is the source of joy, the satisfier of body hungers, the comforter, the protector, the indispensable person of his world. In short, he has learned to love.[32]

Not only Freudians continued to promote the special nature of mother/child relationships; drawing on bioevolutionary theory and neuroscience research sociologist Alice Rossi maintained that it was false to believe that mothers and fathers are interchangeable. Biology and evolution have created a sexual dimorphism for the purpose of reproducing the species. According to Rossi,

Experimental work on response to infants supports the view that the underlying psychophysiological responses to infants are similar in men and women, but their behavioral responses differ in a way consistent with role distancing in the male and role embracing in the female: women show approach behavior of a nurturant kind toward the infant, while men respond by ignoring or withdrawing from the infant.[33]

Other critics argued that the abolition of the tender years doctrine favoring mothers appeared also to eliminate the concept of "tender years" itself. The custodial arrangement was imposed without regard to the age of the children, and without reference to the vast body of developmental research that detailed the changes in children at different points in their maturity.[34]

Although custody orders were theoretically modifiable, this difficult option was rarely exercised, and custody arrangements usually remained fixed no matter what the age of the child. Custody researcher Judith Wallerstein described the unhappy visiting arrangement of Ellen, age fourteen, whose custody arrangement had been set by the court when she was six. Ellen was forced to follow a rigid schedule of weekend and summer visitation with her father, whom she feared, thereby missing out on social activity with her peers. According to Wallerstein,

> In her quiet way, Ellen raises a question about the long-term psychological and social effect of a court order (whether for visiting or custody), which is out of sync with the changing developmental needs of the child. Arguing her own case, with tears in her eyes, eczema on her hands, and yet with moderation, she conceded that the visitng order may have served her best interests at age six, but it has become detrimental and hurtful to her interests as an adolescent.[35]

Also missing was legislative or judicial consideration of the research on gender differences in children and how this may relate to the custodial arrangements; a factor that had been considered by courts since the early nineteenth century. There was, in fact, a substantial body of research that suggested that children, particularly older children, fared better with same-sex parents.[36] Presumably the concept of gender neutrality that prompted the abolition of the maternal preference also forced the elimination of this criteria.

Expert Witness Testimony

The language of many new postmaternal preference laws were psychological in tone. Relationship criteria increasingly dominated the list of factors to be considered in determining the best interests of the child.[37] For example, the North Dakota legislature dictated that among ten factors, the first two to be considered by the court were: "1. The love, affection, and other emotional ties existing between the parents and child. 2. The capacity and disposition of the parents to give the child love, affection, and guidance and to continue the education of the child."[38]

Evidence to support this subjective criteria could only be obtained outside the courtroom by lay eyewitness testimony or by the evaluation of the parties by mental health professionals. Moreover, the lack of objective standards reduced the confidence of the judge in his or her decision-making ability, further encouraging reliance upon outside authorities. Thus, experts were increasingly utilized in child custody cases and were engaged in every step of the proceeding; parents could jointly seek the services of a mental health consultant to aid them with private mediation, or one party, often on the advice of his or her attorney, could employ the consultant with a view to settlement or, potentially, trial testimony. Increasingly the court itself, or the guardian *ad litem* (an attorney, or sometimes a layman or a psychiatrist, appointed by the court to represent the child), could request a psychological evaluation. In addition, the court frequently called for a custody evaluation when disputes arose. These evaluations, usually performed by court social workers, provided a wide range of information about the parents and children, including social and economic data, but they increasingly focused on "psychodynamic" factors.[39]

While mental health experts were prominent in the pretrial procedure, where most disputes were settled, their presence increased dramatically in those cases that found their way to trial. Between 1960 and 1990 the pattern of expert utilization at trial, as reported in appellate court decisions, changed dramatically; the number of experts soared, these experts were more likely to be appointed by the court, rather than by the parties, and they usually were psychologists, rather than psychiatrists or social workers. The nature of their testimony shifted from an evaluation of the sanity of the parent (usually mother) to observations regarding the relationship between parent and child, and in a substantial number of cases these experts testified regarding alleged sexual abuse.[40]

The use of experts in child custody trials, was gradually introduced in the 1940s and 1950s, reflecting, in part, the growth of the mental health profession itself. By the 1960s almost 10 percent of the cases on appeal involved expert testimony. By 1990 more than one-third of the cases on appeal had been tried with the aid of some sort of expert testimony. In 1960 it was the parents who generally employed their own experts in custody battles. By 1990 the court itself appointed the expert in the majority of the cases.[41]

Typically, in the 1960s a psychiatrist was called on to testify regarding the mental stability of one of the parents. Since the maternal presumption was still in effect in the 1960s, it was usually the mother's mental fitness that was at issue. In Vishnevsky v. Vishnevsky[42] the father employed two psychiatrists to testify regarding the mother's emotional illness and how her "emotional disorganization would have bad effects on the children, that they would suffer and have difficulty in school and at home and in adjusting with their playmates."[43] Similarly, in Galbraith v. Galbraith custody of the four children was originally granted to the father; five years later the mother, who suffered from a mental illness, petitioned for modification to receive custody of her two daughters.[44] A psychiatrist testified on the mother's behalf that she was sufficiently mentally competent to care for the children. In this case, however, the court denied her petition.

By 1990 the trend favored psychologists over psychiatrists, and the experts' testimony had more to do with the relationship between the parent and child rather than the mental illness of a parent. This trend reflected the new relationship-oriented laws and the abolition of the maternal presumption. When both mother and father hired mental health professionals to testify as to their relationship with the child, it sometimes became a bitter battle of experts. In an Illinois case the father hired a pediatric psychologist, Dr. Eric Ward, who for ten hours examined the interactions between the three-year-old daughter, Eleanor, the mother, the mother's lesbian partner, and the father.[45] Dr. Ward testified that the best interests of the child would be served by placing custody of the child with the father, based on his observation of child discipline and the instability of the relationship between Miriam (the mother) and Angela (her lesbian lover) and Angela's past and present instability. The mother's expert psychiatrist, on the other hand, a specialist in marital and sexual dysfunctions, testified that Eleanor had prospered under her mother's custodial care and that the father "did not know how to foster independence or treat Eleanor or Miriam with respect," and that based on his clinical evaluations and personality tests Roger had a strong tendency to "distort facts or lie in order to present information in a favorable light." Although it is not possible to ascertain what weight the court gave to these conflicting expert opinions, the trial court granted custody to the father and the decision was upheld on appeal.

More often the court itself appointed the expert, rather than the parent. For example, in Uhls v. Uhls the court relied upon testimony provided by a court-appointed social worker from the county department of social services who had conducted an investigation regarding physical abuse by both the mother and father.[46] And in Palazzo v. Coe the court appointed both a psychologist and a psychiatrist to testify regarding a personality conflict between one of the children and his mother.[47]

The introduction of testimony regarding sexual abuse or physical abuse marked another explicit change in the nature of expert witness testimony between 1960 and 1990.[48] When sexual abuse was at issue frequently more than one expert was called to testify. In Newsom v. Newsom the court heard testimony regarding alleged sexual abuse of the children by the father from four different experts, two of whom were appointed by the court.[49] One court-appointed expert initially decided that there was no indication of abuse, but upon speaking with another counselor who had seen the children, changed his testimony based solely upon the fact that the mother had provided the counselor with explicit details of abuse that were later determined to be untrue. The court decided to disregard the testimony of this expert, and ultimately concluded that there had been no abuse by the father. In S. H. v. B. L. H. the court relied on the testimony of two court-appointed psychologists who testified that the father was sexually abusing the child and awarded sole custody to the mother.[50]

Not all social scientists, nor all judges, were enthusiastic about the entrance of mental health experts into custody proceedings. Social scientists pointed to the imprecise nature of psychological theories and to the unsystematic nature of clinical observations.[51] Other commentators complained that psychologists were incapable of making scientific predictions about which parent would be the better custodian; judges were abdicating their decision-making responsibility in accepting wholesale the judgments of experts. Critics Weithorn and Grisso claimed that while "psychological evidence is sometimes relevant, it is never dispositive because our courts are imbued with the power and responsibility to weigh the social and moral factors that inevitably must be considered in reaching an ultimate judgment."[52]

When surveyed judges tended to discount the weight of expert testimony, especially if the expert were hired by one of the parties, rather than court-appointed. Court-appointed psychologists were rated as moderately important, ranking fourth on eleven items of evidence: psychologists appointed by one of the parties were ranked seventh. However, custody evaluations, usually performed by a court social worker, and, as noted, frequently employing the same kinds of psychological tests employed by a psychologist, were ranked second in importance.[53]

Mediation: From Rights to Relationship Rhetoric

> The dominant rhetoric no longer describes divorce as a process that terminates the relationship between spouses, establishing one as the custodial parent with clear responsibilities. Rather, divorce is now described as a process that, through mediation, restructures and reformulates the spouses' relationship, conferring equal or shared parental rights on both parents, although, in practice, the mother usually assumes the primary responsibility for care of the children.[54]

The judgments of mental health professionals influenced a change in the substantive rules of custody law, forcing courts to abandon legalistic rights in favor of a rhetoric of relationship. But there was also a change in the procedure as well as substance of child custody law. Where adversarial litigation was once the exclusive method of resolving child custody disputes, that model was challenged by the alternative one of mediation.

The trend toward mediation was undoubtedly rooted in the elimination of fault-based divorce. Judges were overwhelmed by the increasing number of divorces, which in turn produced an unprecedented magnitude of custody disputes. Judges in the postmaternal preference era felt ill-equipped to handle the volume and the decision-making burden, and looked to mediation as a substitute for adversarial court proceedings. California set the trend in mediation, as it had in all aspects of the divorce and custody revolution, by requiring mediation in all contested custody disputes before a case could be carried forth to trial.[55] This requirement coincided with the enactment of a preference for joint custody. The cooperative model of mediation was viewed as facilitating the ideal of joint custody in a manner that the adversarial trial process did not. Other states enthusiastically followed California's lead, encouraging a wide variety of mediation efforts, both public and private, often including property and support issues as well as custody arrangements. Only five other states had instituted mandatory mediation in all custody disputes by 1990, but many others permitted courts to order divorcing spouses to undergo mediation.[56]

Whatever form mediation took—public or private, voluntary or involuntary—certain characteristics separated the process ineffably from the legal adversarial process. The goal of a mediator, usually (but not always) a mental health professional, was to achieve agreement between the parents. This agreement was based, theoretically, on the parents' own concept of fairness, not that imposed by state law. A judge, on the other hand, was to apply presumably well-developed principles of the law to the fact situation of a particular family. Mediation sessions were informal and usually short, with parents representing themselves. In contrast, the adversarial system, weighed down by the burden of due process, required the lengthy exercise of a formal hearing, encompassing the right of confrontation and cross-examination. Most often the parties were represented by counsel in court proceedings, they were not in mediation. In neither model was the child likely to be represented or even present. Although some states required the appointment of a guardian *ad litem* in custody trials, most did not, leaving it to the court's discretion. Children were not welcome in mediation, which was considered to be a process of negotiation between the parents, not a democratic family council.

The operation of the Los Angeles conciliation court—one of the first and probably the largest in the nation—provides insight into the results of mandatory mediation. In 1981 4,459 disputed custody cases were handled in Los Angles County, with 55 percent working out an agreement as a result of mediation. No information is available regarding the nature of the settlements in Los Angeles: however, a study of the mandatory mediation process in Alameda County, California, during this same era revealed that 54 percent of the couples agreed to joint custody. In California local courts had the option of requiring mediators to make a recommendation to the court if the parties failed to negotiate an agreement. While Los Angeles elected not to exercise this option, more than half of the other California counties did. In Los Angeles those cases where no agreement was reached were the subject of a thorough review by a court-appointed evaluator whose recommendation was forwarded to the court. Following the evaluation more parties settled, possibly because they realized the salience of this evaluation to the trial outcome. Overall, the conciliation court estimated that the savings in Los Angeles Court directly attributable to mediation was between $990,000 and $1,140,000.[57]

The actual process of mandatory mediation varied widely, but it was always relatively short.[58] In Los Angeles a number of interviews were conducted over a four- to five-hour time period. The counselor first met with the attorneys, then with the parents together, without their attorneys. If the parents requested it, or the counselor deemed it necessary, the counselor would also meet with each parent individually. On some occasions the children were also interviewed, not to elicit their preference but to determine the divorce's effect on them. As the director of Los Angeles conciliation court observed:

> The court does not interfere with marriages and parental relationships prior to the ending of marriage, the theory is that the Court should not interfere following the ending of the marriage unless the child is endangered and the same standard of entry should be applied as prior to the breakup of the marriage.[59]

The informal nature of the proceedings meant that there was no established recipe. While the role of the mediator was deemed that of facilitator rather than director, the individual personality of the mediator could influence the course of the session. The only legal restriction on the process was the prohibition of therapy. Several courts had determined that it was a constitutional violation of liberty to compel therapy. Theoretically mediators were not limited by how a court might decide the issues. Working within the shadow of a looming trial, however, court-appointed mediators were likely to be influenced by a potential trial outcome. This pressure was exacerbated by the fact that in most jurisdictions the mediators' recommendation would be sent to the court; their recommendation, therefore, must adhere to the law.

Voluntary mediation sought by divorcing couples was often of a different nature. The goal of the parties was usually to avoid the long-lasting acrimony and the exorbitant expense they perceived to be part of the adversarial process.

Mediation sessions were likely to extend over a longer period of time and to include other issues in addition to custody.[60] Private mediators usually had either a legal or a mental health background. Since mediators were not appointed by the court, nor obliged to forward a recommendation to the court, they were not tied to solutions that the court might reach. This freedom presumably allowed the couple, facilitated by a mediator, to reach a solution that reflected their own sense of fairness, not that imposed by the law. One mediator, describing his own private practice, observed:

> As a mediator, I soon found out that taking on the role of an odds maker about the outcome in court was not helpful. Although I think couples should have some notion of how courts usually rule in typical dissolution cases, I resist telling them what I think the court's ruling would be and then saying, "Now I think you should construct a settlement that is similar to what our courts would do." Such an approach is commonly taken by beginning divorce mediators with legal background, but I try to refrain from speculating about a court-obtained outcome.[61]

This same mediator described the course of what he termed a typical mediation dealing with the end of a fifteen-year marriage of a husband and wife, Don and Linda. This mediation covered support and property division in addition to custody. The two main custodial issues were visitation and what to call the custody arrangement. The mother claimed that the children, two girls ages nine and thirteen, did not want to visit their father because they feared they would encounter his girlfriend. Clearly, the girlfriend was the sore point of anger for Linda, who did not want the divorce. The mediator, following the mediation gospel of looking forward not backward, not allowing anger to obstruct a settlement, did not allow Linda to talk about the girlfriend, insisting upon focusing on the mechanics of visitation. He recalled,

> Resorting to my conceptual theory of mediation that says people need agreements, not therapy, I asked Linda if she wanted a written temporary agreement that states that Dan will not have his girlfriend stay with him when the children are present. Linda said nothing, and looked at Dan. He said that he does not live with another woman and that such an agreement was unneces-

sary. After a bit more prodding, both agreed that such an agreement was acceptable.[62]

As for the legal designation of the custody arrangement, Don and Linda finally agreed upon joint physical and legal custody. According to the mediator, Linda initially resisted joint physical custody: "When I asked her what she understood by her attorney's admonition that she be designated the physical custodian, she said that she had always been the primary parent, and even though Dan wanted joint custody, it was just not acceptable to her."[63] The mediator argued that these labels become important only in the event that the two of them end up in court, and suggested a binding arbitration clause that would eliminate this concern. The couple then both agreed to joint physical and legal custody and to a binding arbitration clause.

The initial response to mediation was almost universally enthusiastic, but soon a strong negative reaction took form, led principally by feminist legal scholars.[64] While most of the criticism was leveled at mandatory mediation, many of the same points also could be made for voluntary mediation. The essence of the feminist criticism was that mediation favored men. Women were usually the less powerful partner in the marriage, and mediation exacerbated this differential. Women who had real grievances, like Linda, whose husband had left her for another woman, often appeared hysterical or uncooperative in mediation sessions compared with the generally more composed behavior of men. This could influence mediators to consider the husband's wishes as more rational. The forward-looking style of mediation also worked to the disadvantage of mothers with real concerns. One feminist scholar, Tina Grillo, described the case of another mother named Linda who sought to rescind a joint custody agreement. In that case the father refused to return their son, as agreed, at Thanksgiving, and instead placed him until Christmas in a daycare where the teacher frequently relied upon corporal punishment. Linda claimed that the child returned manifesting violent and aggressive behavior. According to Grillo, the mediator's advice was as follows: "The Thanksgiving is past history, and she is sure that they both have complaints about the past. Blaming one another is counterproductive. The mediator tells Linda that she must recognize the parent who has the child is responsible for choosing daycare. Linda must learn to give up control."[65]

Even more problematical for feminist scholars was the battered woman issue. Some social scientists claimed that women who have experienced violence in marriage develop a passive personality.[66] On the other hand, the violent husband is often charming and seemingly forthcoming. Mediators were, according to the critics, too often swayed by the husband, who appeared to be the friendly parent, belying the violence of his domestic behavior. Even for women who had not been beaten, forced engagement with their husbands, without the protection of a lawyer and the legal process, could intimidate them, replicating their powerless mode in marriage.[67]

Most of the feminist critics asserted that the adversarial process, with all of its warts, provided more protection and support for women than did mediation. Granting the patriarchal nature of the legal process and the almost unlimited discretion afforded individual judges, they maintained that the presence of lawyers served women's rights, and that the authority of rules and precedent, neutrally conceived, provided a more empowering alternative for the powerless. As legal scholar Martha Fineman observed:

> The public nature of the legal process means that the basis for decisions will be explained, debated, and publicly considered. This process may not be fool proof, but it is better than one in which substantive rules and standards evolve and are implemented behind closed office doors without any possibility of checks from the political system.[68]

Other critics of mediation, both mandatory and voluntary, claimed that the high percentage of joint physical custody agreements achieved through the process did not fit reality. Very few parents could sustain a sharing arrangement in which the child actually resided with each parent about one-half of the time. Inevitably the child soon drifted toward spending most time with one parent, usually the mother. Child support, however, was usually configured differently for joint custody. A mother could find herself with effective sole custody but less child support than a sole custodian otherwise might receive.[69]

Responding to growing criticism, advocates of mandatory mediation maintained their enthusiasm but revised the model, mostly by making it less mandatory. Some states included exceptions in their statutes exempting cases involving child abuse and spousal abuse.[70] Other states allowed the judge to decide whether mediation was appropriate upon the presentation of evidence to the contrary. The Wisconsin law advised courts to consider "evidence of child or spousal abuse, evidence of alcohol or drug abuse, and any other evidence indicating that a party's health or safety will be endangered by attending the session."[71]

Proponents of mediation offered the straightforward defense that it worked, agreements were achieved, and that the parties liked the process. The limited number of studies evaluating mandatory mediation offered mixed but fairly positive results on these counts. California, which had the oldest mandatory mediation project, received the most attention. In addition to Los Angeles County, where, as already noted, 55 percent of mediation clients reached agreement in 1981, court officials in Santa Cruz County claimed that 75 percent of their 148 mediated cases reached agreement in that same year, and 54 percent of those interviewed one year later maintained their agreement. Still more impressive was San Francisco's experience. Domestic relations judge Donald King reported that before the court instituted mandatory mediation it handled an average of 275 custody or visitation cases per year. The year after mediation was introduced in 1980 only five contested custody/visitation trials or hearings took place.[72]

Clients in mandatory mediation proceedings were somewhat less enthusiastic than judges. While 64 percent of clients in California claimed they would recommend mediation to a friend, only 20 percent in Connecticut and 54 percent in Minneapolis agreed. Twenty-three percent of clients in California felt that the mediator pressured them or their spouse into an agreement. By contrast, clients in Delaware, the second state to compel mediation in disputed cases, found that 94 percent of the participants felt rushed in mediation and 56 percent did not believe that "mediation was better than a hearing with a master or judge."[73]

Voluntary mediation, while not as fully studied as court-mandated mediation, appeared to yield similar results. The rates of agreement were comparable to mandatory rates in California, Connecticut, and Minneapolis, as were the opinions that they would recommend the process to a friend.[74] Still lacking by 1990 were studies comparing the long-term effects of voluntary mediation to those imposed by the legislature or the court—or, for that matter, long-term studies of the lasting results of mediation in either form.

Conclusion

By the last decade of the twentieth century the social sciences had irrevocably involved themselves in child custody disputes, challenging the primacy of the legal system in this critical decision-making area. Judges and legal precedent increasingly gave way to social workers and mental health professionals who based their judgments on social scientific theories. Custody laws were rewritten to stress relationships, rather than rights, and mental health professionals were called upon to evaluate the parent-child relationship in order to make recommendations before trial and, sometimes, to testify at trial. Social workers investigated abuse and neglect allegations and advised the court on when to remove a child from a home or terminate parental rights. Finally, the trial process itself was increasingly replaced by mediation in child custody disputes.

Critics of this intrusion by the social sciences claimed, in part, that social science research could be used selectively for political purposes, as in father custody and shared parenting cases, and that mental health experts could not predict with any accuracy which parent or nonparent would provide better custodial care. Moreover, critics argued that the protections inherent in the judicial process were abdicated in the mediation process. Proponents answered these critics by maintaining, in part, that the social sciences had made important contributions to the understanding of human behavior and that these contributions must be recognized by the law. Proponents also contended that mental health professionals could evaluate child-parent relationships more successfully than judges, and that the legal system had failed to deal in a constructive manner with personal conflicts between parents.

At the end of the twentieth century only two observations could be made with some certainty: the proper role of the social sciences in custody matters was still a subject of controversy but the continuing influence of the social sciences was an established fact.

Afterword

In the fall of 1992 the media focused on the story of a twelve-year-old boy in Florida, Gregory Kingsley, who on his own initiative sought termination of his mother's parental rights so that he might be adopted by his foster family. Assisted by a lawyer, he pursued the suit on his own, since the social service agency that was legally his guardian did not want to cut parental ties even though he had spent only eight months of his life with his mother. The story caught the popular imagination for several reasons. Most Americans fear that all is not going well between parents and children. Those not familiar with the law were shocked to learn that natural parents, even in extreme cases of neglect, still hold rights over their children. Others were heartened that a child had asserted his own rights and did not play the passive role of victim usually allotted to children in custody disputes. A few commentators, rather than cheering Gregory, saw his victory as a dangerous precedent, empowering children to divorce their parents.

Another custody drama caught the public's attention the following year.

The dispute focused on a baby girl in Iowa whose mother gave her up for adoption at birth. The adoptive parents, Jan and Robert DeBoer, named the baby Jessica and took her home to Michigan. Shortly thereafter, the biological father, not married to the mother at the time, appeared and demanded custody of his daughter. The case shuttled back and forth between Iowa and Michigan courts for more than two years. The final judgment, based on Iowa law, awarded the child to the biological father (who had since married the mother). This case poignantly demonstrated that the claim of a biological parent, even an unwed father who had never seen the child, takes legal precedence over the interest of a child remaining with the only family she had ever known.

Clearly, child custody is not an issue that can be put to historical rest. More children today are under the jurisdiction of courts in child custody matters than at any other period since the seventeenth century, when courts supervised the indentures of orphan immigrant children and children whose parents could not care for them. This historical account, I believe, can guide us in a troubled area, informing us of several lessons, but also raising many unanswered questions.

One lesson is that the legal history of child custody is far more about the rights of mothers, fathers, and masters than it is about the welfare of children. For most of our history the interests of a particular child was not an explicit legal concern. The law only began to recognize children's interests in custody disputes a little more than one hundred years ago. First, through the best interests of the child standard, the law focused on the children of divorce, usually middle-class children. Then, at the turn of the century, the law recognized the interests of poor children whose parents could not support them. These interests have not been clearly defined, however, and they have often been interpreted according to the political fortunes of women. Middle-class married women gained moral stature as mothers in the nineteenth century gained some political rights, including the superior right to the custody of their children after divorce. The changing status of women forced gradual acceptance of the concept that children of tender years belonged in the nurturing custody of their mothers. In the early twentieth century social feminists sought to extend this recognition to poor mothers by helping them to retain their children in spite of poverty. At the end of the century the custodial fate of children was once again influenced by the political battles of women—this time by the abolition of the maternal preference in favor of a gender-neutral standard in custody disputes in order to promote gender equality before the law. The best interests of the children were reinterpreted to include either or both parents, not always the mother.

Perhaps this lesson of history is that children, who have no political voice, are too often the political weapons of others' battles or, simply, are not considered at all. To my mind the heroines of this shifting historical panorama are the social feminists and other child welfare advocates of the Progressive era who wholeheartedly campaigned for children's interests, laying a firm foundation for our current child welfare structure. While they have been accused of class bias and of intrusion into the sanctity of the family, their efforts undeniably advanced the quality of life for children, particularly poor children.

The contemporary scene for children is not as salubrious. With regard to child custody there are women's rights advocates, father's rights groups, and grandparents' rights advocates, all pulling in different directions. There are children's advocates, but they are small in number. There is no national coalition of feminists, philanthropists, and lawmakers as there was in the Progressive era, to consider children first. Family law reforms, even those as drastic and far-reaching as the no-fault divorce revolution and the consequent changes in custody, are undertaken with little forethought of the effects on children. Children will not be the first consideration in custody matters unless there are adults who will advocate their interests.

A second lesson that can be gleaned from this historical account is that the law has maintained a two-tiered system in dealing with poor children and relatively rich children in custody matters. This brief recital of the variety of child custody situations demonstrates that child custody law very often involved poor children: those whose parents were dead or those who, in the time before state-supported family support, were too poor to raise their own children. In the colonial period nearly all custodial matters, with the exception of slave children, involved such children. Originally, the nineteenth-century concept of the best interests of the child and the concern for child nurture focusing on the mother applied only to children of divorce whose parents or relatives could support them. Poor children who became dependents of the state were not given such kind consideration. The Progressive era was a major leap forward in child welfare law: poor children finally were also considered worthy of nurturing, and the state initiated a tentative commitment to support them with their families rather than to remove them, usually to work for others.

In the modern era a two-tiered legal approach to child custody persists. Procedurally, dependency and termination of parental rights, more often than not involving poor parents, usually are treated in separate courts from custody following divorce. Moreover, poor families who are dependent upon the state are far more at risk of losing the custody of their children on grounds of abuse and neglect than are self-sufficient families.

A step toward abolishing the two-tiered approach is to unite in one court all matters relating to parents and children, including custody and child support following divorce, removal of children and termination of parental rights, as well as adoption, foster parent and guardianship disputes, and disputes relating to paternity and reproductive technology. This would be a major step toward advancing the interests of all children, not just poor children. While the legal issues in all these proceedings are somewhat different, they all focus on the best interests of the child. The children in all these proceedings could share a support system focused on the needs of families in crisis. Each child should receive his or her own representative, or guardian *ad litem*, to insure that the child's needs are fairly represented and attended to. A child representative should be available even when a case is settled before trial or through mediation. And, finally, the court should not abandon the child after a brief hearing or out of court settlement or foster home placement. All custody arrangements should be periodically reviewed by the court for a number of years to assure their smooth operation. Courts should attend to the changing developmental needs of children and changed family circumstances. Continued counseling should be available for children and their families. While all of these services require a larger staff and a larger budget, much of the cost could be paid by levying court fees on those who can afford to pay.

A third lesson that emerges from this historical account is the changing rights of biological parents. Historically, biological parenthood has been recognized or denied by the law to promote marriage, to protect inheritance rights, and to elicit child support. It was almost never invoked to promote the best interests of the child. In recent times the rights of biological parents have flourished over those of nonparents, but still without regard to the best interests of children. Perhaps because the law no longer attempts to uphold the sanctity of marriage, and there are no longer clear-cut presumptions to determine custody, the biological fact of parenthood is looked on with ever greater favor. An unwed father who has never lived with a child will probably receive custodial preference over a stepfather who raised the child. Surrogate mothers who give birth to a child are deemed incapable of contracting away their biological rights to that child. Foster parents who raise a child have little hope of adopting the child, or even retaining custody of the child, against the wishes of the biological parent, except in exceptional circumstances, like that of Gregory Kingsley.

Does it make sense to recognize biology over clear-cut attachments developed over time? Is it in the best interests of the child? Clearly the law can and does change the rules regarding the rights of biological parents. In the recent swing toward biological parents large populations of adults who raise children, most notably stepparents, relatives, and foster parents, have been largely ignored. A reevaluation of the custodial rights of nonbiological parents is in order, as granting custody to these parties can be—and often is—in the best interests of the children.

Finally, the role of social science, a latecomer to the child custody world, must be examined and defined. We have seen that social scientific concepts and practitioners have been granted tremendous influence, sometimes at the expense of established laws and legal procedures. The centrality of social workers, grounded in social science principles, was established in matters of dependency and abuse or neglect during the Progressive era. More recently social scientific theory has changed substantive laws. Experts from the mental health profession are frequently called as expert witnesses in custody disputes following divorce, and the model of mediation, a form of dispute resolution developed by the social sciences, has replaced legal proceedings in many custody disputes.

Without doubt, social science can inform us about human behavior in a manner that the law cannot. Studies of child development and of parent-child relationships could provide important information to decision makers. There are, however, two important problems with the application of social science to custody issues, as it has developed. The first is that social science sometimes is utilized selectively to promote arrangements, like shared custody and father custody, that are politically inspired and do not accurately reflect the range of social scientific research. In that instance mother-infant studies and gender studies, which might have promoted different solutions, are ignored. Also ignored are developmental studies suggesting that different arrangements, or different sex parents, are more appropriate at different stages of development.

The second pitfall in the application of the social sciences is the risk inherent in taking away the court's ultimate decision-making power. Critics have pointed out that expert witnesses do not have infallible, or even very accurate, rates of predicting which parent will do a better job of raising a child. In addition, when they are hired by a parent rather than the court, the objectivity of expert witnesses is questionable. The judge must be the decision maker, because he or she applies a wide range of social and moral factors rather than a single psychological assessment. Likewise, with mediation, the court could abandon important procedural safeguards of the trial process for the individuals involved, including the children. Lack of impartiality is also a concern. The mediator, while assuming a neutral posture, is, in fact, making the decisions.

Social science can be a complement to the law, without taking away its ultimate responsibility. First, both judicial and legislative reformers should strive to carefully and systematically consult with a wide range of scientists who are working on various aspects of child development and parent-child relations; currently, legislators too often hastily replicate another state's law or too quickly succumb to one interest group's lobbying efforts. Second, expert witnesses should be appointed only by courts, and the experts should testify only to what they have observed, not to what they have concluded. The scientific basis for their observations should also be explained to the court. For instance, if a psychologist describes a high degree of conflict between mother and father, he or she must discuss the relevant research that describes the effects of parental conflict on children. Expert testimony should be only one element in a larger range of testimony about the parents and the children. Third, mediation should be available, but not mandatory. Rather than determining the initial custodial arrangement, the mediator could fill the larger role of monitoring the arrangement. If courts oversee the custody arrangement for several years the mediator may help to work out any difficulties that might develop in the relationship. Finally, as a long-term service available to all children and their parents, mental health professionals can provide therapy to help both children and parents cope with the trauma of divorce, removal, or termination of parental rights. The decision-making role of the court is critical, but the best interests of the child demand a supportive transition.

Notes

1. Fathers/Masters: Children/Servants

1. Va. Co. Records (1933), 3:259, in Robert Bremner, *Children and Youth in America*, 4 vols. (Cambridge, 1970), 1:7.

2. *Acts of the Privy Council of England, 1619–1621* (London, 1930), p. 118, in Bremner, *Children and Youth in America*, 1:8.

3. Richard B. Morris, *Government and Labor in Early America* (New York, 1946), p. 391.

4. For a full discussion of the demographics for seventeenth-century New England and the Chesapeake colonies, see R. W. Beales, "The Child in Seventeenth-Century America," in Joseph M. Hawes and N. Ray Hiner, eds., *American Childhood: A Research Guide and Historical Handbook* (Westport, Ct., 1985), pp. 15–57.

5. In spite of these common themes it is by no means an easy task to generalize about child custody law and practice in colonial America. One can certainly point to dozens of differences among the developing colonies over the more than 150-year period before the founding of the new republic in 1790. While paying attention to the most important differences, it is still possible to consider the finite subject of child custody over the colonial

period as a whole, rather than focusing on each colony and dividing the experience into two centuries, because, first, the law developed similarly in all colonies, and, second, child custody was not an innovative (except for slavery) or fluid area of the law during this era. According to legal historian Lawrence Friedman, there were significant legal mutations among the thirteen colonies, yet the theme of unity remained strong because of the similarities in the colonial experience. "The texture of social and economic life was open: there was abundant land, the home government exerted weak but growing control, English tradition gave way to something uniquely American, different in the various colonies, but generally moving in parallel directions." Lawrence L. Friedman, *A History of American Law* (New York, 1973), p. 37.

6. See, generally, John Demos, *A Little Commonwealth: Family Life in Plymouth Colony* (New York, 1970), and P. Greven, *Four Generations: Population, Land, and Family in Colonial Andover, Massachusetts* (Ithaca, 1970).

7. A. E. Smith, *Colonists in Bondage* (New York, 1947), p. 12.

8. For a full discussion of the demographics for seventeenth-century New England and the Chesapeake colonies, see R. W. Beales, "The Child in Seventeenth-Century America," in Joseph M. Hawes and N. Ray Hiner, eds., *American Childhood: A Research Guide and Historical Handbook* (Westport, Ct., 1985), pp. 15–57.

9. Ibid., p. 19.

10. "Laws and Ordinances of New England," in *An Abridgement of the Laws in Force and Use in Her Majesty's Plantations* (London: Parker and Smith, 1704), p. 23.

11. Doris Foster and Henry Freed, "Life with Father: 1978," *Family Law Quarterly* (Winter 1978), 11(4):322

12. See, for example, Michael Grossberg, *Governing the Hearth: Law and Family in Nineteenth-Century America* (Chapel Hill, 1985), p. 235, and Andre P. Derdeyn, "Child Custody Contest in Historical Perspective," *The American Journal of Psychiatry* (December 1976), 133(12):369

13. James Kent, *Commentaries on American Law*, 2d. ed., 4 vols. (Boston, 1826–1830), 2:193.

14. Foster and Freed, "Life With Father: 1978," p. 322.

15. As quoted in William Forsyth, *Custody of Infants* (Philadephia, 1850), p. 8.

16. Mass. Records (1853), 2:8–9, in Bremner, *Children and Youth in America*, 1:39–40.

17. Ibid.

18. "Laws and Ordinances of New England," p. 23.

19. Samuel E. Morison, ed., "Records of the Suffolk County Court, 1671–1680," CSM Publications (1933), 30:599, in Bremner, *Children and Youth in America*, 1:41–42.

20. W. W. Hening, Statutes at Large (Virginia) 1:156, 157, 311–312, 336–337 (1823 ed.), as quoted in Marcus W. Jernegan, *Laboring and Dependent Classes in Colonial America, 1607–1783* (New York, 1931), p. 48.

21. As quoted in Jernegan, *Laboring and Dependent Classes*, p. 151.

22. Ibid., p. 153.

23. Watertown Records (Watertown, 1894), p. 64, as quoted in Edmund S. Morgan, *The Puritan Family* (New York, 1944, rpt., 1966), p. 65.

24. Suffolk County Records, p. 231, as quoted in Morgan, *The Puritan Family*, p. 65.

25. Jernegan, *Laboring and Dependent Classes*, p. 151–155.

26. "Laws of Virginia," in *An Abridgement of the Laws in Force and Use in Her Majesty's Plantations*, p. 32.

27. Mass. Records (1853), 2:8–9, in Bremner, *Children and Youth in America*, 1:39–40.

28. Max Ferrand, ed., *Laws and Liberties of Massachusetts*, reprinted from a copy of the 1648 edition (Cambridge, 1929), p. 11, in Bremner, *Children and Youth in America*, 1:41.

29. Mass. Records (1854), 3:101.

30. John. R. Sutton, "Stubborn Children: Law and the Socialization of Deviance in the Puritan Colonies," *Family Law Quarterly* (Spring 1981), 15:31–64.

31. Franklin B. Dexter, ed., *Ancient Town Records* (New Haven, 1917), 1:88–89, in Bremner, *Children and Youth in America*, 1:38.

32. Ferrand, *Laws and Liberties of Massachusetts*, p. 11.

33. Records and Files of the Quarterly Courts of Essex County, Massachusetts, 1:188.

34. Ibid., 2:262.

35. John Demos, *Past, Present, and Personal: The Family and Life Course in American History* (New York, 1986), p. 46.

36. As quoted in Morgan, *The Puritan Family*, p. 45.

37. William Blackstone, *Commentaries on the Law of England*, 3d ed. (New York, 1900), 1:453.

38. W. W. Hening, Statutes at Large (Virginia) (New York, 1823), 1:157.

39. Ibid., pp. 311–312.

40. Tapping Reeve, *The Law of Baron and Femme, of Parent and Child, of Guardian and Ward, of Master and Servant, and of the Powers of Courts of Chancery* (New Haven, 1816), pp. 70–72.

41. Richard B. Morris, *Studies in the History of American Law, with Special Reference to the Seventeenth and Eighteenth Centuries* (New York, 1930), pp. 126–155; Mary Beard, *Women as a Force in History: A Study in Traditions and Realities* (New York, 1962 [1946]).

42. Marylynn Salmon, "Women and Property in South Carolina: The Evidence from Marriage Settlements, 1730–1831," *William and Mary Quarterly* (1982), 39:684–685.

43. See chapter 2 of this volume for a full discussion of the legislative campaign for married women's property rights.

44. See Nancy F. Cott, "Divorce and the Changing Status of Women in Eighteenth-Century Massachusetts," *William and Mary Quarterly*, 3d ser. (1976), 33:586–614, for a study of Massachusetts divorce records. See also Linda Kerber, *Women of the Republic:*

Intellect and Ideology in Revolutionary America (Chapel Hill, 1980), pp. 158–183, for an analysis of eighteenth-century Connecticut divorces.

45. Connecticut Records, 2:328, as discussed in Morgan, *The Puritan Family,* p. 37.

46. Morgan, *The Puritan Family* , p. 37.

47. See Henry S. Cohn, "Connecticut Divorce Mechanism: 1636–1969," *American Journal of Legal History* (1970), 44:35–54; Morgan, *The Puritan Family,* pp. 37–38; Nancy F. Cott, "Eighteenth-Century Family and Social Life Revealed in Massachusetts Divorce Records," *Journal of Social History* (Fall 1976), 3:29–30; Kerber, *Women of the Republic,* pp. 158–183.

48. Cott, "Eighteenth-Century Family Life," pp. 29–30.

49. "The Superior Court Diary of William Samuel Johnson, 1772–73" (Connecticut), in John Farrel, ed., *American Legal Records* (New York, 1942), 4:38.

50. Kerber, *Women of the Republic,* p. 183.

51. Lofft 748, 98 Eng. Rep. 899 (K.B. 1774).

52. 10 Ves. 5, 32 Eng. Rep. 762 (Ch. 1804).

53. Beales, "The Child in Seventeenth-Century America," pp. 19, 22.

54. Hasseltine B. Taylor, *Law of Guardian and Ward* (Chicago, 1935), p. 34.

55. 12 Charles II, c. 24 (1660), as quoted in Taylor, *Law of Guardian and Ward,* p. 36.

56. Va. Statutes at Large (Philadelphia, 1823), 2:92–94; Md. Archives (1884), 2:325–329; Bremner, *Children and Youth in America,* 1:58–59.

57. Mary A. Greene, *The Woman's Manual of Law* (New York, 1902).

58. Berthod Fernow, ed. and trans., *The Minutes of the Orphanmasters of New Amsterdam, 1655 to 1683* (New York, 1902), pp. 3–9, in Bremner, *Children and Youth in America,* 1:56.

59. Lois G. Carr, "The Development of the Maryland Orphans' Court, 1654–1715," in R. Land, L. Carr, and J. Papenfuse, eds., *Law, Society, and Politics in Early Maryland* (Baltimore, 1977), pp. 50–51.

60. Richard B. Morris, ed., *Select Cases of the Mayor's Court of New York City, 1674–1784* (Washington, D.C., 1935), pp. 184–185.

61. See Bremner, *Children and Youth in America,* 1:64.

62. Md. Archives, 53:136–137, in Bremner, *Children and Youth in America,* 1:58.

63. Chester G. Vernier, *American Family Laws,* 4 vols. (Stanford, 1936), 4:485.

64. Records and Files of the Quarterly Courts of Essex County, Massachusetts (1672–74), 5:103

65. In the Matter of Pierce, 12 How. Pr. 532 (N.Y. 1856); Gilmore v. Kitson, 165 Ind. 402, 74 N. E. 1083.

66. Carr, "The Development of the Maryland Orphans' Court," p. 54.

67. As quoted in Helena M. Wall, *Fierce Communion* (Cambridge, 1990), p. 90.

68. Ibid., pp. 89–92.

69. Ibid., p. 90.

70. Blackstone, *Commentaries on the Law of England*, 1:454–60.

71. Kent, *Commentaries on American Law*, 2:214.

72. Colonial Laws of Massachusetts, reprinted from the edition of 1660 (Boston, 1889), p. 257, in Bremner, *Children and Youth in America*, 1:50.

73. Richard Semmes, *Crime and Punishment in Early Maryland*, (New York, 1938), p. 196.

74. W. W. Hening, ed., *Statutes at Large of Virginia* (New York, 1823), 2:115, in Bremner, *Children and Youth in America*, 1:51.

75. Ibid., p. 168.

76. Joseph H. Smith and Philip A. Crowl, eds., *Court Records of Prince George's County, Maryland, 1696–1699*, (Washington, D.C., 1964), p. vi.

77. Ibid., p. 188.

78. Ibid., p. vi.

79. Ibid., p. 434.

80. There is evidence that this law was superseded in 1681, by a statute that instead placed a heavy fine on masters who allowed such unions. Md. Archives (1889), 7:29, in Bremner, *Children and Youth in America*, 1:54.

81. Md. Archives (1883), 1:533–534, in Bremner, *Children and Youth in America*, 1:53.

82. Virginia Statutes at Large (Philadelphia, 1823), 3:453, in Bremner, *Children and Youth in America*, 1:54.

83. Virginia Statutes at Large (Richmond, 1820),˙204:453, in Bremner, *Children and Youth in America*, 1:53.

84. Carr, "The Development of the Maryland Orphans' Court," p. 49.

85. Grossberg, *Governing the Hearth*, p. 199.

86. Hening, Statutes at Large (Virginia), 12:688.

87. Grossberg, *Governing the Hearth*, 1:219.

88. Blackstone, *Commentaries on the Law of England*, 1:453.

89. Wall, *Fierce Communion*, p. 113.

90. Richard B. Morris, *Government and Labor in Early America* (New York, 1946), p. 391.

91. Smith, *Colonists in Bondage*, p. 148.

92. Great Britain, Privy Council, Acts of the Privy Council of England, 1619–1621 (London, 1930), p. 118, in Bremner, *Children and Youth in America*, 1:8.

93. As quoted in Smith, *Colonists in Bondage*, p. 149.

94. Documents Relative to the Colonial History of New York, (Albany, 1856–1887), 2:52, in Bremner, *Children and Youth in America*, 1:23.

95. Smith, *Colonists in Bondage*, p. 73.

96. Virginia Statutes at Large, 1:441–442, quoted in Bremner, *Children and Youth in*

America, 1:23.

97. Walter Clark, ed., No. Car. Records (Goldsboro, N.C., 1904), 23:62–66, in Bremner, *Children and Youth in America*, 1:116.

98. Reeve, *The Law of Baron and Femme*, p. 209.

99. C. G. Chamberlayne, *The Vestry Book of St. Paul's Parish* (Richmond, 1940), pp. 202–205, 324–327, 332–333, in Bremner, *Children and Youth in America*, 1:263.

100. Jernegan, *Laboring and Dependent Classes in Colonial America*, pp. 165–170.

101. Chester County Court Records, in John S. Futhey and Gilbert Cope, *History of Chester County, Pennsylvania* (Philadelphia, 1881), pp. 430–431, in Bremner, *Children and Youth in America*, 1:118.

102. Maryland Archives, 70:33.

103. As quoted in Wall, *Fierce Communion*, p. 113.

104. Thomas Cooper, ed., *Statutes at Large of South Carolina* (Columbia, 1838), 3:544–546, in Bremner, *Children and Youth in America*, 1:150.

105. James T. Mitchell and Henry Flaners, eds., *The Statutes at Large of Pennsylvania from 1682 to 1801* (Harrisburg, 1896), 2:54–55.

106. Ibid.

107. Records of Essex County (1921), 8:302–303.

108. "Rev. John Eliot's Records of the First Church in Roxbury, Massachusetts," in *Sixth Report of Boston Record Commissioner* (Boston, 1881), p. 187.

109. Morgan, *The Puritan Family*, p. 77.

110. Records of the Suffolk County Court, 1671–1680 (1933), 30:915, in Bremner, *Children and Youth in America*, 1:40.

111. Records and Files of the Quarterly Courts of Essex County, Massachusetts, 1:113.

112. Bremner, *Children and Youth in America*, 1:105.

113. Cotton Mather, *A Christian at His Calling: Two Brief Discourses, One Directing a Christian in His General Calling: Another Directing Him in His Personal* (Boston, 1701), pp. 36–45.

114. Records of New Amsterdam, 5:243.

115. Plymouth Colony Records, 2:58–59.

116. "An Act for the Gradual Abolition of Slavery," 1780–ch. 881, Pennsylvania Statutes at Large (Harrisburg, 1904), 10:68–69, in Bremner, *Children and Youth in America*, 1:324.

117. Baker (of Color) v. Winfrey, 15 B. Mon 499 (1855), in Bremner, *Children and Youth in America*, 1:390.

118. Jernegan, *Laboring and Dependent Classes in Colonial America*, pp. 187–188.

119. Virginia Statutes at Large (Richmond, 1820), 4:433, in Bremner, *Children and Youth in America*, 1:54

120. Winthrop Jordan, *White Over Black: American Attitudes Toward the Negro, 1550–1812* (Chapel Hill, 1968), p. 89.
121. Virginia Statutes at Large (Richmond, 1820), 4:433, in Bremner, *Children and Youth in America*, 1:54.
122. Maryland Provincial Court Proceedings (1658), 41:262.
123. Virginia Colonial Decisions (1728–41), 2:236.
124. Jacqueline Jones, "Race, Sex, and Self-Evident Truths: The Status of Slave Women During the Era of the American Revolution," in Albert Hoffman, ed., *Women in the Age of the American Revolution* (New York, 1989), p. 302.
125. Virginia Statutes at Large, 2:170, in Bremner, *Children and Youth in America*, 1:53.
126. Allan Kulikoff, "The Beginnings of the African-American Family in Maryland," *Law Society and Politics in Early Maryland*, p. 176.
127. Jones, "Race, Sex, and Self-Evident Truths," p. 302.
128. Lawrence v. Speed, 2 Bibb 401 (1811), in Bremner, *Children and Youth in America*, 1:332.
129. Kulikoff, "The Beginnings of the African-American Family in Maryland," p. 177.
130. Ibid. pp. 179–180.
131. Jones, "Race, Sex, and Self-Evident Truths," pp. 314–315.

2. From Fathers' Rights to Mothers' Love

1. People v. Gates, 57 Barb. 291, 296 (N.Y. 1869).
2. Ibid., p. 296, quoting People v. Mercein, 3 Hill 399 (N.Y. 1842).
3. Many states had laws that allowed the child to reject a voluntary indenture, but only after the age of fourteen.
4. People v. Gates, 57 Barb. 291, 297 (N.Y. 1869).
5. Foulke v. People, 4 Colo. App. at 528 (1894), quoting the leading doctrine of Lord Mansfield in Blisset's Case, 1 Lofft 748, 98 Eng. Rep. 899 (K.B., 1774).
6. See, generally, Michael Grossberg, *Governing the Hearth: Law and Family in Nineteenth-Century America* (Chapel Hill: 1985); Jamail S. Zainaldin, "The Emergence of a Modern American Family Law: Child Custody, Adoption, and the Courts, 1796–1851," *Northwestern University Law Review* (1979), 73:1038, 1085. These historians all note the cult of motherhood, or the cult of domestication, as it is sometimes called, but they fail to analyze how this social phenomenon is translated into changes in custody law. In addition, there has been no examination of the complicated and sometimes contradictory relationship of the women's rights movement and the cult of motherhood, and its effect on custody law in the legislature and the judiciary respectively.

An older, now considered traditional school of thought and scholarship placed the change away from the father toward the best interests of the child and its nurturing mother in the later Progressive era. According to this school, reformers and the new helping professions (educators and social workers) brought about changes in both private and public law that emphasized the interests of women and children. See, e.g., June Axinn and Herman Levin, *Social Welfare: A History of the American Response to Need* (New York, 1975), pp. 75–99, 115–143. For a discussion of the scholarship of this school, see Zainaldin, "The Emergence of a Modern American Family Law," p. 1039.

7. Maxine Margolis, *Mothers and Such: Views of American Women and Why They Changed* (Berkeley, 1984), p. 33.

8. There is a rich historical literature on the cult of domesticity. See, for example, Barbara Welter, "Cult of True Womanhood: 1820–1860," in Linda Gordon, ed., *The American Family in Social Historical Perspective* (New York, 1973), pp. 372–392; Nancy Cott, *The Bonds of True Womanhood: Women's Sphere in New England, 1780–1835* (New Haven, 1977); Kathryn Kish Sklar and Catherine Beecher, *A Study in American Domesticity* (New Haven, 1973).

9. Historian Mary Ryan, in *Cradle of the Middle Class: The Family in Oneida County, New York, 1790–1865* (Berkeley, 1981), p. 232, claims that "mother love was the linchpin in a new method of socializing children." The emphasis on nurturing rather than patriarchal well-being better prepared children, particularly sons, for the new individualism of the capitalist world.

10. There is a significant controversy among demographers about the drop in fertility since it preceded rather than coincided with significant urbanization. For a full account of this controversy, see Carl N. Degler, *At Odds: Women and the Family in America from the Revolution to the Present* (New York, 1980), pp. 181–188.

11. Margolis, *Mothers and Such*, p. 36.

12. Ansley J. Coale and Melvin Zelnick, *New Estimate of Fertility and Population in the United States* (Princeton, 1963), pp. 34–35.

13. Degler, *At Odds*, p. 377.

14. For a description of the life of women in small-town nineteenth-century America see Mary Ryan, *Cradle of the Middle Class: The Family in Oneida County, New York* (Berkeley, 1981).

15. According to legal historian Maxwell Bloomfield, "The legal profession had come of age in most colonies by the middle of the eighteenth century. Lawyers shared political power with mercantile and landed elites: study in a law office (or, for the favored few, the English Inn of Court) had become an established norm for practitioners; courts and some local bar assocations, as in New York, helped to control admissions standards and internal police." Maxwell Bloomfield, *American Lawyers in a Changing Society* (Cambridge, 1976), p. 33.

16. Quoted in Margolis, *Mothers and Such*, p. 38.

17. Bradwell v. Illinois, 83 U.S. [16 Wall.] 130, 141, 21 L. 3d 442 (1873) (J. Bradley concurring).

18. Eleanor Flexnor, *Century of Struggle* (Cambridge, 1959), p. 85.

19. Ibid.

20. Ellen C. Dubois, ed., *Elizabeth Cady Stanton, Susan B. Anthony: Correspondence, Writings, Speeches* (New York, 1981), document 8, p. 49.

21. Ibid. note 16, p. 88.

22. The *Century Digest*, which covers the years 1658–1896, lists approximately three hundred child custody cases that are related to divorce or separation.

23. Nancy F. Cott, "Eighteenth-Century Family and Social Life Revealed in Massachusetts Divorce Records," *Journal of Social History* (Fall 1976), 10:29–30.

24. Dept. of Commerce and Labor, *Bureau of the Census: Special Reports: Marriage and Divorce, 1867–1906*, part 1 (Washington, D.C.: GPO, 1909), p. 41.

25. Ibid. p. 42.

26. Degler, *At Odds*, p. 166.

27. Historian Mary Beard received a popular following in the 1930s for her interpretation that the idea of women's legal subjugation was a myth originating with the nineteenth-century feminists themselves. See Mary Beard, *Woman as a Force in History* (New York: Collier, 1971); for a discussion of the controversy over the origins of the women's rights movement, see also Peggy Rabkin, *Fathers to Daughters: The Legal Foundations of Female Emancipation* (Westport, Ct., 1980), pp. 4–12.

28. According to Peggy Rabkin, it was the heady taste of property rights that inspired the first women's rights convention in America at Seneca Falls in 1848. Rabkin, *Fathers to Daughters*, p. 12.

29. Andrew Sinclair, *The Emancipation of the American Women* (New York, 1965) p. 87.

30. Rabkin, *Fathers to Daughters*, p. 109.

31. Modeled after the Declaration of Independence, the Declaration of Rights and Sentiments used the pronoun *He* to represent a generic legislative and judicial patriarchy, rather than George III.

32. Seneca Falls Women's Rights Convention of 1848, Declaration of Rights and Sentiments, reprinted in Susan B. Anthony and Ida Hustead Harper, eds., *The History of Women's Suffrage*, 4 vols. (Rochester, N.Y., 1902), 1:70.

33. Degler, *At Odds*, p. 332.

34. Rheta Dorr, *What Eight Million Women Want* (Boston, 1910), p. 94.

35. Ibid., p. 96.

36. Seneca Falls Women's Rights Convention of 1848, reprinted in *The History of Women's Suffrage*, 1:686–687.

37. Quoted in Grossberg, *Governing the Hearth*, p. 246.

38. People v. Brooks, 35 Barb. 85, 87 (N. Y. 1861).

39. Grossberg, *Governing the Hearth,* p. 247.

40. Dorr, *What Eight Million Women Want,* p. 111.

41. Dubois, *Elizabeth Cady Stanton, Susan B. Anthony,* document 9, p. 129.

42. Quoted in Dubois, *Elizabeth Cady Stanton, Susan B. Anthony,* p. 97.

43. Grossberg, *Governing the Hearth,* p. 236.

44. Judges in the early republic also relied on Blackstone's commentaries and Kent's commentaries. James Kent, *Commentaries on American Law,* 2d ed., 4 vols. (Boston, 1826–1830); William Blackstone, *Commentaries on the Law of England* (New York, 1976 [1915 ed.]). Contemporary American legal treatise writers gradually became incorporated into judicial decisions as well. See Tapping Reeve, *The Law of Baron and Femme, of Parent and Child, of Guardian and Ward, of Master and Servant, and of the Powers of Courts of Chancery* (New York, 1816), and James Schouler, *Treatise on the Law of Domestic Relations* (Boston, 1870).

45. 10 Ves. 5, 32 Eng. Rep. 762 (Ch. 1804).

46. Lofft 748, 98 Eng. Rep. 899 (K.B. 1774).

47. Ibid.

48. Ex parte Hewitt, 11 Rich. Law 326, 329 (S.C. 1858).

49. Ibid., p. 330; see also Commonwealth v. Briggs, 16 Pick. 203 (Mass. 1834).

50. See, for example, State v. Payne, 23 Tenn. 523 (1843).

51. 4 Desau. 33 (S. C.1809).

52. Ibid., p. 44.

53. Mercein v. People ex rel. Barry, 25 Wend. 64,101 (N.Y.) 1840.

54. Ibid., p. 104.

55. People v. Mercein, 3 Hill 399, 418 (N.Y. 1842).

56. Ibid., p. 422.

57. The rule in England, up until 1839, that the father was entitled to the sole custody of his child unless he was clearly unfit was altered significantly by the passage of stat. 2 & 3 Vict. ch. 54, known as Justice Talfourd's Act, which officially introduced the notion of the child's interests. This act, however, retained the primacy of the father's interest, leaving uncertain how the child's interests would be considered. Schouler, *Treatise on the Law of Domestic Relations,* p. 389.

58. 91 App. Div. 322, 325 (N.Y. 1904). See also Matter of Pray, 60 Howard Pr. 194 (N.Y. 1881); McKim v. McKim, 12 R.I. 462 (1879) (male children more likely to be awarded to fathers).

59. Carr v. Carr, 22 Gratt. 168, 174 (Va. 1872); Anonymous, 55 Ala. 428 (1876); Mckim v. Mckim, 12 R.I. 462 (1879).

60. Anonymous, 55 Ala. at 432 (1876). For some examples of the application of the tender years doctrine, see Goodrich v. Goodrich, 44 Ala. 670 (1870); Wand v. Wand, 14 Cal. 512 (1860); Miner v. Miner, 11 Ill. 43, (1849); Umlauf v. Umlauf, 27 Ill. App. 375

(1888); Landis v. Landis, 39 N.J. Law 274 (1877); Scoggins v. Scoggins, 80 N.C. 318 (1879); Cariens v. Cariens, 50 W. Va. 113, 405 S.E. 335 (1901).

61. People ex rel. Sinclair v. Sinclair, 47 Misc. Rep. 230, 231 (N.Y. 1905); see also Landis v. Landis, 39 N.J. Law 274 (1877).

62. Bennett v. Bennett 43 Conn. 313 (1876); Darnall v. Mullikin, 8 Ind. 152 (1856); State v. Flint, 63 Minn. 187 (1895).

63. Schouler, *Treatise on the Law of Domestic Relations*, p. 336.

64. Stigall v. Stigall, 22 N.J. Law 286, 288 (1847).

65. Ibid., p. 289. For examples of the best interests standard, see also State v. Baird and Torrey, 21 N.J Eq. 384 (1869), Gishwiler v. Dodez, 4 Ohio St. 615 (1855).

66. Joseph R. Long, *A Treatise on the Law of Domestic Relations* (St. Paul, 1905), p. 321.

67. Lindsay v. Lindsay, 14 Ga. 657 (1854); Kremelberg v. Kremelberg, 52 Md. 553 (1879); Crimmins v. Crimmins, 64 How. Prac. 103 (N.Y. 1882); Jackson v. Jackson, 80 Ore. 402 (1880); Helden v. Helden, 7 Wis. 256 (1858).

68. This rule most often worked in favor of the mother since women were three times as likely than fathers to be granted a divorce where children were reported. The most prominent ground for divorce was desertion (about 30 percent), followed by cruelty (20 percent) and adultery (20 percent).

69. See, for example, Ore. Code, Subd. 1 Sec. 402 (1888): "Whenever a marriage shall be declared void or dissolved, the court shall have power to further decree, among other things, the care and custody of the minor children of the marriage, as it may seem just and proper, having due regard to the age and sex of such children, and unless manifestly improper, give the preference to the party not in fault."

70. Lindsay v. Lindsay, 14 Ga. at 660 (1854).

71. Crimmins v. Crimmins, 64 How. Prac. at 105 (N.Y. 1882). See also Commonwealth v. Briggs, 16 Pick 203 (Mass. 1834); Kremelberg v. Kremelberg, 52 Md. 553 (1879); Jackson v. Jackson, 8 Ore. 402 (1880); Helden v. Helden, 7 Wis. 256 (1858). Occasionally, however, courts held that the tender years doctrine prevailed over mother's adultery. See People v. Hickey, 86 Ill. App. 20 (1898) and Commonwealth v. Addicks, 5 Bin. 520 (Pa. 1813).

72. Bryan v. Bryan 34 Ala. at 519 (1859). See also Olmstead v. Olmstead, 27 Barb. 9 (N.Y.1832); People v. Rhoades, 24 Barb. 521 (N.Y. 1857); Uhlmann v. Uhlmann, 17 Abb. N. C. 236 (N.Y. 1885).

73. Sherwood v. Sherwood, 56 Ia. 608 (1881).

74. People v. Nickerson, 19 Wend. 16 (N.Y. 1837).

75. Levering v. Levering, 16 Md. 213 (1860)

76. Codd v. Codd, 2 Johns. Chan. 141; Bedell v. Bedell, 1 John's Chanc. 605 (N.Y. 1815)

77. In an unusual case, Lambert v. Lambert, 16 Ore. 485 (1988), the court ignored two

fit parents and awarded the child to the paternal grandfather, in part because of the rivalry of the parents over the control of the child.

78. Commonwealth ex rel. Goerlitz v. Barney, 4 Brewster 408 (Pa. 1872).

79. Degler, *At Odds,* p. 173.

80. 12 Charles II, c. 24 (1660), as quoted in Hasseltine B. Taylor, *Law of Guardian and Ward* (Chicago, 1935).

81. Taylor, *Law of Guardian and Ward,* p. 36.

82. Mary A. Greene, *The Woman's Manual of Law* (New York, 1902)

83. In the Matter of Pierce, 12 How. Pr. 532 (N.Y. 1856); Gilmore v. Kitson, 165 Ind. 402, 74 N. E. 1083.

84. As quoted in Rabkin, *Fathers to Daughters,* p. 112.

85. Greene, *The Woman's Manual of Law,* p. 93.

86. Farrer v. Clark, 19 Miss. 195 (1855).

87. The states that recognized the continuing guardianship of others following remarriage were California, Kentucky, Minnesota, Mississippi, Montana, Ohio, New Hampshire, Rhode Island, and Vermont. Cited in Greene, *The Woman's Manual of Law,* p. 99.

88. Lea v. Richardson, 8 La. Ann. 94, 95 (1853).

89. Ibid.

90. Striplin v. Ware, 36 Ala. 87 (1860). For granting continuing custody rights upon remarriage, see also State v. Scott, 30 N.H. 274 (1855); Baily v. Morrison, 4 La. Ann. 523 (1849).

91. Copp v. Copp, 20 N.H. 284, 286 (1850); see also Fitzgerald v. Fitzgerald, 24 Hun.370 (N.Y. 1881).

92. O'Connor v. Barre, 3 Mart. 446 (La. 1814); Webb v. Webb, 5 La. Ann. 595 (1850); Swartwout v. Swartwout, 2 Redf. Sur. 52 (N.Y. 1871); Field v. Torey, 7 Vt. 372 (1835).

93. Grossberg, *Governing the Hearth,* p. 219.

94. Elizabeth Cady Stanton et al., *History of Women's Suffrage,* 6 vols. (New York, 1872–1922), 3:419.

95. 12 Henning 688 (1785).

96. Both mother and father were routinely whipped for the act of fornication in colonial times. Father was required to pay support. See Suffolk County Records as quoted in Robert Bremner, *Children and Youth in America,* 4 vols. (Cambridge, 1970), 1:51–52.

97. Reeve, *The Law of Baron and Femme,* p. 277.

98. Hudson v. Hills, 8 N.H. 417, 418 (1836).

99. Friesner v. Symonds, 46 N. J. Eq. 521 (1890).

100. Olson v. Johnson, 23 Minn. 301, 303 (1877).

101. Lawson v. Scott, 9 Tenn. 92 (1825).

102. Lawrence Stone, *Family, Sex, and Marriage* (London, 1977), pp. 517–548.

103. Graham v. Benner 2 Ca. 503, 506 (1852). For a contrary result see Wright v. Wright, 2 Mass. 109 (1806).

104. Kent, *Commentaries on American Law,* 2:214.

105. The extreme poverty of the mother could sometimes play a role in custody disputes between mother and putative father. See People v. Kling, 6 Barb. 366 (N.Y. 1849). More likely, however, the poor officials would bring an action against the available father for support.

106. Susan Tiffin, *In Whose Best Interests? Child Welfare Reform in the Progressive Era* (Westport, Ct., 1982), p. 39.

107. Adams v. Adams, 59 Vt. 158, 161 (1877).

108. Bremner, *Children and Youth in America,* 2:137.

109. For a discussion of how the adoption laws reflected the new quasi-contractual nature of child-parent ties, see Zainaldin, "The Emergence of a Modern American Family Law."

110. People v. Erbert, 17 Abb. Prac. 395, 400 (N.Y. 1864).

111. Ibid.

112. The New York state adoption law, 1873, as quoted in Bremner, *Children and Youth in America,* 2:137.

113. Ibid.

114. Ferguson v. Jones, 17 Or. 204 (1888).

115. In re Williams, 102 Ca. 70 (1894).

116. Bremner, *Children and Youth in America,* 2:137.

117. Fouts v. Pierce, 64 Iowa 71 (1884).

118. Grossberg, *Governing the Hearth,* p. 266.

119. People v. Gates, 57 Barb 291 (N.Y. 1869); State v. Reuff, 29 W. Va. 751 (1887).

120. Grossberg, *Governing the Hearth,* p. 261.

121. As quoted in Dubois, *Elizabeth Cady Stanton, Susan B. Anthony,* p. 49

122. See, for instance, People ex rel. Brooks v. Brooks, 35 Barb. 85 (N.Y. App. Div. 1861).

123. Osborn v. Allen, 26 N.J. Law 388, 392 (1857).

124. Ibid., p. 394.

125. Jaquelyn Hall, James Leloudis, Robert Korstad, Mary Murphy, Lu Ann Jones, Christopher B. Daly, *Like a Family: The Making of a Southern Cotton Mill World* (Chapel Hill, 1987), p. 56.

126. David Smith, Sandra Smight, Fred Doolittle, "How Children Used to Work," *Law and Contemporary Problems* (1975), 39(3):99.

127. Tiffin, *In Whose Best Interests?* p. 90.

128. Charles L. Brace, "What is the Best Method for the Care of Poor and Vicious Children?" in Bremner, *Children and Youth in America,* 2:291.

129. Bremner, *Children and Youth in America,* 2:291.

130. Lyman P. Alden, "The Shady Side of the Placing-Out System," in Bremner, *Children and Youth in America,* 2:298.

131. Tiffin, *In Whose Best Interests?* p. 92.

132. For a complete discussion of the legal uncertainties attending the Proclamation of Emancipation and subsequent constitutional amendments, see G. J. Randall and David Donald, *Civil War and Reconstruction* (Lexington, Mass., 1969), pp. 394–395.

133. Comas v. Reddish, 35 Ga. 236, 237 (1866). In this case the father sued and won back the custody of his son since it was determined that he could support him.

134. Grossberg, *Governing the Hearth,* p. 266.

135. Miss. Laws 1865–66, c. 40, sec. 5, cited in Wallace v. Godfrey (C.C.) 42 Fed. 812, 813 (Miss. 1890).

136. Ibid. See also Gregley v. Jackson, 38 Ark. 487 (1882).

137. Branch v. Walker, 102 N.C. 34, 8 S.E. 896 (1889).

3. The State as Superparent

1. Moore v. Dozier, 128 Ga. 90, 57 S.E. 110, 96–97 (1907).

2. Ibid., p. 94.

3. Ibid., p. 92.

4. For a thorough discussion regarding the the impact of the social sciences on child custody during this era, see chapter 5.

5. For a discussion of the laws regulating the activities of the selectment of Massachussets, see chapter 1.

6. Susan Tiffin, *In Whose Best Interests? Child Welfare Reform in the Progressive Era* (Westport, Ct. 1982), p. 200.

7. Walter S. Trattner, *From Poor Law to Welfare State: A History of Social Welfare* (New York, 1974), p. 200.

8. As quoted in Jane Addams, *My Friend Julia Lathrop* (New York, 1935), p. 213.

9. William O'Neill, in his book, *Everyone Was Brave: The Rise and Fall of Feminism in America* (Chicago, 1969), used the term *social feminists* to describe those women whose primary concern was the service to others and to society. He contrasted this groups to the first wave of feminists whose primary objective was the achievement of individual opportunities for women.

10. O'Neill, *Everyone Was Brave,* pp. 143–144.

11. Jane Addams, "Why Women Should Vote," in Christopher Lasch, ed., *The Social Thought of Jane Addams* (New York, 1965), p. 151.

12. For a discussion of the fight for women's property rights see chapter 2.

13. As quoted in Tiffin, *In Whose Best Interests?* p. 46.

14. Christopher Lasch, *Haven in a Heartless World: The Family Besieged* (New York, 1977), p. 14.

15. For the American colonial version of the Elizabethan Poor Laws, see *Laws and Ordinances of New England, An Abridgement of the Laws in Force and Use in Her Majesty's Plantations* (London, Parker and Smith, 1704), p. 23.

16. Proceedings of the Conference on the Care of Dependent Children, 1909, p. 41, in Robert Bremner, *Children and Youth in America*, 4 vols. (Cambridge, 1970), 2:358, 359.

17. Tiffin, *In Whose Best Interest?* pp. 122–128.

18. Juvenile Courts—Funds to Parents, Laws of Illinois, vol. 47 (Springfield, 1911), in Bremner, *Children and Youth in America*, 2:370.

19. Ibid., p. 130.

20. This widow-biased policy seems highly discriminatory against other mothers who acted as single parents, but there is some scholarly evidence that indicates that widows were not always what they called themselves. A recent study of African-American marriage patterns in relation to the 1910 census reveals that widowhood was seriously overreported, presumably in an attempt to explain births outside of marriage. Samuel H. Preston, Sue Lim, S. Philip Morgan, "African-American Marriage in 1910: Beneath the Surface of Census Data," *Demography* (February 1992), 29:1.

21. U.S. Children's Bureau, *Mother's Aid* (Washington, D.C., 1933), pp. 6–24, in Bremner, *Children and Youth in America*, 2:395.

22. Tiffin, *In Whose Best Interest?* p. 131.

23. U.S. Children's Bureau, *Mother's Aid*, pp. 6–24, in Bremner, *Children and Youth in America*, 2:395.

24. For an illuminating discussion of the problems of poor mothers, see Linda Gordon, "Child Abuse, Gender, and the Myth of Family Independence: Thoughts on the History of Family Violence and Social Control," *Review of Law and Social Change*, 12:523–537, and *Heroes of Their Own Lives: The Politics and History of Family Violence* (New York, 1988).

25. Gordon, *Heroes of Their Own Lives*, no. 2503, p. 87.

26. Tiffin, *In Whose Best Interests?* p. 148.

27. See chapter 1 for a disucssion of colonial support obligations.

28. James Kent, *Commentaries on American Law*, 2d ed., 4 vols. (Boston, 1826–1830), 1:32.

29. Lillian Brandt, *574 Deserters and Their Families* (New York, 1905), pp. 24–38.

30. Chester G. Vernier, *American Family Laws*, 4 vols. (Stanford, 1936), 4:66–86.

31. Hunter v. State, 10 Okl. 119, 134 P. 1134 (1913).

32. Vernier, *American Family Laws*, 4:61.

33. Tiffin, *In Whose Best Interest?* p. 159.

34. Brandt, *574 Deserters*, p. 49.

35. U.S. Children's Bureau, *Mother's Aid*, p. 6–24, in Bremner, *Children and Youth in America*, 2:395.

36. See earlier discussion of colonial treatment of unwed mothers, chapter 1.

37. See earlier discussion of illegitimacy in the nineteenth century, chapter 2.

38. Emma O. Lundberg and Katharine Lenroot, *Illegitimacy as a Child Welfare Problem*, part 1, U. S. Children's Bureau Publication no. 66 (Washington, D.C.: GPO, 1920), p. 26.

39. Louise de Koven Bowen, *A Study in Bastardy Cases* (Chicago: Juvenile Protective Association, 1914) pp. 9–10.

40. Tiffin, *In Whose Best Interest?* p. 173.

41. All states by 1930 offered some form mitigation of the harsh common law rule of *filius nullius* and allowed legitimation by a subsequent marriage, and nineteen offered legitimation by acknowledgement by the father. Vernier, *American Family Laws*, 4:154–155.

42. North Dakota, Comp. L. 1913, Secs. 4421, 4450, 5745, Supp. 1913–1925, in Vernier, *American Family Laws*, 4:170.

43. Vernier, *American Family Laws*, 4:24–52.

44. Doughty v. Engler, 112 Kan. 583 (1923).

45. Ibid., p. 207.

46. Ex parte Gambetta 145 P. 1005 (1915).

47. Cal. Pen. Code, Sec. 270 (1924).

48. Grace Abbott, *The Child and the State* (Chicago, 1938), 2:552–67.

49. U.S. Children's Bureau, *Mother's Aid*, pp. 6–24.

50. Tiffin, *In Whose Best Interest?* p. 169.

51. Lundberg and Lenroot, *Illegitimacy as a Welfare Problem*, pp. 47–48.

52. Unpublished report by the U.S. Children's Bureau on the Minnesota law, in Abbott, *The Child and the State*, 2:570–571.

53. Gordon, *Heroes of Their Own Lives*, p. 159.

54. As previously noted, the first state mothers' aid act was passed in 1911, and by 1939 they were available in thity-nine states, including Georgia.

55. For a discussion of the special plight of single mothers see Gordon, *Heroes of Their Own Lives*, pp. 82–115.

56. Blisset's Case, 98 Eng. Rep. 899 (K.B. 1773). See also Cave v. Tincher, 166 S.W. 1028, 258 Mo. (1914).

57. *Extract from the Ninth Annual Report of the State Board of Charities of the State of New York, Relating to Orphan Asylums and Other Instituitons for the Care of Children* (Albany, 1876), pp. 306–308, in Bremner, *Children and Youth in America*, 2:192.

58. William J. Shultz, *The Humane Movement in the United States, 1910–1922* (New York, 1924), p. 185, in Bremner, *Children and Youth in America*, 2:217.

59. Tiffin, *In Whose Best Interest?* p. 219.

60. State v. Jones, 84 N. C. 584, 599 (1886).

61. Ibid., p. 600. See also State v. Koonse, 123 Mo. App. 655, 101 S. W. 139 (1907), State v. Washington 104 La. 443 (1900), Haydon v. State 5 Ala. App. 61, 72 So. 586 (1916).

62. Elizabeth Pleck, *Domestic Tyranny* (New York, 1987), pp. 84–85.

63. South Carolina Code of Law, 1922, in Vernier, *American Family Laws*, 4:46.

64. South Dakota, comp. l. 1929, in Vernier, *American Family Laws*, 4:46.

65. Commonwealth v. Dee, 110 N.E. 287, 222 Mass. 184, 185 (1915).

66. Purinton v. Jamrock, 195 Mass 187 (1907).

67. "Abandonment and Other Acts of Cruelty to Children, 1881," ch. 676, *Laws of New York* (Albany, 1881).

68. Charles E. Faulkner, in Bremner, *Children and Youth in America*, 2:195.

69. Gordon, *Heroes of Their Own Lives*, pp. 93, 130.

70. MPSCC no. 3026, as reported by Gordon, *Heroes of Their Own Lives*, p. 132.

71. For a more complete discussion of *binding out* see chapter 1, and for *placing out* see chapter 2. Parental rights were extremely limited under both systems. Parents could insist on the performance of the master's obligation in an indenture contract, but could not take back their child. With a "placed out" child, parents could retrieve their child if their situation grew better, but, in fact, this rarely happened.

72. Purinton v. Jamrock, 195 Mass 187 (1907).

73. Vernier, *American Family Laws*, 4:340.

74. In re Cozza, 163 Cal. 514, 126 P.161 (1912).

75. Vernier, *American Family Laws*, 4:282.

76. "The Delineator Child Rescue Campaign," *Delineator* (November 1907), 70:715–718, in Bremner, *Children and Youth in America*, 2:391.

77. Homer Folks, "Family Life for Dependent Children," in Spencer and Bartwell, eds., *Care of Dependent, Neglected, and Wayward Children*, pp. 75–80, in Bremner, *Children and Youth in America*, 2:321.

78. Tiffin, *In Whose Best Interest?* p. 105.

79. William O'Neill, *Divorce in the Progressive Era* (New Haven, 1967), pp. 19–20.

80. U.S. Department of Commerce, Bureau of the Census, Historical Statistics of the United States: Colonial Times to 1970, part 2. Not until 1965 did divorce actually lead death as a cause for losing a parent. Kingsley Davis, "The American Family in Relation to Demographic Change," in Charles R. Westoff and Robert Parke, Jr., eds., *Demographic and Social Aspects of Population Growth* (Washington D.C., 1972), 1:255.

81. Harmon v. Harmon, 208 P. 647, 111 Kan. 786 (1922).

82. Sorge v. Sorge 112 Wash. 131, 191 Pac. 817 (1920); Twohig v. Twohig, 176 Wis. 275, 186 N.W. 592 (1922); State ex rel. Henry v. Lyons, 71 So. 507, 139 La. 243 (1916). See also Buseman v. Buseman, 98 S.E. 574 (1919); Hunter v. State, 10 Okl. 119, 134 P.

1134 (1913); Payne v. Graham, 102 S. 729 (1925).

83. John W. Morland, ed., *Keezer on the Law of Marriage and Divorce,* 3d. ed. (New York, 1946), p. 752.

84. Crabtree v. Crabtree, 154 Ark. 401, 242 S. S. 804 (1922).

85. McNeir v. McNeir, 76 Misc. 661, 129 N.Y.S. 481 (1911).

86. Smith v. Frates, 107 Wash. 13, Pac. 880 (1919).

87. Vernier, *American Family Laws,* 4:18.

88. Ibid., see tables of all state laws, pp. 24–54.

89. California, Montana, North Dakota, and South Dakota, while offering a best interests of the child standard as the primary rule, also offered a presumption regarding either parents. "As between parents adversely claiming the custody or guardianship, neither parent is entitled to it as of right, but other things being equal, if the child be of tender years, it should be given to the mother: if it be of an age to require education and preparation for labor or business, then to the father." See Vernier, *American Family Laws,* 4:53.

90. New Mexico, St. Ann. 1929, Secs. 35(33319), 62(9104), 62(202), 68(303), as cited in Vernier, *American Family Laws,* 4:40.

91. Vernier, *American Family Laws,* 4:24–51.

92. See chapter 2 for a discussion of this issue.

93. Only Alabama and California specifically include noncustodial parents. California law reads, "Not excused because mother entitled to custody." Vernier, *American Family Laws,* 4:66.

94. For a good discussion of the split in courts on this issue, see State v. Langford, 176 P. 197, 90 Or. 251 (1918). At least one court awarded the custody of a fifteen-year-old boy to his father on the ground that the father's obligation to support gave him the right of custody; see Payne v. Grahm, 102 So. 729 (1925).

95. Pacific Gold Dredging Co. v. Industrial Accident Commission 194 P. 1, 184 Ca. l. 462 (1920).

96. Milburn v. Milburn, 254 S.W. 121 (Texas, 1923).

97. Vernier, *American Family Laws,* 4:485.

98. See also Norman v. Norman (1921) 107 S.E. 407; Grant v. Grant (1920) 110 A. 70; In re Morhoff's Guardianship (1919) 178 P. 294; Waters v. Gray (1921) 193 S.W. 33; Cecacci v. Martelli (1922) 235 S.W. 951; Strangeway et al. v. Allen (1922) 240 S.W. 384. Cf. State v. Bienek (1923) 193 N.W. 452 (appellate court awarded child to blood relative despite the fact that this arrangement would disrupt stability of child's environment).

99. Mary Ann Mason, "Patterns of Appellate Court Decisions in Custody Cases: 1920, 1960, 1990," paper delivered at Law and Society, Philadelphia, May 1992.

100. Jaques v. Jacques, 58 Utah 265, 198, 770 (1921).

101. Buseman v. Buseman, 98 S.E. 574 (1919).

102. See also State ex rel. Rosenstein et al. v. Hoover, 229 S.W. 15 (1921).

4. In the Best Interests of the Child?

1. All divorce settlements, including the custody of the children, were under the jurisdiction of the court; only a small percentage of custody determinations were decided by the judge at trial, the remainder were agreed upon by the parties.

2. Demographers predicted that at least half of American marriages entered into in the 1980s would end in divorce. Lenore Weitzman, *The Divorce Revolution: The Unexpected Social and Economic Consequences for Women and Children in America* (New York, 1985), p. xiv.

3. In two decades families maintained by women alone increased from 36 percent to 50 percent of all poor families. Of the net increase of 129,000 poor families in 1983, 95 percent were headed by women. U.S. Bureau of the Census, *Money Income and Poverty: Status of Families and Persons in the United States: 1983* (1984).

4. The use of expert witness testimony and mediation will be discussed fully in the following chapter.

5. Some states did provide for the appointment of a child advocate in custody disputes. The duty of the advocate was to speak for what he or she determined were the child's best interests.

6. State ex rel. Watts v. Watts, 350 N.Y.S. 2d. 285 (1973).

7. Margaret Mead, "Some Theoretical Considerations of the Problems of Mother-Child Separation," *American Journal of Orthopsychiatry* (1954), p. 24, as quoted in State ex rel. Watts v. Watts, 350 N.Y.S. 2d. 285 (1973).

8. By 1982 only seven remaining states gave mothers a preference over fathers for children of tender years. They were Alabama, Florida, Kentucky, Louisiana, Mississippi, Utah, and Virginia. Jeff Atkinson, "Criteria for Deciding Custody in the Trial and Appellate Courts," *Family Law Quarterly* (1984), 18(1):11 .

9. The Uniform Marriage and Divorce Act, put forth by the commissioners on uniform state laws, defines the child's best interests as a composite of the following factors: "(1) The wishes of the child's parent or parents as to his custody; (2) the wishes of the child as to his cutodian; (3) the interaction and interrelationship of the child with his parent or parents, his siblings and any other person who may significantly affect the child's best interest; (4) the child's adjustment to his home, school and community; (5) the mental and physical health of all individuals involved. The court shall not consider conduct of a present or proposed custodian that does not affect his relationship to the child." UMDA Sec. 402.

10. For a full discussion of state legislation and case law regarding custody see the biennial articles by Doris Jonas Freed and Henry H. Foster, Jr., "Divorce in the Fifty States: An Overview," in *Family Law Quarterly* (1986, 1988, 1990).

11. Harry Krause, *Family Law*, 2d ed. (St. Paul, 1986), p. 337.

12. Weitzman, *The Divorce Revolution*, p. xvii.

13. Mary Ann Mason, *The Equality Trap* (New York, 1988), chapters 1 and 2.

14. For a full discussion of the activities of the social feminists see chapter 3.

15. For a thorough discussion of ERA symbolism and strategy, see Jane J. Mansbridge, *Why We Lost the ERA* (Chicago, 1986), and Mason, *The Equality Trap*, pp. 19–48.

16. "National Organization for Women, Statement of Purpose (1966)" in Aileen S. Kraditor, ed., *Up From the Pedestal* (Chicago, 1970), p. 368.

17. Weitzman, *The Divorce Revolution*, p. 231.

18. Brief for California Fed. Sav. and Loan Assn. at 10, 12. California Fed Sav. and Loan Assn. v. Guerra, 758 F. 2d 390 (9th Cir. 1985), aff'd. 479 U. S. 272 (1987) (nos. 84–5843 and 84–5844). For a full treatment of the legal controversy surrounding pregnancy, see Mary Ann Mason, "Motherhood vs. Equal Treatment," *Journal of Family Law*, 29(1):2–12, 45–48.

19. California Fed Sav. and Loan Assn. v. Guerra, 479 U.S. 272 (1987)

20. Doris J. Freed and Henry J. Walker, "Family Law in the Fifty States: An Overview," table 9, *Family Law Quarterly* (1990), 22(4):57.

21. Mary Ann Mason, "Patterns of Appellate Court Decisions in Custody Disputes: 1920, 1960, and 1990," paper delivered at Law and Society, Philadelphia, May 1992

22. Barbara Bergman, *The Economic Emergence of Women* (New York, 1986), tables 2–3, p. 25.

23. In re Stevens, 183 Ill App. 3d. 160, 538 N.E. 2d. 1279 (1989).

24. Smith v. Frates, 107 Wash. 13 (1919).

25. The data from my own comparative study of one hundred appellate court decisions from 1960 and one hundred from 1990 indicate that while moral fitness was mentioned thirty-six times in 1960 as a factor in the decision, it was mentioned only six times in 1990. Mary Ann Mason, "Patterns of Appellate Court Decisions."

26. See, e.g., Roe v. Roe, 324 S.E. 2d 6691 (Va. Sup. Ct. 1985).

27. See, e.g., Doe v. Coe, 452 N.E. 2d 293 (1983); S.N.E. v. R.L.B., 699 P 2d 875 (Alaska 1985). This position is also promoted by the influential Uniform Marriage and Divorce Act, Sec. 402, which states, "The court shall not consider conduct of a present or proposed custodian that does not affect his relationship to the child."

28. D.H. v. J.H., 418 N.E. 2d 286 (Ind. App. 1981).

29. Ibid., p. 296.

30. Weitzman, *The Divorce Revolution*, pp. 226, 227.

31. Mary Ann Mason, "Patterns of Appellate Court Decisions."

32. Thomas J. Reidy, Richard M. Silver, Alan Carlson, "Child Custody Decisions: A Survey of Judges," *Family Law Quarterly* (1991), 23(75):110.

33. Lenore Weitzman notes that about one-third of divorced women reported that their husbands threatened to ask for custody as a ploy in negotiations. Weitzman, *The*

Divorce Revolution, pp. 310, 311. See also Doris Foster and Henry Freed, Law and the Family: "Politics of Divorce Process-Bargaining Leverage, Unfair Edge," *New York Law School Review* (1984), 192:6.

34. For a general discussion of the pros and cons of joint custody see Jay Folberg, ed., *Joint Custody and Shared Parenting* (New York, 1984).

35. For an analysis of the primary caretaker preference see J. Neely, "The Primary Caretaker Parent Rule: Child Custody and the Dynamics of Greed," *Yale Law and Policy Review* (1984), 3:168, and David Chambers, "Rethinking the Substantive Rule for Custody Disputes in Divorce," *Michigan Law Review* (1984), 83:477.

36. The wording of the statute was ambiguous. It could be construed as giving sole custody equal footing with joint custody, when there was a dispute, or giving joint custody first preference [Cal. Civ. Code, Sec. 4600 (West, 1983)], but the statute unambiguously stated that when the parents agree to joint custody, there "shall be a presumption . . . that joint custody is in the best interest of the child" [Cal. Civ. Code, Sec. 4607 (West Supp. 1989)]. As part of the reform package, the legislature required mandatory mediation in contested custody cases. Later an appellate court clarified the intent of this legislation by agreeing, in In re Marriage of Wood, that a trial court could impose a joint custody arrangement against the wishes of one parent. Cal. Civ. Code, Sec. 4607 (West Supp. 1989). In re Marriage of Wood, 141 Cal. App. 3d 671, 683–840, 190 Cal. Rptr. 469, 477–78 (1983).

37. Freed and Walker, "Family Law in the Fifty States," table 9.

38. Dodd v. Dodd, 403 N.Y. S. 2d 401 (1978).

39. Taylor v. Taylor, 306 Md. 290, 508 A. 2d 964 (1986).

40. McCann v. McCann, 167 Md. 167, 172, 173, A. 7 (1934).

41. Taylor v. Taylor, 306 Md. 290, 508 A. 2d 964, 975 (1986).

42. Robert H. Mnookin, Eleanor E. Maccoby, Catherine R. Albiston, Charlene E. Depner, "Private Ordering Re-Visited," p. 73, in Stephen D. Sugarman and Herma Hill Kay, eds., *Divorce Reform at the Crossroads* (New Haven, 1990).

43. Carol Bruch, "And How Are the Children? The Effects of Ideology and Mediation on Child Custody Law and Children's Well-Being in the United States," *International Journal of Law and the Family* (1988), 2:106, 116–121.

44. In response to concerns that joint custody might be inappropriately applied, the California legislature once again amended its child custody law, asserting: "This section establishes neither a preference nor a presumption for or against joint legal custody, joint physical custody, or sole custody, but allows the court and the family the widest discretion to choose a parenting plan which is in the best interests of the child or children." Mnookin, Maccoby, Albiston, and Depner, "Private Ordering Re-Visited," p. 73.

45. Ibid., pp. 72, 73.

46. See, generally, Lenore Weitzman, *The Divorce Revolution*, pp. 244–45; David Chambers, "Rethinking the Substantive Rule for Custody Disputes in Divorce," *Michigan*

Law Review (1984), 83:477; L. Singer and D. Reynolds, "A Dissent on Joint Custody," *Maryland Law Review* (1988), 47:497.

47. Chambers, "Rethinking the Substantive Rule," p. 562.

48. Pikula v. Pikula, 374 N. W. 2d 705 (Minn. 1985); Garska v. McCoy, 278 S. E. 2d 357 (W. Va. 1981).

49. Kennedy v. Kennedy, 376 N. W. 2d 702 (Minn. App. 1985).

50. Ibid., p. 706.

51. Ibid., p. 708.

52. There is some evidence that judges are critical of working mothers who no longer play the full-time caretaker role. See Nancy Polikoff, "Why Mothers are Losing," *Women's Rights Law Reporter* (1982), 7:235.

53. Mary Ann Mason, "Patterns of Appellate Court Decisions."

54. Santosky v. Kramer, 455 U. S. 745 (1982).

55. Cal. Civil Code Sec. 4600 subd. (c), and Cal. Probate Code Sec. 1514 subd. (b).

56. Henrikson v. Gable, 162 Mich. App. 248, 412 N.W. 2d 702 at 704 (1987).

57. Painter v. Bannister, 258 Iowa 1390, 140 N.W. 2d 152 (1966).

58. Krause, *Family Law*, p. 257.

59. After 1980 a custody determination would no longer be overturned by a court in a different state. To forestall parental kidnapping and changes in custody orders, the Uniform Child Custody Jurisdiction Act, which recognized the judgement of the court with the closest connection to the child, was passed by all states by 1986. In addition, Congress, in 1980, passed the Federal Parental Kidnapping Prevention Act, which mandated that all states follow the court that originally rendered the decree. This act also set up a parent locator service to track parents suspected of kidnapping a child.

60. U.S. Con. Res. 45, April 19, 1983, and see Krause, *Family Law*, p. 270.

61. Ex Parte Bronstein, 434 So. 2d 780, 784 (Ala. 1983).

62. Demographer Frank Furstenberg estimated that about 25 percent of all children born in the eighties would live with a stepparent before they reached majority. Frank Furstenberg, "The New Extended Family: The Experience of Parents and Children After Remarriage," in Pasley and Ihinger-Tallman, eds., *Remarriage and Stepparenting: Current Research and Theory* (New York, 1987), pp. 42, 44. Other researchers predicted that 40 percent of those who marry when one or both has children are likely to divorce within five years. Given these two predictions, a very large percentage of children would both live with a stepparent and experience the divorce of that stepparent from their natural parent.

63. For a full discussion of stepparent rights and obligations see David Chambers, "Stepparents, Biologic Parents, and the Law's Perception of 'Family' after Divorce," in Kay and Sugarman, eds., *Divorce Reform at the Crossroads* (New Haven, 1990), pp. 102–129.

64. Henrikson v. Gable, 162 Mich. App. 248, 412 N.W. 2d 702.

65. Henrikson v. Gable, 162 Mich. App. 248, 412 N.W. 2d 702 at 704 (1987).

66. In re Custody of N.M.O., 399 N.W. 2d 700, at 703, quoting Wallin, 290 Minn. at 265, 187 N.W. 2d at 630.

67. See Chambers, "Stepparents, Biologic Parents," p. 118.

68. Ibid.

69. Application of Slochowsky, 73 Misc. 2d 563, 342 N.Y. S. 2d 525 (Sup. Ct. 1973).

70. The Omnibus Reconciliation Act of 1981 determined that the stepparents' income must be taken into account. 42 U.S. C. A. Sec. 602 (a) (31).

71. Chambers, "Stepparents, Biologic Parents," p. 116.

72. In the landmark California case, Marvin v. Marvin, 18 Ca. 3d 660, 134 Cal. Rptr. 825, 557 P. 2d 106 (1976), the court proceeded "on the principle that adults who voluntarily live together and engage in sexual relations are nonetheless as competent as any other persons to contract respecting their earnings and property rights."

73. People v. Sorenson, 66 Cal. Rptr. 7, 10 (1968).

74. Uniform Parentage Act, Sec. 5.

75. In the Matter of Baby M., 537 A. 2d 1227, 1241 (1988).

76. Ibid., pp. 1258, 1263.

77. Krause, *Family Law,* pp. 187–188.

78. In the Matter of Baby M., 537 A. 2d 1227 (1988).

79. Trial court opinion cited in Davis v. Davis, 1992 WL 115574, *1 (Tenn.) slip opinion, not yet released for publication.

80. Davis v. Davis, 1992 WL 115574, *15,*16.

81. 1986 L. Acts R. S. 9:121 et seq.

82. *New York Times,* July 20, 1992, p. 1, col 5.

83. Stanley v. Illinois, 405 U.S. 645 (1971).

84. Ibid.

85. In Cabban v. Mohammed, 441 U. S. 380 (1979), where the father had lived with the mother and two children for five years the court allowed the father to block the adoption, while in Quilloin v Walcott, 434 U.S. 246 (1978), the court denied an unmarried father a "veto power" over the adoption of his nonmarital child, when for eleven years he supported the child only irregularly and never lived with the child.

86. Lehr v. Robertson, 463 U.S. at 261–262.

87. Michael U. v. Jamie B., 218 Ca. Rptr. 39 (1985)

88. Michael U. v. Jamie B., 218 Cal. Rptr. 39 at 43.

89. Michael U. v. Jamie B., 218 Cal. Rptr. 39 at 46.

90. Uniform Parentage Act, Sec. 4(a)

91. Uniform Parentage Act, Sec. 14(a)

92. Lewis v. Martin, 397 U.S. 552 (1970). The Supreme Court in this case decided the income could only be considered if the stepparent had an obligation of "general applicability." Congress changed this requirement in the Omnibus Reconciliation Act of 1981,

determining that the stepparents' income must be taken into account. 42 U.S.C.A. Sec. 602(a)(31).

93. Lewis v. Martin, 397 U.S. 552 (1970).

94. 42 U.S.C.A. Sec. 5101–5106. The act was renamed the Child Abuse Prevention Adoption and Family Services Act of 1988.

95. Douglas Besharov, "Doing Something About Child Abuse: The Need to Narrow the Grounds for State Intervention," *Harvard Journal of Law and Public Policy* (1985), 8:545.

96. Legal scholar Michael Wald, analyzing the research on children in foster care placement, concluded that social, emotional, and academic development were negatively affected by removal of children and placement in foster care. Michael Wald, *Protecting Abused and Neglected Children: A Comparison of Home and Foster Placement* (Stanford, 1985), pp. 9–13.

97. In the Matter of Deobrah G., Georgia G., Bruce G., and Elizabeth G. 2d Civil No. 40391, Ca. Ct. App. June 29, 1973 (unpublished opinion).

98. Ibid.

99. The statute specifying criteria for abuse and neglect was later modified, removing mention of unsanitary conditions. See Cal. Welf & Inst Code, Secs. 300, 361.

100. In re Amber B., 191 Cal. App. 3d 682 (1987).

101. In re Amber B., 191 Cal. App. 3d 682 (1987), at 685.

102. In a letter sent to the court before the hearing, Amber's mother reported that her son had described instances of possible sexual abuse of Amber by an aunt. Footnote 1, at 685.

103. Mary Ann Mason, "A Judicial Dilemma: The Use of Expert Witness Testimony in Child Sex Abuse Cases," *Journal of Law and Psychiatry* (1992), 21:35–65.

104. See chapter 3 for a full discussion of the cultural conflicts relating to the new child labor and school attendance laws.

105. In re P. 71 Misc. 2d 965, 337 N.Y.S. 2d 203 (1972).

106. Wyman v. James, 400 U.S. 309.

107. Santosky v. Kramer, 455 U.S. 745 (1982).

108. Santosky v. Kramer, 455 U.S. 745 (1982), at 754.

109. Lassiter v. Dept. of Social Services of Durham County, 452 U.S. 18 (1981).

110. See L. Posner, "The Regulation of the Market in Adoptions," *Buffalo University Law Review* (1987), 67:59, 64–72.

111. Homer Folks, "Family Life for Dependent Children," in Spencer and Bartwell, eds., *Care of Dependent, Neglected, and Wayward Children*, pp. 75–80, in Bremner, *Children and Youth in America*, 2:321.

112. Robert Mnookin, "Foster Care—In Whose Best Interest?" *Harvard Educational Review* (1973), 43:599

113. Smith v. Organization of Foster Families for Equality and Reform, 431 U.S. 816 (1977).

5. The Ascendancy of the Social Sciences

1. As quoted in Edmund S. Morgan, *The Puritan Family* (New York, 1944; rpt. 1966), p. 45.

2. See chapter 1 for a complete analysis of the father's role.

3. John Monahan and Laurens Walker, *Social Science and the Law* (St. Paul, 1984), p. 1.

4. Lofft 748, 98 Eng. Rep. 899 (K.B. 1774).

5. Foulke v. People, 4 Colo. App. 528 (1904).

6. People v. Mercein, 3 Hill 399, 418 (N.Y. 1842). For a full discussion of this case, see chapter 2.

7. Monahan and Walker, *Social Science and the Law*, pp. 1–3.

8. Muller v. Oregon, 208 U. S. 412, 421 (1908).

9. Mary Ann Mason, "Patterns of Appellate Court Decisions in Custody Disputes: 1920, 1960, and 1990," paper delivered at Law and Society, Philadelphia, May 1992.

10. Carl Degler, *At Odds: Women and the Family in America From the Revolution to the Present* (New York, 1980), p. 403.

11. Walter I. Trattner, *From Poor Law to Welfare State*, 4th ed. (New York, 1989), p. 216.

12. As quoted in Trattner, *From Poor Law to Welfare State*, p. 114, note 6.

13. For a full discussion of the Chicago school, see Christopher Lasch, *Haven in a Heartless World: The Family Besieged*, pp. 29–36; see also Trattner, *From Poor Law to Welfare State*, pp. 217–220.

14. "Letter to the President of the United States Embodying the Conclusions of the Conference on the Care of Dependent Children," Proceedings of the Conference on the Care of Dependent Children, 1909, pp. 192–197, in Bremner, *Children and Youth in America*, 2:368–379.

15. In the Westlaw Family Law state database, the work of Goldstein, Freud, and Solnit is mentioned 177 times.

16. Joseph Goldstein, Anna Freud, and Albert Solnit, *Beyond the Best Interests of the Child* (New York, 1973), p. 38. See also Joseph Goldstein, Anna Freud, and Albert Solnit, *Before the Best Interests of the Child* (New York, 1979), and Joseph Goldstein, Anna Freud, and Albert Solnit, *In the Best Interests of the Child* (New York, 1986).

17. Pierce v. Yerkovich, 363 N.Y.S. 2d 403, 410 (1976).

18. Stell v. Stell, 783 P. 2d 615, 622 (Wash. App. 1989). See also In Re Navajo County Juvenile Action, 831 P. 2d 368 (Ariz. 1992), a motion to set aside an adoption.

19. Burfening v. Burfening, 440 N.W. 2d 496, 501 (N.D. 1989).

20. Richard Neely, "The Primary Caretaker Parent Rule: Child Custody and the Dynamics of Greed," *Yale Law and Policy Review* (1984), 3:168, 170.

21. David M. v. Margaret M. 385 S.E. 2d 912, 916 (1989).

22. Dinius v. Dinius, 448 N.W. 2d 210, 212.

23. As quoted in Maxine Margolis, *Mothers and Such* (Florida, 1984), p. 90.

24. Very few, if any, researchers would claim that there are no differences between the responses of mothers and fathers to children, even if these responses are considered minor. For example, Michael Lamb found that fathers engaged infants in more rough and tumble play and invented new and unusual games. Mothers were more inclined to conventional games such as peek-a-boo and pat-a-cake. Michael F. Lamb, "Father Infant and Mother Infant Interaction in the First Year of Life," *Child Development* (1977), 48:167–81. See also Berman, "Are Women More Responsive Than Men to the Young? A Review of Developmental and Situation Variables,"*Psychological Bulletin* (1980), 88:688. This article reviews almost sixty studies over twenty years. The research takes many forms, including measuring the pulse rate of mothers and fathers in response to pictures and observations of real interactions between mothers, fathers, and children.

25. David L. Chambers, a leading proponent of a primary caretaker preference, contended, following a review of the literature, that there is no reason, based on gender alone, to prefer placing the child with the mother. David L. Chambers, "Rethinking the Substantive Rule for Custody Disputes in Divorce," *Michigan Law Review* (1984), 83:477. On the other hand, legal scholar Martha Fineman criticized Chambers's analysis of the father studies, claiming that the observations upon which the researchers relied represented only minimal parenting skill—"skills that would be inadequate if we were talking about mothers rather than fathers." Moreover, she claimed that research findings were based on small, select, or unrepresentative samples. Martha L. Fineman and Anne Opie, "The Uses of Social Science Data in Legal Policymaking: Custody Determinations at Divorce," *Wisconsin Law Review* (1987), pp. 107–157, p. 145.

26. For a thorough discussion of father parenting studies see Ross A. Thompson, "Fathers and the Child's `Best Interests': Judicial Decision Making in Custody Disputes," in Michael F. Lamb, *The Father's Role* (New York, 1986), chapter 3.

27. Watts v. Watts, 350 N.Y. S. 2d 285, 289 (N.Y. Fam. Ct. 1973)

28. Frank Furstenberg, J. Address to the American Association of the Advancement of Science (AAAS), May 1986, p. 18.

29. Zummo v. Zummo, 394 Pa. Super. 30, 44, 574 A. 2d 1130, 1137, nn. 8, 11, 12. Some of the studies cited are Allison and Furstenberg, "How Marital Dissolution Affects Children," *Developmental Psychology* (1989), 25:540, 540–49; Fishel, "Children's Adjustment in Divorced Families," *Youth and Society* (1987), 19:173, 173–96; McCant, "The Cultural Contradiction of Fathers as Nonparents," *Family Legal Quarterly* (1987), 21:127,

127–43; Wooley, "Shared Parenting Arrangements," *Family Advocate* (1978), 1:6; Grote and Weinstein, "Joint Custody," *Journal of Divorce* (1977), 1:43, 43–53; Coysh et al., "Parental Postdivorce Adjustment in Joint and Sole Physical Custody Families,"*Journal of Family Issues* (1989), 10:52, 52–71; Tschann, Johnston, and Wallerstein, "Resources, Stressors, and Attachment as Predictors of Adult Adjustment After Divorce: A Longitudinal Study," *Journal of Marriage and Family* (1989), 51:1033, 1033–46; Guttmann, "The Divorced Father," *Journal of Comparative Family Studies* (1989), 20:247, 247–61; Bowman and Ahrons, *Marriage and the Family* (1985), pp. 481–88; Koch and Lowery, "Visitation and the Non-Custodial Father," *Journal of Divorce* (1984), 8:47, 47–65; Greif, "Fathers, Children, and Joint Custody," *American Journal Orthopsychology* (1979), 49:311, 311–19; Seltzer, Schaeffer, and Chang, "Family Ties After Divorce: The Relationship Between Visiting and Paying Child Support," *Journal of Marriage and the Family* (1989), 51:1013, 1013–32; J. Pearson and N. Thoennes, "Supporting Children After Divorce: The Influence of Custody on Child Support Levels," *Family Law Quarterly* (1988), 22:319, 319–39.

30. Zummo v. Zummo, 394 Pa. Super. Crt., 44, 574 A. 2d 1130, 1137.

31. Sigmund Freud, *An Outline of Psychoanalysis* (New York, 1949), p. 48.

32. Selma Fraiberg, *Every Child's Birthright: In Defense of Mothering* (New York, 1977). For a neo-Freudian look at mother-infant attachment see also M. Mahler, F. Pine, and A. Bergman, *The Psychological Birth of the Human Infant* (New York, 1975).

33. Alice Rossi, "Gender and Parenthood," *American Sociological Review* (1984), 49(1):8.

34. Jean Piaget, considered the father of experimental developmental psychology, carefully detailed the development of the child's thought processes. He believed that children do not consistently differentiate between the subjective and objective until the age of seven or eight. The tender years doctrine usually encompassed this time frame as well. See, e.g., Jean Piaget and B. Inhelder, *The Psychology of the Child* (New York, 1969).

35. Judith S. Wallerstein, Presentation to the American Bar Association, August 9, 1992. For an analysis of the longterm effects of custody on children, see also Judith S. Wallerstein and Sandra Blakeslee, *Second Chances* (New York, 1989).

36. Thompson, "Fathers and the Child's 'Best Interests.' "

37. Likewise, the laws defining grounds for removal of children from their parents expanded to include psychological criteria. The California statute citing grounds for removal included: "The minor is suffering severe emotional damage, as indicated by extreme anxiety, depression, withdrawal, or untoward aggressive behavior toward self or others, and there are no reasonable means by which the minor's emotional health may be protected without removing the minor from the physical custody of his or her parent or guardian." Cal. Civil Code Sec. 361.

38. N.D.C.C. Sec. 14.

39. For a critical interpretation of custody evaluations, see J. R. Levy, "Custody Inves-

tigations as Evidence in Divorce Cases," *Family Law Quarterly* (1987), 21:149.

40. These figures are taken from my comparative study of appellate court decisions, 1920, 1960, and 1990. Mary Ann Mason, "Patterns of Appellate Court Decisions."

41. Ibid.

42. Vishnevsky v. Vishnevsky 105 N.W. 2d 314 (Wis. 1960).

43. Ibid., at 318.

44. Galbraith v. Galbraith 356 P. 2d 1023 (1960).

45. Williams v. Williams, 563 N.E. 2d 1195 (Ill. App. 3 Dist. 1990).

46. Uhls v. Uhls 794 P. 2d 894 (Wyo. 1990).

47. Palazzo v. Coe 562 So. 2d 1137 (La. App. 4 Cir. 1990).

48. This fact is mentioned by twelve of the experts at trial in 1990, while never mentioned in 1960. Mary Ann Mason, "Patterns of Appellate Court Decisions."

49. Newsom v. Newsom 557 So. 2d 511 (Miss. 1990).

50. S.H. v. B.L.H. 572 A. 2d 730 (Pa. 1990).

51. See, for example, Shirley Opaku, "Psychology: Impediment or Aid in Child Custody Cases?" *Rutgers Law Review* (1976), 29:1117.

52. Lois A. Weithorn and Thomas Grisso, "Psychological Evaluations`20in Divorce Custody: Problems, Principles, and Procedures," in L. Weithorn, ed., *Psychology and Child Custody Determinations* (New York, 1987), p. 46.

53. Thomas Reidy, Richard M. Silver, and Alan Carlson, "Child Custody Decisions: A Survey of Judges," *Family Law Quarterly* (1989), 23:75 (1989).

54. Martha L. Fineman, "Dominant Discourse, Professional Language, and Legal Change in Child Custody Decision-Making," *Harvard Law Review* (1988), 101(4):727–730.

55. Cal. Civil Code, Sec. 4607.

56. The five other states were Delaware, Maine, Florida, Washington, and Wisconsin.

57. Hugh McIsaac, "Court-Connected Mediation," *Conciliation Courts Review* (December 1983), 21(2):3.

58. A study of Connecticut, Los Angeles, and Minneapolis court-related custody mediations revealed that cases averaged 1.5 sessions and 2.3 hours in Connecticut, 1.7 sessions and 3 hours in Los Angeles, and 3.3 sessions and 4.3 hours in Minneapolis. In Maine mediations are usually held in a single session. Tina Grillo, "The Mediation Alternative: Process Dangers for Women," *Yale Law Journal* (1991), 100(1545):1583, note 180.

59. Hugh McIsaac, "Court-Connected Mediation," *Conciliation Courts Review* (1983), 21(2):5.

60. Joan Kelly found that private sessions averaged ten hours. Joan Kelly, "Mediated and Adversarial Divorce: Respondents' Perceptions of Their Processes and Outcomes," *Mediation Quarterly* (Summer 1989), 22(77):74.

61. Stephen K. Erickson, Marilyn S. Mcknight, Erickson, "Don and Linda: A Typical Divorce Case," *Mediation Quarterly* (1988), 21(3):10.

62. Ibid., p. 14.

63. Ibid., p. 20.

64. See, e.g., Fineman, "Dominant Discourse," p. 727, and Grillo, "The Mediation Alternative," p. 1545.

65. Grillo, "The Mediation Alternative," p. 1563.

66. The concept of the battered woman is credited to Lenore Walker, *The Battered Woman* (New York, 1979).

67. Grillo, "The Mediation Alternative," pp. 1605–1607.

68. Fineman, "Dominant Discourse," p. 769.

69. See, e.g., Randy Klaff, "The Tender Years Doctrine: A Defense," *California Law Review* (1982), 70:335.

70. Minnesota and Oregon, for example, excluded cases of child and spousal abuse from court-ordered mediation: Minn. Stat. Ann. Sec. 518–619; Or. Rev. Stat. Ann. Sec. 107.755–795.

71. Wis. State. Sec. 767.11(3) (West Supp. 1990).

72. Nicole Sideris, "Divorce Mediation: Must It Be Voluntary?" *Conciliation Courts Review* (1988), 26(2):68.

73. Ibid.

74. J. Pearson and N. Thoennes, "Mediating Litigation Custody Disputes: A Longitudinal Evaluation," *Family Law Quarterly* (1984), 17:479–524.

Index

Abbot, Grace and Edith, 91
Abortion rights, 139
Abuse, *see* Battered women; Child abuse and neglect
Act of 1642 (Mass.), 10
Act of 1672 for Suppressing of Vagabonds and Disposing of Poor Children to Trades (Va.), 10
Adams, Jeremiah, 35
Addams, Jane, 89, 91, 166
Adoption: colonial stepparents and, 22, 24; late twentieth century, 135, 137–38, 147, 156–59; nineteenth century, 73–75, 79; Progressive-era, 109–11
Adultery: colonial era, 16, 17, 18; late twentieth century, 127; nineteenth century, 63, 64, 205n71; 1920s, 112–13

African slave trade, 44, 45; *see also* Slave fathers
Aid to Families with Dependent Children (AFDC), 138, 148–49, 151, 154
Aid to Needy Children program (Calif.), 140
Alabama, 62, 67, 135, 212n93
Alameda County (Calif.), 179
Alden, Lyman P., 79–80
Allington, William, 42, 43
Amber B. (abused child), 152–53, 218n102
American Bar Association, 129
American Journal of Sociology, 97
Amsterdam (Netherlands), 32
Anatomically correct dolls, 153
Angela (lesbian), 176

Animal protection, 101, 102
Anna (adoptee), 74
Apprentices, *see* Indentured servants
Artificial insemination, 139–40, 142
Ashbees, Stephen, 28
Asian immigrant families, 154
Association rights, 6, 14

B. (social worker), 94
B., Amber (abused child), 152–53, 218*n*102
B., K. (lesbian), 128
Baby M., 141
Bar associations, 202–3*n*15
Barbour, Maria, 49–50
Battered women, 183, 184
Beard, Mary, 15, 203*n*27
Best interests standard, xi, xii, 59, 86; late twentieth century, 121–60, 174, 190, 191; nineteenth century, 61–62, 67, 74, 75, 76, 82
Beyond the Best Interests of the Child (Goldstein, Freud, Solnit), 168–69
Binding out, *see* Indentured servants
Biological parenthood, x, xii, 191; adoptive parents and, 188; grandparent rights and, 135; "psychological parent" concept and, 169–70; U.S. Supreme Court on, 134, 146–47 ; *see also* Blood relatives
Birthrate, 51–52, 202*n*10
Biseck family, 137
Black freemen, 41, 80–81
Black illegitimacy, 145
Black marriage, 209*n*20
Blackmun, Harry A., 134, 154–55
Black parents, 154
Black slave children, *see* Slave children

Blackstone, William, 14, 25, 31, 59, 90, 204*n*44
Blisset's Case (1774), 17, 59, 101, 163
Blood relatives, 24, 31, 134; *see also* Biological parenthood
Bloomfield, Maxwell, 202–3*n*15
Boston, 99
Brace, Charles Loring, 79, 108
Brandeis, Louis, 164, 165
Bronstein, Alvin, 135
Brooklyn Bureau of State Charities, 91–92
Bryan v. Bryan (1859), 64
Burgess, Ernest, 166
Burr, Aaron, 17
Buseman v. Buseman (1919), 117

Cabban v. Mohammed (1979), 217*n*85
California:
—court cases: Graham v. Benner, 72; In the Matter of Deborah G., 151–52; In re Amber B., 152–53; In re Cozza, 109–10; In re Marriage of Wood, 215*n*36; Marvin v. Marvin, 217*n*72; Michael U. v. Jamie B., 147; Pacific Gold Dredging Co. v. Industrial Accident Commission, 115–16; Painter v. Bannister, 135; People v. Sorenson, 140, 141
—legislation on: equal guardianship, 57; joint custody, 130, 131–32, 215*n*36, 215–16*n*44; maternity leave, 126; mediation, 178–79; no-fault divorce, 124, 125; noncustodial parents, 212*n*93; nonparental custody, 134; removal of children, 222*n*37; unmarried fathers, 98–99
—mediation in, 131–32, 179–80, 184
California Federal Savings and Loan

Association, 126
California Supreme Court, 140, 147
Canon law, 15
Chambers, David L., 132, 220*n*25
Chancery courts, 58
Charitable organizations, 91, 94, 96, 99, 108, 157
Chattels, 6, 7, 35, 40, 44
Chesapeake colonies, 4–5, 8–9, 18, 26–28
Chicago Juvenile Court, 88
Chicago School of Social Work, 166
Chichester family, 37
Child abuse and neglect: colonial era, 12, 36; late twentieth century, 151, 152–53, 175, 177, 184; Progressive era, 100, 101–8
Child Abuse Prevention, Adoption and Family Services Act (1988), 218*n*94
Child Abuse Prevention and Treatment Act (1974), 150
Child advocates, 213*n*5; *see also* Guardians *ad litem*
Childbirth, 125–26, 142
Child development, 173–74, 192, 202*n*9
Child discipline, 11, 12, 102–3, 104
Child labor, x, xi, 78, 106–7, 110
Child placement, *see* Adoption; Foster home care; Indentured servants; "Placing out" system
Child removal: colonial era, 4; late twentieth century, 149–56, 159, 190, 222*n*37; Progressive era, 90–91, 100–8, 166, 167; *see also* Lost custody
Children's Aid Society, 108
Childsavers, 87–92, 149
Child sexual abuse, 152–53, 175, 177
Child support: colonial era, 27; late twentieth century, 138–39, 147–48, 183;

Progressive era, 87, 94–96, 98–99, 115–16, 119; *see also* Public support
Child welfare legislation, 86–87
Child welfare workers, 100–1, 114, 151
Chrisian (Plymouth resident), 39
Civil codes, 24–25, 73
Civil War, 64, 65
Clark, Edward, 24
Cohabitation, 139, 170, 217*n*72
Colonial era, xi, 1–47, 104, 188, 195–96*n*5; culture of, 52; divine right theory in, 162; divorce in, 15–18, 54; households in, 4–5, 51, 76; illegitimacy in, 2, 3–4, 22, 24–30, 33, 34, 70, 96; paternal desertion in, 94
Comas v. Reddish (1866), 80, 208*n*133
Common law, xi, 3, 58, 59–60, 90, 118; best interests standard and, 62; on blood relationships, 134; on divorce, 15; grandparent rights and, 135; on guardianship, 18; on illegitimacy, 24–25, 72, 98; on married women's status, 14–15; natural law and, 163; on parents, 14, 94; on paternal rights, 6–7, 115; on remarriage, 67; slavery and, 3, 43; state interventionism and, 87; on stepfathers, 21, 136
Community property, 56
Connecticut, 11–12, 16, 35, 184
Cook County Juvenile Court (Ill.), 102
Cooley, Charles, 166
Cope, William, 35
Copp, Elizabeth Adelaide, 67–68
Corporal punishment, 102–3, 104, 182; *see also* Whipping
Court of Equity (England), 17
Coverture status, 14–15, 19, 22, 23, 55–56
Cozza, Linda, 109–10

Crabtree v. Crabtree (1922), 113

Criminal class, 166; *see also* Juvenile delinquents

Criminal punishment, 68, 152

"Cruelties" (organizations), 101–4, 108

Cruelty, *see* Battered women; Child abuse and neglect

Cult of motherhood, 51, 53, 66, 69, 71, 201–2n6

D. H. v. J. H. (1981), 127–28

Daphne (slave), 45

Davis v. Davis (1992), 143–44

Daycare, 182

Death: maternal, 145, 146; paternal, 18, 20, 64–68, 115

Death penalty, 11

DeBoer family, 188

Deborah G. (neglected child), 151–52

Declaration of Rights and Sentiments (1848), 56, 89, 203n31

Dee, William, 105

Delaware, 184

Delineator (periodical), 110

Demos, John, 13

Desertion, 16, 18, 64, 92, 94–96

Deuteronomy (Biblical book), 11

Dionysius of Halicarnassus, 7

District of Columbia, 95

Divine law, 11, 61, 95, 116, 162

Divorce: colonial era, 15–18; late twentieth century, 123–29, 138–39, 167–74, 178, 213nn1, 2, 217n62; nineteenth century, 54–55, 63, 74, 86, 205n68; Progressive era, 87, 92, 109, 111–17; *see also* No-fault divorce

Dod, Richard, 21

Don (husband), 181–82

Donor parenthood *see* Artificial insemination; Surrogate mothers

Dorr, Rheta, 56, 57

Dreiser, Theodore, 110

Dutch children, 32

Eastman, Elizabeth, 22

Education: colonial era, 7, 8, 9, 14, 34, 37–38; Progressive era, 87, 106–7, 154

Elizabethan poor laws, 7, 10, 91

Ellenborough, Edward Law, Lord, 18, 59

Ellen (fourteen-year-old child), 174

Emancipation Proclamation, 80

Empson, Elenor and Mary, 21

England: chancery courts, 58; Court of Equity, 17; Inn of Court, 202n15; parliamentary law, 19, 65, 139; poor laws, 7, 10, 91; Privy Council, 1–2

English common law, *see* Common law

Enlightenment, the, 162

Equal Rights Amendment, 125

Every Child's Birthright (Fraiberg), 173

Expert witnesses, 162, 167, 174–78, 191, 192–93

Families: conflict in, 131, 132, 192–93; farm, 79–80, 110; immigrant, 90, 154; privacy of, 88, 90, 101, 150, 151, 154–55; slave, 42–46; social feminists and, 89; U.S. Supreme Court on, 53

Family Law Act (Calif.: 1969), 124, 125

Farm families, 79–80, 110

Father-child studies, 171, 220nn24, 25

Fathers' custody, *see* Paternal custody

Faulkner, Charles E., 107

Federal Parental Kidnapping Prevention Act (1980), 216n59

Feminism: adoption law and, 73; apprenticeships and, 77–78, 81–82; bastardy laws and, 68–69; cult of motherhood and, 53–54, 202*n*6; late twentieth century, 124–26, 149; nineteenth century, xiii, 15, 90, 203*n*27; Progressive era, 88, 89; testamentary rights and, 66; *see also* Social feminists; Women's status

Feminist criticism, 182–83

Femme couvert status, 14–15, 19, 22, 23, 55–56

Fenwick, Cuthbert, 42–43

Filius nullius, see Illegitimate children

Fineman, Martha, 183, 220*n*25

Florence Crittendon Missions, 99

Folks, Homer, 111, 157

Fornication, *see* Sexual transgression

Fort New Amsterdam, 19–20, 32

Foster home care: late twentieth century, 122, 156–59, 191, 218*n*96; Progressive era, 86, 110, 111

Fourth Amendment, 154, 155

Fowler, Philip, 36

Fraiberg, Selma, 173

Frances (Plymouth resident), 39

Franklin, William, 36

Frates (defendant), 114

Frazier, E. Franklin, 166

Free blacks, 41, 80–81

Freud, Anna, 168–69, 170

Freud, Sigmund, 173

Friedman, Lawrence, 196*n*5

Frozen embryos, 142–44

"Funds to Parents" (Ill.), 92

Furstenberg, Frank, 172, 216*n*62

G., Deborah (neglected child), 151–52

Gable (Mich. stepfather), 136, 137

Galbraith v. Galbraith (1960), 176

Gambetta (putative father), 98

Games, 220*n*24

Gandy, Eric and Danielle, 158

Gender equality before the law, 114–15, 122, 159, 167–68, 171

Gender of children, 62, 174

Gennings, John, 35

Georgia, 80, 85–86, 98, 100, 208*n*133

Glenn, Mary Wilcox, 91–92

Godey's Ladies Book, 52

Goerlitz, Marion, 64–65

Goldstein, Joseph, 168–69, 170

Gordon, Linda, 93

Grandparents, 23, 117, 135

Green, Anola, 107–8

Grillo, Tina, 182

Grisso, Thomas, 177

Grossberg, Michael, 58

Guardians *ad litem*, 175, 179, 190; *see also* Child advocates

Guardianship: colonial era, 18, 19–20, 23; late twentieth century, 149–50; nineteenth century, 64–68, 156–57, 206*n*87; Progressive era, 114, 115

Gustin, Walter and Betty, 17

Habeas corpus actions, 58

Hall, Joseph, 22

Harmon v. Harmon (1922), 112–13

Harnett (N.Y. justice), 138

Harper, Thomas, 35

Hawaii, 93

Helping professions, 202*n*6

Henrikson v. Gable (1987), 136–37

Home industry, 51

Home placements, *see* Adoption; Foster home care; "Placing out" system

Home privacy, 88, 90, 101, 150, 151,

Home Privacy (*Cont.*)
154–55
Homicide, 104
Homosexuality, 127, 128
How (colonial girl), 11–12
Hudson, Jonathan, 22
Humphrey, Ellis, 35

Illegitimate children: colonial era, 2, 3–4, 22, 24–30, 33, 34; late twentieth century, 144–45; nineteenth century, 68–73; Progressive era, 93, 96–100
Illinois, 92, 98, 127, 146, 176
Illinois Board of Public Charities, 88
Immigrant families, 90, 154
Indentured servants, 2, 30–39; adoption and, 24; education of, 9; illegitimate children as, 29; illegitimate children of, 26–28; Maryland colony, 29; Massachusetts Bay Colony, 10, 30–31; New England colonies, 8; nineteenth century, 76–80; orphans as, 20, 21, 31, 32, 34; paternal responsibilities and, 7; "placing out" and, 108–9, 110, 211*n*71; poor laws on, 72–73; stepchildren as, 22; Virginia colony, 1–2, 10; women's rights movement and, 54, 77–78, 82; *see also* Involuntary apprenticeships; Voluntary apprenticeships
Indiana, 127–28
Indians, 41, 42
Industrialization, 78
Inheritance: colonial era, 20, 29–30; nineteenth century, 69, 71, 73, 75, 81; Progressive era, 97; *see also* Wills
Inn of Court (England), 202*n*15
In re Amber B. (1987), 152–53
In re Marriage of Wood (1989), 215*n*36

In the Matter of Baby M. (1988), 141–42, 157
In the Matter of Deborah G. (1973), 151–52
In vitro fertilization, 142–44
Involuntary apprenticeships, 31–36, 38, 74, 76, 78–81
Involuntary mediation, 179–80, 183–84
Iowa court cases, 64, 75, 135, 188
Iowa Supreme Court, 135
Ipswich Quarterly Court, 12

Jacques v. Jacques (1921), 117
James, Barbara and Maurice, 154–55
Jamrock, Mary, 106, 109
Jernegan, Marcus, 34
Joint custody, 123, 126, 129–32, 215*n*36, 215–16*n*44; adverse effects of, 170; mediation and, 178, 182, 183; studies of, 172
Jones, Mary C., 103
Justice Talfourd's Act (England: 1839), 204*n*57
Juvenile courts, 102
Juvenile delinquents, 80
Juvenile Protection Association of Chicago, 97

K. B. (lesbian), 128
K. R. (lesbian), 128
Kaus (Calif. justice), 147
Keezer on the Law of Marriage and Divorce, 113
Kelley, Florence, 89, 90, 91, 165
Kelly, Joan, 223*n*60
Kennedy v. Kennedy (1985), 132–33
Kent, James, 7, 94, 204*n*44
Kent County (Md.), 35

Kentucky court decisions, 41
Kidnapping, 32, 216*n*59
King, Donald, 184
Kingsley, Gregory, 187, 191
Kotelchuck, Milton, 171
Kramer (social services commissioner), 155–56
Kulikoff, Allan, 44, 45

Ladies' Magazine, 52–53
Lambert v. Lambert (1988), 206*n*77
Lamb, Michael, 220*n*24
Langford family, 116–17
Lasch, Christopher, 90
Lathrop, Julia, 88–89, 91, 166
Legal profession, 202–3*n*15
Legitimization, 25, 71–72, 81, 210*n*41
Lehr v. Robertson, 146–47
Lesbian mothers, 128, 176
Lewis v. Martin (1970), 218*n*92
Lincoln, Abraham, 80
Linda (wife), 181–82
Lindsay v. Lindsay (1854), 63
Livingston, Nancy Shippen, 17
London City Council, 1, 32
Los Angeles County, 179–80, 184, 223*n*58
Lost custody, 115–16, 149–56; *see also* Child removal
Louisiana, 67, 144, 177
Love, 173, 174

M., Baby, 141
Mackintosh, Jane, 20–21
McNeil v. McNeil (1911), 113
Magbee, Matthew, 24
Maine, 223*n*58
Mandatory mediation, 179–80, 183–84

Mansfield, William Murray, Lord, 17, 59
Margolis, Maxine, 51
Marriage settlements, 14–15
Married former slaves, 81
Married Woman's Property Act (N.Y.: 1860), 55
Married women, 14–15, 53–54, 56, 66, 69
Marvin v. Marvin (1976), 217*n*72
Maryland, 130–31
Maryland colony: apprentices, 29; court cases, 24; legislation, 28–29, 43; orphans, 8–19, 21, 23; plantations, 45; slavery, 39
Maryson, Jane, 42
Massachusetts, 73–74, 92, 105, 106
Massachusetts Bay Colony: court cases, 22; divorce, 16; legislation, 10, 11, 25–26, 30, 34; paternal responsibilities, 6, 7–8; selectmen visits, 88
Massachusetts Society for the Prevention of Cruelty to Children, 93–94, 96, 106–7, 108
Maternal custody, 128–29, 159–60, 165
Maternal custody presumption, xi, xiii, 173; late twentieth century, 122, 123, 124, 126, 127, 176, 213*n*8; nineteenth century, 61–62, 205*n*71; 1920s, 113; Progressive era, xii, 87, 97–98, 118–19, 165
Maternal death, 145, 146
Maternal idealization, 51, 53, 66, 69, 71, 201–2*n*6
Maternal mental health, 176
Maternal parenting, 172–73, 220*n*24
Maternal status, 13–21, 42–46, 50–54, 114
Mather, Cotton, 38
Mattock, Samuel, 9–10
Mead, Margaret, 123

Mediation, 162, 178–85; California, 131–32, 179–80, 184; legal proceedings and, 191, 192, 193; session length in, 223n58

Medical care, 154

Mental health professionals: as expert witnesses, 162, 167, 175–78, 185, 191; as mediators, 179; as therapists, 193

Mercein v. People (1842), 60, 61, 63

Michael U. v. Jamie B. (1985), 147

Michigan, 93, 136–37, 188

Middle-class culture: late twentieth century, 154; nineteenth century, 52, 58, 82; Progressive era, 90, 101, 114, 119

Middle-class women, 69

Milburn (Tex. father), 116

Minneapolis, 184, 223n58

Minnesota, 99, 100, 132–33, 223n70

Minnesota State Board of Control, 99

Minorities, 154, 157

Miscegenation, 41

Mississippi, 81

Molestation, 152–53, 175, 177

Moore, Mrs., 85–86, 100

Moral considerations: in appellate court decisions, 214n25; in child removal, 101; cohabitation as, 139; maternal custody and, 100; mothers' pensions and, 92–93; parental unfitness and, 104, 107, 127; poverty and, 91; slaveholders and, 44; *see also* Sexual transgression

Morgan, Edmund, 37

Morris, Richard B., 2, 15

Mother-infant research, 172–73, 220n24

Mothers' pensions, 92–100, 148, 149, 210n54

Mulattoes, 28–29, 41–42

Murder, 104, 113

Murphy, John and Nancy, 135

Mutuality, 7, 115–16

National Humane Review, 97

National Organization for Women, 125, 126

National Women's Political Caucus, 126

Natural law, 60, 61, 71, 162–64, 165

Natural parenthood, *see* Biological parenthood

Naunton, Robert, 1

Nebraska mothers' pensions, 93

Neglect, *see* Child abuse and neglect

New Amsterdam, 19–20, 32

New England colonies: divorce, 15–17; emigration to, 2; households, 4–5; paternal death, 18; paternal responsibilities, 8, 9–10; "stubborn child" laws, 10–11

New Hampshire, 11, 67–68, 70

New Jersey court cases, 62, 70–71, 77, 141–42, 157

New Mexico legislation, 114

New Netherland, 32

Newsom v. Newsom (1990), 177

New York Charity Organization Society, 91

New York Children's Aid Society, 79

New York City, 20–21, 79

New York Constitutional Convention (1846), 55

New York Society for the Prevention of Cruelty to Children, 101–2

New York State:

—bar associations, 202–3n15

—colonial era, 15, 32

—court cases, 57; Application of Slochowsky, 138; Crimmins v. Crimmins, 63–64; Dodd v. Dodd, 130; In re P. 71,

154; Mercein v. People, 60, 61; People v. Erbert, 74; People v. Nickerson, 64; Pierce v. Yerkovich, 169; Santosky v. Kramer, 134, 136, 155–56; Watts v. Watts, 123, 171
—desertion, 94
—foster care, 159
—legislation, 55–56, 57, 74, 75, 106
New York State Women's Suffrage Society, 69
New York Supreme Court, 57, 60, 61
No-fault divorce, 124, 127, 144, 167, 178
Nonmarital partners, 139, 170, 217*n*72
Nonparental custody, 117, 122, 133–39, 159, 169, 191
Nonsupport, *see* Child support
North Carolina, 33, 103
North Dakota, 97, 170, 171, 174
Northern colonies, 40, 45

Ohio Humane Society, 102
Oklahoma, 95, 116
Old Testament, 11, 12
Olson, Odell, 137
Omnibus Reconciliation Act (1981), 217*n*70, 218*n*92
O'Neill, William, 89, 208*n*9
Oregon: court cases, 75, 116–17, 164–65, 206*n*77; legislation, 136, 205*n*69, 223*n*70
Orphanages, 111, 157
Orphans, 18–21, 31, 32, 34
Orphan's Home of the South Georgia Conference of the Methodist Episcopal Church South, 100

Palazzo v. Coe (1990), 177
Parens patriae doctrine, 58, 101

Parental conflict, 131, 132, 192–93
Parental consent, 109
Parental fitness, 63–64, 74, 104–5, 107, 127
Parental incompetence, 104, 149
Parental kidnapping, 216*n*59
Parental poverty, *see* Poor parents
Parental rights termination, *see* Child removal; Lost custody
Park, Richard, 36
Parsons, Hugh, 9
Paternal custody, 6–13, 64, 87, 97–98, 129
Paternal death, 18, 20, 64–68, 115
Paternal desertion, 16, 18, 64, 92, 94–96
Paternal parenting, 171, 220*nn*24, 25
Paternal rights: divine right theory and, 162; Justice Talfourd's Act and, 204*n*57; late twentieth century, 135, 145, 159; nineteenth-century, 60–61, 163; Progressive era, 114, 115, 118–19
Paternity trials, 70
Payne, Tom, 42, 43
Payne v. Grahm (1925), 212*n*94
Pennsylvania, 35, 36, 40, 65, 172, 177
Pennsylvania Society to Protect Children from Cruelty, 103–4
People ex rel. Sinclair v. Sinclair (1904), 61
Perry, John, 12
Phelps, Henry and John, 12
Philadelphia Society for Organizing Charity, 91
Piaget, Jean, 221*n*34
"Placing out" system, 78–80, 108–9, 110, 111
Planters, 44, 45
Play, 220*n*24
Pleck, Elizabeth, 103
Plymouth Colony, 39

Polygamy, 81
Poor children, x, 189–90; colonial era, 9, 31, 32; nineteenth century, 78–80, 82–83; Progressive era, 86
Poor Law Act (England: 1576), 25
Poor Law Act (England: 1601), 10, 91
Poor-law officials: involuntary apprenticeships and, 31, 34, 81; responsibilities of, 44, 74, 82, 101; Virginia colony, 27
Poor laws, 7, 10, 25, 72, 90–91
Poor mothers, 25, 207*n*105, 213*n*3
Poor parents: late twentieth century, 149, 153–54; nineteenth century, 62, 72–73; Progressive era, 90–91, 104–5, 166, 167
Popular culture, *see* Middle-class culture
Prather v. Prather (1809), 60
Preembryos, 143–44
Pregnancy, 125–26, 142
Pregnancy Discrimination Act (1978), 125–26
Prenuptial agreements, 14–15
Primary caretaker preference, 123, 129, 132–33, 170–71
Prince George County (Md.), 20, 21, 27
Privacy rights, 88, 90, 101, 150, 151, 154–55
Private charities, 91, 94, 96, 99, 108, 157
Privy Council (England), 1–2
Progressive era, xi–xii, 85–119, 161, 189, 190; helping professions, 202*n*6; immigrant families, 90, 154; maternal adultery, 127; social workers, 88, 90, 101, 102, 191; third-wave feminists and, 124, 149
Property rights: colonial fathers, 6–7; former slaves, 81; married women, 53–54, 55–56, 66, 69, 203*n*28; slaveholders, 40
Property settlements, 16

Prostitution, 107
Protective agencies, *see* Social service agencies
Prother, Aaron, 23
Psychiatrists, 175–76
"Psychological parent" concept, 168, 169–71
Psychologists, 175, 176, 177–78, 192–93
Psychology, 168, 173, 177
Public officials, 8–9; *see also* Poor-law officials; State interventionism
Public support, 25, 91, 138, 148–49, 154; *see also* Aid to Families with Dependent Children (AFDC); Child support; Mothers' pensions
Public whipping, 12, 27, 29, 206*n*96
Punishment, *see* Corporal punishment; Criminal punishment
Puritanism, 11, 37, 38
Putative fathers, *see* Unmarried fathers
Putting out, *see* Indentured servants

Quilloin v. Walcott (1978), 217*n*85

R. K. (lesbian), 128
Rabkin, Peggy, 203*n*28
Raming, Henry, 153
Reeve, Tapping, 70
Relatives, *see* Blood relatives
Religious education, 7, 8, 9, 14
Remarriage, 19, 21, 22, 67, 68, 116–17
Removal of children, *see* Child removal
Reporting laws, 150
Reproductive technology, xii, 139–44, 157
Rex v. DeManneville (1804), 17–18, 59, 64
Rhode Island colony, 11, 29
Richmond, Mary, 91
Robertson family, 146

Rochester Women's Rights Convention (1853), 66
Roman law, 7
Ron (abusive father), 152–53
Roosevelt, Theodore, 91
Rose, Ernestine, 55
Rossi, Alice, 173
Rural population, 52
Ryan, Mary, 202*n*9

S. H. v. B. L. (1990), 177
Salem (Mass.), 12, 36
Salmon, Marilyn, 15
San Francisco, 184
Sansbury, Ruth, 28
Santa Cruz County (Calif.), 184
Santosky v. Kramer (1982), 134, 136, 155–56
Scant, William, 8
Scerry, Frances, 37
School attendance, 106–7, 154; *see also* Education
Searches and seizures, 154, 155
Seneca Falls Women's Rights Convention (1848), 56, 89, 203*n*28
Separation, 54, 55
Settlement place, 33, 72
Sex equality before the law, 114–15, 122, 159, 167–68, 171
Sex of children, 62, 174
Sexual transgression: colonial era, 25, 206*n*96; inheritance laws and, 69–70; late twentieth century, 144; maternal, 113–14, 128; parental unfitness and, 107, 127; *see also* Adultery; Child sexual abuse
Shaw, Josephine Lowell, 91
Shea, Felicia K., 130

"Sheep Fund" (Ohio), 102
Simpson, Cora, 93–94, 96
Slave children, 2, 5, 6; English common law and, 3, 43; families of, 42–46; freed, 80–81; indentured servitude and, 39–42
Slave fathers, 28, 29, 41, 43
Slochowsky family, 138
Small, Albion, 166
Smith, Madeline, 158
Social feminists, 89–90, 189; in aid debate, 91–92; O'Neill on, 208*n*9; social sciences and, 165; third-wave feminists and, 124, 149
Socialization, 202*n*9
Social sciences, 161–85, 191–92
Social Security System, 148
Social service agencies, 99, 148, 149, 150, 151, 154–55; *see also* Private charities
Social workers: Progressive era, 88, 90, 101, 102, 191; twentieth century, 149, 158, 175, 178, 185; *see also* Child welfare workers
Social work profession, 165–66
Sociology, 165–66
Solnit, Albert, 168–69, 170
Sorenson family, 140, 141
South Carolina, 15, 39, 60, 104
South Dakota, 104
Southern colonies: free black children, 41; indentures, 35; mulatto children, 41–42, 43; plantations, 45; slavery, 3, 5, 39
Southern textile industry, 78
Spanish law, 67
"Spiriters," 32–33
Stabbing, 104
Stanford Child Custody Study, 131, 132
Stanley v. Illinois (1971), 145–46
Stanton, Elizabeth Cady, 55, 56, 57, 77

State courts, 58

State government, 55

State interventionism: early, 101; late twentieth century, 122, 149–51; Progressive era, xi–xii, 85–119; social sciences and, 164, 166

State legislatures: late twentieth century, 129; nineteenth century, 55–57; Progressive era, 86–87, 95, 97, 114, 115

State v. Langford, 116–17

Statute of Artificers (England: 1562), 37

Stell vs. Stell (1989), 169–70

Stepparents, 122, 135–39, 216–17n62, 217n70; female, 23–24;

male, 19, 21–23, 116, 149

Stern, William, 141

Stevens, John Paul, 146–47

Stigall v. Stigall (1847), 62

Stone, Lucy, 57

Stratton, Lucy, 26

"Stubborn child laws," 11

Styles, Robert, 37

Suffolk County Court (Mass.), 8, 9–10

Suffrage, 89

Surrogate mothers, 140–42, 191

Taft, Howard, 88

Taylor v. Taylor (1986), 130–31

Tender years doctrine, see Maternal custody presumption

Tennessee court cases, 71, 143–44

Tennessee Supreme Court, 143

Testamentary guardianship, see Guardianship

Texas, 116

Textile industry, 78

Therapy, 180, 193

Third-party custody, 117, 122, 133–39,
159, 169, 191

I Timothy (Biblical book), 95, 116

Town officials, see Poor-law officials; Public officials

Trattner, Walter, 165–66

Turner, Arthur, 26

Uhls v. Uhls (1990), 177

Ulster County (N.Y.), 155–56

Uniform Adoption Act, 137

Uniform Child Custody Jurisdiction Act, 216n59

Uniform Marriage and Divorce Act, 136, 213–14n9, 214n27

Uniform Parentage Act, 140, 142, 148

University of Chicago, 88, 166

Unmarried fathers: colonial era, 25–26, 27, 28; late twentieth century, 145–48; nineteenth century, 70; Progressive era, 98–99

Unmarried mothers: colonial era, 29; late twentieth century, 148–49; nineteenth century, 71–72, 73; Progressive era, 93, 97, 99, 100, 101, 105, 107

Unmarried partners, 139, 170, 217n72

Unreasonable searches and seizures, 154, 155

Unworthiness, see Moral considerations

Urban culture, see Middle-class culture

U.S. Census Bureau, 54, 78, 111

U.S. Children's Bureau, 88, 96

U.S. House of Representatives, 135

U.S. Supreme Court opinions, 53, 126, 150; Lehr v. Robertson, 146–47; Lewis v. Martin, 218n92; Muller v. Oregon, 164–65; Santosky v. Kramer, 134, 155–56, 156; Smith v. Organization of Foster Families for Equality and

Reform, 158–59; Stanley v. Illinois, 145–46
Utah, 117

Van Hoesem, Jan, 39
Virginia colony:
—divorce, 15
—indenture records, 34
—legislation, 9; English poor laws and, 10; on illegitimacy, 26–27, 29; on indentures, 33, 34; on inheritance, 69; on mulattoes, 29, 43; on religious education, 14
—London children, 32
—orphans, 18–19, 21
—slavery, 39, 43
Virginia Company, 1–2, 32
Vishnevsky v. Vishnevsky (1960), 176
Visitation rights, 136, 154, 168–69, 169, 181–82
Vocational education, 8, 37–38
Voluntary apprenticeships, 36–39, 76, 201*n*3
Voluntary mediation, 180–82, 184–85
Volunteer workers, 101, 149

Wald, Lillian, 89
Wald, Michael, 218*n*96
Wallerstein, Judith, 174
Ward, Eric, 176
Ward, Lester Frank, 165
Washington Board of Children's Guardians, 108
Washington State court cases, 113–14, 169–70
Watertown (Conn.), 9
Watts, William, 29
Watts v. Watts (1973), 123, 171

Weithorn, Lois A., 177
Weitzman, Lenore, 215*n*33
Welsh law, 139
Wesselson, Joachim, 39
Western states, 104, 110
West Virginia, 132, 170–71
Whipping, 12, 27, 29, 206*n*96
White, Byron R., 146
White family, 147
Whitehead, Mary Beth, 141, 142
White House Conference on the Care of Dependent Children (1909), 91, 166–67
"Why Women Should Vote" (Addams), 89
Widowed mothers: colonial era, 3, 20; nineteenth century, 65–66, 67, 68, 77; Progressive era, 92, 96, 209*n*20
Willard, Samuel, 13–14, 162
Williams family, 176
Wills, 19, 43; *see also* Inheritance
Wirth, Louis, 166
Wisconsin, 137, 184
Women's Rights Convention (Rochester: 1853), 66
Women's Rights Convention (Seneca Falls: 1848), 56, 89, 203*n*28
Women's status, x, xii–xiii, 50–54, 89; *see also* Feminism; Maternal status
Worcester Central District Court (Mass.), 105, 106
Workhouses, 9
Working women, 125, 126–27, 164–65, 216*n*52
Worthiness, *see* Moral considerations
Wright, Paulina, 55

Zainaldin, Jamail, 73–74
Zummo v. Zummo, 172

Designer: Teresa Bonner
Text: Adobe Caslon Regular
Compositor: Columbia University Press
Printer: Edwards Brothers
Binder: Edwards Brothers